Best of the Best from the

Northeast

Cookbook

Selected Recipes from the
Favorite Cookbooks of
**NEW YORK, PENNSYLVANIA, MASSACHUSETTS,
CONNECTICUT, VERMONT, NEW HAMPSHIRE,
RHODE ISLAND and MAINE**

The American lobster, also known as Maine lobster, is found on the Atlantic coast of North America. They are caught primarily using lobster traps. Nearly 90 percent of the nation's lobster supply is caught off the coast of Maine. Maine lobsters have won international fame for their flavor and contribution to the culinary world.

Best of the Best from the
Northeast
Cookbook

Selected Recipes from the
Favorite Cookbooks of
NEW YORK, PENNSYLVANIA, MASSACHUSETTS,
CONNECTICUT, VERMONT, NEW HAMPSHIRE,
RHODE ISLAND and MAINE

EDITED BY
Gwen McKee
AND
Barbara Moseley

QUAIL RIDGE PRESS
Preserving America's Food Heritage

Library of Congress Cataloging-in-Publication Data

Best of the best from the Northeast cookbook : selected recipes from the favorite
cookbooks of New York, Pennsylvania, Massachusetts, Connecticut, Vermont,
New Hampshire, Rhode Island, and Maine / edited by Gwen McKee and
Barbara Moseley — 1st ed.
      p. cm..
Includes index.
ISBN-13: 978-1-934193-38-9
 ISBN-10: 1-934193-38-0
1. Cooking, American--New England style. 2. Cook books. I. McKee, Gwen.
II. Moseley, Barbara.
TX715.2.N48B485 2011
641.5974--dc22   2010039698

ISBN–13: 978–1-934193-38-9 • ISBN–10: 1-934193-38-0
Book design by Cyndi Clark
Cover photo by Greg Campbell • Illustrated by Tupper England

Printed in Canada
First edition, January 2011
On the cover: Lobster Thermidor, page 194

QUAIL RIDGE PRESS
P. O. Box 123 • Brandon, MS 39043
info@quailridge.com • www.quailridge.com

Contents

PHOTO BY BARBARA MOSELEY

In November 1620, the Mayflower landed at Plymouth, Massachusetts, with 102 Pilgrims aboard. Many of the people and events surrounding Plymouth Colony have become part of American folklore, including the tradition of Thanksgiving and the monument known as Plymouth Rock.

Quest for the Best Regional Cooking

Of all the places Barbara and I have traveled, the beautiful Northeast stands out as a place we always recommend people do not miss. Since my daughter lives south of Boston, we go there often, and are never without awe at the sights, sounds, history, feeling, and yes, tastes of this glorious part of our country. Pennsylvania is also a state we love tooling around in on frequent trips to be on QVC, as well as walking the streets of Manhattan when we visit friends. Though the touristy places are numerous in every state, it seems there is always something to see at every turn that catches your eye and your fancy. There are so many big cities to explore, so many small off-the-beaten-path roads to take you to an Amish farm or a lighthouse or an old country store, or lure you into an old diner or a cozy bed and breakfast.

Traveling to every state in the United States in search of the best cookbooks and recipes took Barbara Moseley and me the better part of 27 years. What started in our home state of Mississippi with one cookbook, grew to include our neighboring states, then as each one neared completion, we reached out farther and farther away from home to explore the cuisines of states far and wide. The experience has been one that has enabled us to bring home each new state's recipes to become ours forever.

But nothing seems so special and dear as when you share it with others who you know will enjoy it as much as you do. Our BEST OF THE BEST STATE COOKBOOKS feature chosen favorite recipes that we are proud to have brought from each state home to you, wherever you are. I wish we could introduce you to the many people we have met in every state who were proud of their cooking heritage and eager to show us just how good their recipes were, and are! Sometimes it was a particular local ingredient, or the way they kneaded the dough, or browned the flour, or marinated the meat, or maybe a secret method they used to make something particularly unique to their way of cooking. It has truly been a delicious experience!

Of course, the local food and fare are a big part of the entire experience. From Boston Cream Pie to New York Cheesecake to Philly Cheese Steak, traditions in food are alive through the recipes and stories and historical facts within these pages that take you to the incomparable Northeast. Enjoy the journey.

Gwen McKee

Gwen McKee and Barbara Moseley, editors of the
BEST OF THE BEST STATE COOKBOOK SERIES

Beverages and Appetizers

The Liberty Bell is perhaps one of the most prominent symbols associated with the American Revolution. It has been described as an international icon of liberty. Its most famous ringing occurred on July 8, 1776, to summon citizens of Philadelphia for the reading of the Declaration of Independence. The Liberty Bell Center in downtown Philadelphia, Pennsylvania, now houses the bell.

Mint Meadow Tea

1 cup sugar
1 pint water
1 cup fresh tea leaves, either
   peppermint or spearmint

Juice of 1 lemon
Water

Stir sugar and pint of water together in a saucepan and bring to a boil. Pour boiling syrup over tea leaves and let steep for 20 minutes. Remove the leaves and let tea cool. Add the lemon juice and enough water to make ½ gallon of tea. Serve either hot or cold.

From Amish and Mennonite Kitchens (Pennsylvania)

Sparkling Strawberry Punch

1 heaping quart fresh
   strawberries, or
   2 (10-ounce) packages
   frozen strawberries
1 (6-ounce) can frozen
   lemonade concentrate,
   slightly thawed
1 (⅘-quart) bottle rosé wine,
   chilled

2 (28-ounce) bottles ginger ale,
   chilled
1 (28-ounce) bottle club soda,
   chilled
2 trays ice cubes
¼ cup sugar
Orange slices for garnish

About 10 minutes before serving, in blender on high, blend strawberries and lemonade concentrate. Pour mixture into punch bowl. Add remaining ingredients, except orange slices. Stir until sugar is dissolved. Garnish with orange slices. Makes 18 (1-cup) servings or 36 (½-cup) servings.

What's Cooking at Trinity (Pennsylvania)

Irish Cream

A delicious after-dinner drink, it makes a great gift.

1 teaspoon coffee powder
2 tablespoons boiling water
1 (14-ounce) can sweetened
　condensed milk

2 cups coffee creamer
1 teaspoon vanilla flavoring
6 shots whiskey or to taste

Combine ingredients in blender container; blend well. Chill. May be stored in refrigerator several weeks. Yields 1¼ quarts.

Connecticut Cooks II (Connecticut)

Iced Coffee

4 tablespoons instant coffee
¾ cup sugar
1 cup water
2 quarts milk

½ gallon vanilla or
　vanilla/chocolate ice cream
2 scoops vanilla sugar

In a pot, heat coffee, sugar, and water until boiling. Add milk. Add ice cream and vanilla sugar, and combine with hand blender.

Optional: Ice chips may be used to keep coffee cold for longer periods of time.

Note: To make vanilla sugar, bury two vanilla beans in one pound of granulated or powdered sugar. Store in airtight container for about a week.

Culinary Creations (New York)

Hot Mulled Cider

You can use a crockpot, but it will take longer to heat. This is the recipe we use at the annual Harvest Craft Fair.

1 quart hot tea	3 sticks cinnamon
1 gallon cider	1 teaspoon allspice
Juice of 5 lemons	1 teaspoon whole cloves
Juice of 5 oranges	½ teaspoon salt (optional)
1¼ cups brown sugar	Pinch of mace

Simmer all, uncovered, for 15 minutes in a large 10–12-quart pan, stirring from time to time. Serve hot with thin slices of oranges in each cup. Makes 20–30 servings. This cannot be frozen, but it can be refrigerated and reheated.

Tasty Temptations from the Village by the Sea (Massachusetts)

Brew

2 cups cranberry juice	2 cups apple juice
4 cups decaffeinated or regular tea	1 cup orange juice
½ teaspoon cloves	Honey to taste
½ cup lemon juice	1 teaspoon cinnamon

Combine all ingredients in saucepan. Heat until warm.

Hasbro Children's Hospital Cookbook (Rhode Island)

Hot Punch

Great for good winter nights.

3 cups cranberry juice	6 allspice
3 cups apple juice	4 cloves
1 stick cinnamon	½ cup brown sugar

Put juices in coffee percolator. Place remaining ingredients in coffee filter. Perk and serve.

Our Volunteers Cook (New York)

Harvard-Yale Hot Buttered Rum Mix

Some hearty tailgaters we know served this with smashing results one freezing afternoon prior to the annual Ivy League football game. The game turned out to be rather humdrum, but everyone was clamoring for the hot rum recipe. A hint: save any leftovers for the holidays and skating parties. Here's to the lads in crimson and blue . . . .

½ cup (1 stick) butter, slightly softened
1 cup brown sugar
1 heaping teaspoon ground cinnamon
1 heaping teaspoon ground nutmeg

⅛ teaspoon ground allspice
¼ teaspoon powdered ginger
½ teaspoon Angostura bitters (in the condiments section)

To make the mix, place the softened (but not melted) butter in a medium bowl. Add the brown sugar gradually, and cream the butter and the sugar together, mixing well. Mix in the spices and bitters. Store tightly covered in the refrigerator for up to several months, or use immediately.

To use the mix, stir 1–2 teaspoons of the butter/spice mix into 2 ounces of dark rum and 4 ounces boiling water for each serving. Yields enough for 20 servings.

J. Bildner & Sons Cookbook (Massachusetts)

"The Game" is a name given to the football game between Harvard University and Yale University. The first meeting between the teams occurred on November 13, 1875, at Hamilton Field in New Haven, Connecticut. The venue alternates between Harvard Stadium and the Yale Bowl. For many students and alumni of Harvard and Yale, "The Game" is an important event. The schools are located only a few hours' travel from one another; and, perhaps because they are among the nation's most prestigious and oldest universities, the rivalry is intense. Beating the rival is often considered more important than the team's season record. As of 2010, Yale leads the series 65–54–8.

The Harvard-Yale Regatta is another rivalry between the schools.

Delish Dip

1 (8-ounce) package cream
  cheese (lite)
2 tablespoons milk
½ cup sour cream
1 (2½-ounce) jar dried beef,
  chopped
2 tablespoons minced onion

2 tablespoons chopped
  green bell pepper
Dash of pepper
½ teaspoon horseradish
(optional)
Crushed walnuts

Soften and mix cream cheese, milk, and sour cream. Mix in dried beef. Add onion, green pepper, pepper, and horseradish. Place in greased baking dish. Sprinkle with crushed walnuts. Bake at 350° for 15 minutes, covered. Serve with crackers or vegetables.

Cooking with H.E.L.P. (Maine)

Cucumber Dip

(Tzatziki)

". . . great as a dip, salad dressing, or sauce for shish kebob or rice."

1 teaspoon salt
2 pints plain yogurt
1 cup finely chopped
  cucumbers
Salt (to sprinkle)

1 clove garlic, crushed
2 teaspoons olive oil
1 tablespoon fresh dill or mint
1 tablespoon lemon juice

Yogurt should be thick for this recipe. Add 1 teaspoon salt to yogurt and let stand uncovered about 2 hours; keep draining off water until remaining yogurt thickens.

Sprinkle cucumber with salt and let stand at least 20 minutes. Press dry in a strainer.

Combine thickened yogurt, cucumber, and remaining ingredients. Mix well. Chill. Makes 3 cups.

Treasured Greek Recipes (New York)

Turkey Tidbits with Cranberry Dip

½ cup sour cream
1 teaspoon lemon juice
1 teaspoon horseradish
¼ teaspoon salt
1 pound uncooked turkey
  breast, cut into pieces

⅔ cup dry bread crumbs
⅔ cup ground walnuts
2 tablespoons margarine,
  melted
Cranberry Dip

Combine sour cream, lemon juice, horseradish and salt in non-metal bowl; blend well. Add uncooked turkey breast pieces. Toss to coat. Cover; marinate in refrigerator 2–24 hours. In shallow pan, combine bread crumbs and ground walnuts. Remove turkey from marinade. Roll in crumbs. Place on greased 10x15-inch pan. Drizzle melted margarine over turkey. Bake at 350° for 35 minutes or until golden brown. Serve warm or cold with Cranberry Dip.

CRANBERRY DIP:
1 (8-ounce) can jellied
  cranberry sauce

¼ cup sour cream
2 tablespoons horseradish

Mix all ingredients.

Savor the Flavor (New York)

The Ivy League is an athletic conference comprising eight private institutions of higher education in the Northeastern United States. The eight institutions are Brown University (Providence, Rhode Island), Columbia University (New York City), Cornell University (Ithaca, New York), Dartmouth College (Hanover, New Hampshire), Harvard University (Cambridge, Massachusetts), Princeton University (Princeton, New Jersey), the University of Pennsylvania (Philadelphia, Pennsylvania), and Yale University (New Haven, Connecticut). Seven of the eight schools were founded during America's colonial period; the exception is Cornell, which was founded in 1865. The use of the phrase is not limited to athletics, and the term also has connotations of academic excellence.

English Muffin-Crab Dip

1 stick butter
1 (5-ounce) jar Old English
  cheese spread
1½ teaspoons mayonnaise
½ teaspoon garlic powder

½ teaspoon seasoned salt
1 (6-ounce) can crabmeat,
  drained
6 English muffins, split

Cream together all ingredients except English muffins. Spread creamed mixture on 12 halves of English muffins. May place on cookie sheet and freeze, then place muffins back in bag wrapper. Store in freezer until ready to use. When ready to serve cut each muffin in 6 wedges. Place on cookie sheet. Broil approximately 5 minutes or until bubbly.

Our Daily Bread, and then some... (New York)

Amber Glow

1 (8-ounce) package cream
  cheese, softened
1 (10-ounce) jar apricot
  preserves (¾ cup)
1½ teaspoon dry mustard

1 teaspoon prepared
  horseradish
¼ cup chopped salted
  peanuts
Crackers

Press cream cheese into an 8-ounce plastic margarine tub or a small bowl. Loosen edges with a spatula and invert onto the center of a shallow serving dish. Smooth surface with a spatula.

In a small bowl, mix preserves, mustard, and horseradish until well blended. Pour over cheese. Sprinkle with nuts. Serve with crackers.

Chefs and Artists (Pennsylvania)

Roasted Red Pepper Pesto Cheesecake

1 cup butter-flavored cracker crumbs (about 40 crackers)
¼ cup (½ stick) butter or margarine, softened
2 (8-ounce) packages cream cheese, softened
1 cup ricotta cheese
3 eggs
½ cup Parmesan cheese
½ cup DiGiorno Pesto Sauce
½ cup drained roasted red peppers, puréed

Mix crumbs and butter. Press onto bottom of 9-inch springform pan. Bake at 325° for 10 minutes. Mix cream cheese and ricotta cheese with electric mixer at medium speed until well blended. Add eggs, one at a time, mixing well after each addition. Blend in remaining ingredients. Pour over crust. Bake at 325° for 55 minutes to one hour. Run knife or metal spatula around rim of pan to loosen cake; cool before removing rim of pan. Refrigerate 4 hours or overnight. Let stand 15 minutes at room temperature before serving. Garnish, if desired. Serve with crackers. Also great served with fresh fruit for brunch. Makes 12–14 servings.

Recipes from the Children's Museum at Saratoga (New York)

Chipmunk Pie

1 (8-ounce) package cream cheese, softened
1 cup sour cream
3 tablespoons green pepper, finely chopped
1 small jar dried chipped beef, cut finely with scissors
½–1 cup coarsely chopped walnuts

Mix all ingredients. Place in pie plate. Heat in 325° oven for about 15 minutes. Serve as dip or spread.

Cooking Down the Road, and at home, too (New York)

Lucia's Boursin

1 (8-ounce) package cream
  cheese, softened
4 tablespoons butter, softened
4 teaspoons heavy cream
¼ teaspoon garlic powder
⅛ teaspoon dried oregano

⅛ teaspoon dried thyme
⅛ teaspoon dried marjoram
⅛ teaspoon dried dill
⅛ teaspoon dried basil
⅛–¼ cup coarsely cracked
  peppercorns

With an electric mixer, beat together cream cheese, butter, and heavy cream on low speed until well blended. Add herbs; blend on low speed. Remove both ends of a clean tuna fish can to use as a mold. Place on wax paper; fill completely with cheese mixture, leveling top of can. Chill in mold for at least 1 hour; remove mold and roll in peppercorns. Serve boursin with crackers. Serves 6–10.

The Heart of Pittsburgh (Pennsylvania)

Cold Salmon Mousse

1 (16-ounce) can red salmon;
  drain, remove bones, and
  flake
1 (8-ounce) package cream
  cheese (room temperature)
1 tablespoon lemon juice
¼ teaspoon salt

1 tablespoon grated
  horseradish
2 tablespoons grated onion
½ tablespoon liquid smoke
  (optional)
6 tablespoons chopped pecans
½ cup chopped fresh parsley

Blend all ingredients except pecans and parsley. Chill for at least 4 hours. Make 2 balls by dividing mixture in half. Roll each ball in 3 tablespoons of chopped pecans mixed with 3 tablespoons of chopped parsley just before serving. Serve with French bread. Garnish with small pickles, tomatoes, cucumbers, and whatever you have. Flavors improve if made the day before.

Note: This dish is also great molded in individual molds (line molds with plastic wrap) and used as a first course. Press pecans and parsley on molded salmon.

Seafood Expressions (Rhode Island)

Red Pepper Bruschetta with Feta

1 (7-ounce) jar roasted red peppers, drained and chopped
¼ cup chopped green onions
1 (4-ounce) package tomato basil feta cheese
1 clove garlic, minced
1 tablespoon olive oil
1 tablespoon lemon juice
1 loaf French bread, cut into ½-inch slices

Mix peppers, onions, cheese, garlic, olive oil, and lemon juice. Set aside. Brush bread lightly with olive oil. Place on cookie sheet. Broil until lightly toasted. Top each slice with 1 tablespoon pepper mixture. Broil lightly. Yields 1½ dozen slices.

Trinity Catholic School Cookbook (New York)

Olives in Cheese Pastry

2 cups (8 ounces) grated Cheddar cheese
1¼ cups flour
1 stick butter, melted
About 40 pimiento-stuffed olives, drained

Work the cheese, flour, and butter together to form a smooth dough. Mold about 1 teaspoon of dough around each olive and shape into balls. At this point you can freeze the balls on a cookie sheet, then transfer to a plastic bag for indefinite storage in the freezer. When ready to serve, bake the frozen balls on a cookie sheet in a 400° oven for 15–20 minutes. If you don't wish to freeze them, just prepare, chill for an hour, and bake as above.

Bucks Cooks II (Pennsylvania)

Cherry Tomato Bites

2 pints cherry tomatoes
1 (8-ounce) package cream
  cheese, softened
6 bacon strips, cooked and
  crumbled

¼ cup minced green onions
¼ cup minced fresh parsley
¼ teaspoon Worcestershire

Cut a thin slice off the top of each tomato. Scoop out and discard pulp. Invert the tomatoes on a paper towel to drain.

Meanwhile, combine remaining ingredients in a small bowl; mix well. Spoon into tomatoes. Refrigerate until serving. Yields 4 dozen.

Sharing Our Bounty Through 40 Years (New York)

Grape Meatballs

MEATBALLS:

2 pounds ground beef
⅓ cup chopped onion
2 eggs, beaten
1 cup Italian bread crumbs
⅓ cup grated Romano
  cheese

¼ cup parsley flakes
½ cup milk
2 dashes pepper
Olive oil

Combine all ingredients except olive oil; mix well. Shape into bite-size balls and brown in olive oil. Simmer in Sauce about 1 hour.

SAUCE:

1 (12-ounce) bottle chili sauce
Juice of 1 lemon

1 (10-ounce) jar Pennsylvania
  grape jelly

Combine ingredients and add to Meatballs.

Divine Recipes Fit for a Pennsylvania Grape Queen
(Pennsylvania)

Spinach Cheese Balls

2 (10-ounce) packages frozen chopped spinach
1 tablespoon minced dried onion
2 cups herb-seasoned stuffing mix
1 cup grated Parmesan cheese
2 eggs, beaten
3 tablespoons melted butter

In a saucepan, cook spinach according to package directions. Drain and add dried onion. In mixing bowl, combine spinach mixture, stuffing, and cheese. Stir in eggs and melted butter. Let stand for 15 minutes. Shape into 1-inch balls. Place in a shallow ovenproof pan. Bake at 375° for 10–15 minutes or until heated through. Yields 48.

Note: This can also be spread in a 9-inch pie pan and cut into wedges as a luncheon dish.

It's Our Serve (New York)

Pepperoni Stuffed Mushrooms

12 large mushrooms
1 medium onion, finely chopped
½ cup diced pepperoni
¼ cup finely chopped green pepper
1 small clove garlic, minced
2 tablespoons butter or margarine
½ cup finely crushed snack crackers (Ritz)
3 tablespoons grated Parmesan cheese
1 tablespoon finely chopped, fresh parsley
½ teaspoon salt
¼ teaspoon dried oregano
Dash pepper
⅓ cup chicken broth

Set aside mushroom caps. Chop stems. Sauté onion, pepperoni, green pepper, garlic, and mushroom stems in butter. Combine crackers, Parmesan cheese, parsley, salt, oregano, and pepper and add to sautéed vegetables and pepperoni. Spoon mixture into caps and place in baking dish. Add broth to baking dish and bake uncovered at 325° for 25 minutes. Serves 6.

It's Our Serve (New York)

Hidden Valley Ranch Sausage Stars

2 cups (1 pound) cooked, crumbled sausage
1½ cups grated sharp Cheddar cheese
1½ cups grated Monterey Jack cheese
1 cup prepared Hidden Valley Ranch Original Salad Dressing Mix
1 (2.25-ounce) can sliced ripe olives
½ cup chopped red pepper
1 package fresh or frozen wonton wrappers, cut in fourths
Vegetable oil

Preheat oven to 350°. Blot sausage dry with paper towels and combine with the cheeses, salad dressing, olives and red pepper. Lightly grease a miniature (or regular) muffin tin and press 1 wrapper in each cup; brush with oil. Bake 5 minutes, until golden. Remove from tins; place on a baking sheet. Fill with sausage mixture. Bake 5 minutes, until bubbly. Yields 4–5 dozen.

Fortsville UMC Cookbook (New York)

Sausage Quiches

1 (8-ounce) package refrigerated crescent rolls
½ pound hot sausage, crumbled
2 tablespoons dried onion flakes
2 tablespoons minced chives
4 eggs, lightly beaten
1 pint cottage cheese, small curd
2 cups grated Swiss or Cheddar cheese
⅓ cup grated Parmesan cheese
Paprika

Generously grease 4 miniature muffin tins. Separate dough pieces and cut up to fit into tins about ⅔ way up the sides. Brown sausage lightly with onion. Drain well. Add chives. Spoon equally over dough. Mix eggs and cheeses. Fill tins with mixture. Sprinkle top with paprika. May be frozen at this point, tightly covered. Bring to room temperature. Bake at 375° for 20 minutes. Makes 48 small quiches.

Connecticut Cooks (Connecticut)

Glazed Bacon

While I served on the board of directors of Nationwide Life Insurance Company, I discovered this unbelievable glazed bacon. This is my version, and be sure to make plenty. Normally I prepare five pounds of bacon for a party of thirty. It should not be refrigerated or tightly covered. If it does get a bit limp, refresh it by placing in broiler until it bubbles again.

½ pound bacon, sliced
½ cup light brown sugar,
  packed

1 tablespoon Dijon mustard
2 tablespoons red or white
  wine

Put the bacon in a large cake pan and bake in a preheated 350° oven for 10 minutes. Drain off the fat. At this point, before you add the glaze, the bacon should be almost crisp—be sure not to underbake it.

In a small bowl, mix the sugar, mustard, and wine until smooth. Pour half of this glaze over the bacon and return to the oven. Bake at 350° for 10 minutes. Turn the bacon; cover with the remaining glaze and continue to bake until golden brown. Remove and place on wax paper. Serve warm or cooled. Makes 6 servings.

Betty Groff's Country Goodness Cookbook (Pennsylvania)

Bow House Brochettes

Flavor lives up to its wonderful aroma!

½ pound sliced bacon
1 pound sea scallops, rinsed
  and drained
2 tablespoons unsalted
  butter, melted

1½ tablespoons firmly
  packed brown sugar
1 teaspoon ground cinnamon

Cut bacon slices in half. Wrap bacon around scallop and secure with wooden toothpick. Combine butter, brown sugar, and cinnamon. Brush on bacon-wrapped scallops. Broil, turning as necessary, until bacon is crisp on all sides.

Scallops and bacon may be assembled early in day and chilled. Recipe may be doubled. Yields 1½ dozen.

Connecticut Cooks II (Connecticut)

Scallop Puffs

One of the great pleasures of living at the eastern end of Long Island Sound is the scallops, both the bay scallops from the waters at Niantic, and the large sea scallops. This recipe is a splendid way to use them.

½ pound sea scallops
2 tablespoons butter
1 teaspoon grated lemon
 rind
1½ garlic cloves, minced
½ teaspoon dried dill weed

1 cup shredded Swiss cheese
1 heaping cup mayonnaise
⅛ teaspoon black pepper
6 dozen 1½-inch bread
 rounds, lightly toasted
Paprika

Cut scallops in quarters. Melt butter. Add scallops, grated lemon rind, and garlic. Cook for 2–3 minutes. Add dill and cook 30 seconds more. Cool to room temperature. Add cheese, mayonnaise, and pepper and mix well. (Can be prepared up to a week in advance; cover and refrigerate.)

Place mixture on toast rounds, sprinkle with paprika, and run under broiler for 2–3 minutes. Serve hot. Puffs can be frozen after broiling. Makes 72 puffs.

The Lymes' Heritage Cookbook (Connecticut)

Lobster Tarts

1 pie crust
2 tablespoons butter
1 (6-ounce) can frozen
 lobster, or 8 ounces fresh
 lobster
2 tablespoons finely
 chopped onion
1 tablespoon finely chopped
 parsley

2 tablespoons lemon juice
1 tablespoon flour
½ cup warm light cream
1 egg yolk
2 tablespoons brandy
Cheddar cheese

Make 36 mini tarts using either tart pan or small muffin pan. Lightly bake. Melt butter; add lobster, onion, and parsley. Sprinkle with lemon juice and flour. Add cream, which has been blended into yolk and brandy. Fill tarts with mixture and sprinkle with cheese. Bake at 375° for about 20 minutes.

A Taste of New England (Massachusetts)

Crab Rangoons

1 (8-ounce) package cream
  cheese, softened
8 ounces crabmeat or surimi
  (imitation crab)
¼–½ teaspoon cayenne
  pepper, or crushed dried
  red pepper flakes, to taste

2–3 tablespoons water
Oil for frying
1 pound wonton wrappers or
  1 pound egg roll wrappers,
  cut in quarters

Combine all ingredients except wonton wrappers. Place ½–1 teaspoon crab mixture in a corner of the wonton and roll up on the diagonal. Moisten tips of wonton wrappers with water to seal. Place seam-side-down in 1½–2 inches hot oil and fry until golden on one side. Turn over and fry until second side is golden. Remove from oil and drain on paper towels. Yields approximately 64 rangoons.

Hint: Serve with duck sauce or hot mustard. These may be frozen. To reheat, place frozen rangoons in a 350° oven and bake until hot, about 10 minutes. You can substitute a 6½-ounce can of tuna for the crab.

From Ellie's Kitchen to Yours (Massachusetts)

Mustard Seed Shrimp

A different twist to marinated shrimp.

1½ cups mayonnaise
⅓ cup lemon juice, freshly
  squeezed
¼ cup sugar
½ cup sour cream
1 large red onion, finely
  chopped

4 tablespoons chopped fresh
  dill, or 2 teaspoons dry dill
1 tablespoon mustard seed
1 tablespoon Worcestershire
2 pounds medium shrimp,
  cooked and peeled

In a large bowl, mix mayonnaise, lemon juice, sugar, sour cream, onion, and seasonings. Stir in the shrimp; cover and refrigerate overnight. Spoon into a crystal bowl or family heirloom and serve with wooden picks. Serves 6–8. Must be made ahead.

Seafood Secrets Cookbook (Connecticut)

Basil Shrimp

16 jumbo shrimp (thawed if
  frozen), peeled, deveined
16 fresh basil leaves
  (preferably purple)
16 slices apple-smoked bacon
  or regular bacon

2 cups vegetable oil
1 (12-ounce) jar barbecue
  sauce
4 teaspoons grated horseradish
2 dashes hot pepper sauce

Preheat oven to 375°. To butterfly shrimp, make a deep slit along
the back of each, but not all the way through. Rinse shrimp; pat dry.
Place one basil leaf inside slit in each shrimp. Wrap each shrimp in
a slice of bacon and secure with a toothpick (flavorless).

In a medium stockpot or saucepan, heat oil over high heat to
350°; when hot, carefully add shrimp a few at a time. Deep-fry 2–3
minutes, until crisp. Using a slotted spoon, remove shrimp from oil
and place on a tray lined with paper towels to absorb any excess oil.

In a skillet, combine barbecue sauce, horseradish, and pepper
sauce. Add precooked shrimp to sauce and heat in oven 5 minutes,
basting shrimp often, until shrimp is heated through. Serve on a platter garnished with lemon wedges and extra basil leaves. Serves 4.

City Tavern Cookbook (Pennsylvania)

Coconut Chicken

4–5 whole boneless, skinless,
  chicken breasts
3 eggs
1 (7-ounce) package shredded
  coconut

¾ cup flour
½ cup milk
Vegetable oil
Duck sauce*

Cut chicken into bite-size pieces. Combine eggs, coconut, flour,
and milk to make batter. Dredge chicken in batter to coat. Fry
chicken pieces in oil until golden brown, turning often. Serve with
duck sauce. Makes 80–100 pieces.

*Duck sauce is a Cantonese dipping sauce; it is a thick sweet-and-sour
sauce made of plums, apricots, vinegar, and sugar.

Note: May be made ahead and frozen. When ready to serve, reheat at
350° for 10 minutes.

Family & Company (New York)

Chinese Chicken Wings

3 cloves garlic, minced
1 small onion, minced
3 tablespoons chopped
  fresh parsley
1 cup soy sauce
½ cup vegetable oil

1 tablespoon Dijon mustard
1 tablespoon honey (or ½
  tablespoon sugar)
3–5 pounds chicken wings,
  disjointed

Combine garlic, onion, parsley, soy sauce, oil, mustard, and honey. Mix thoroughly in food processor or with wire whisk. Marinate wings for several hours at room temperature or overnight (covered in refrigerator).

Bake wings on a cookie sheet or jellyroll pan at 300° for 45 minutes, turning once, and broil for approximately 5 minutes or until wings are brown and bubbly.

A Taste of Salt Air & Island Kitchens (Rhode Island)

Chinese Barbecued Spareribs

2 pounds lean spareribs, cut
  into 2-inch lengths
Salt
½ cup water
⅓ cup soy sauce
⅓ cup light brown sugar
2 tablespoons cider vinegar

¼ teaspoon freshly grated
  ginger root
1–2 cloves garlic, very
  finely minced
1 tablespoon cornstarch
2 tablespoons water

Place the lightly salted ribs in a roasting pan with the ½ cup of water. Cover and bake at 350° for 1¼ hours. Drain off all water and grease, cool slightly, and cut into individual ribs. Can do this several days ahead.

Combine the soy sauce, sugar, vinegar, ginger, and garlic in a saucepan and bring to a boil stirring constantly. Boil 1 minute. Combine cornstarch and water well and add to the sauce. Cook over medium heat stirring constantly until sauce is thick and clear. Cool slightly and then pour over ribs to coat completely. Place coated ribs in a flat baking dish and bake for 20 minutes at 350°. Yields about 20 ribs.

RSVP (Maine)

Tasty Toasts

I always keep these wonderful herb toasts in my freezer. They are a good accompaniment for soups, salads, or any beverage. Quite my favorite canapé and possibly my most popular.

1 cup (2 sticks) margarine, softened
½ teaspoon dried oregano
½ teaspoon dried basil
½ teaspoon dried rosemary
½ teaspoon dried thyme
4 tablespoons minced fresh parsley
24 slices melba-thin white bread, crusts removed

Cream margarine with all seasonings; blend well. Spread bread slices generously with mixture. Cut each slice into 4 even pieces and place on 2 cookie sheets. Bake in a preheated 250° oven for 1 hour. Cool, pack in closed container, and store in freezer. Use them as needed, served at room temperature. Makes 96 toasts.

The Lymes' Heritage Cookbook (Connecticut)

Bread and Breakfast

WIKIPEDIA.ORG

Liberty Enlightening the World, familiarly known as the Statue of Liberty, has greet-ed generations of newcomers to the shores of the United States from its home in New York Harbor since 1886. The statue was a gift from the people of France in honor of American independence.

Feather Beds

⅓ cup sugar
1 teaspoon salt
¾ cup hot potato water
¼ cup margarine

4–4½ cups flour
1 package yeast
½ cup warm mashed potatoes
1 egg

Stir together sugar, salt, hot potato water, and margarine. Let cool. Add the rest of the ingredients and knead well. Let rise until double in bulk. Then roll out and cut into circles. Put close together on a baking sheet. Let rise again until double. Bake at 350° for 30 minutes until golden.

Note: These may also be made into crescent rolls and clover rolls. They are very light and most delicious.

Grandmother's Cookbook (Pennsylvania)

Clover-Leaf Rolls

¾ cup scalded milk
¼ cup sugar
3 tablespoons shortening
1½ teaspoons salt

1 cake compressed yeast
¼ cup lukewarm water
1 egg, beaten
3½ cups all-purpose flour

Pour scalded milk over sugar, shortening, and salt. Soften yeast in lukewarm water. Add egg. Add yeast mixture to milk that has cooled to lukewarm temperature. Add flour gradually, mixing well after each addition. Knead lightly for several minutes. Place in greased bowl, cover and let rise in warm place until double in bulk. Pinch off pieces of dough the size of a marble, roll into round balls, and place 3 balls in greased muffin tins. Let rise until double in bulk. Bake at 425° for 20 minutes. Makes 15–18 rolls.

Mennonite Community Cookbook (Pennsylvania)

Quick Brown Bread

A traditional New England bread that is especially good with chicken, ham, and baked beans. Hard to go wrong making this.

2 cups whole-wheat flour	1 egg
1 teaspoon salt	1 cup buttermilk
½ teaspoon baking soda	½ cup molasses
1½ teaspoons baking powder	¼ cup shortening

Mix the flour, salt, soda, and baking powder thoroughly. Beat the egg and add to it the buttermilk, molasses, and shortening. Add the liquid to the dry ingredients and stir only enough to barely mix. Bake in a well-greased loaf pan at 350° for 30 minutes. Cut in slices and serve hot. Makes 1 loaf.

The Country Innkeepers' Cookbook (Maine)

Cooperstown B&B Banana Jam Bread

½ cup margarine	1 tablespoon baking powder
1 cup sugar	½ teaspoon salt
2 eggs	½ cup strawberry jam
1 cup mashed banana	1 cup chopped pecans or walnuts
1 teaspoon lemon juice	1 cup raisins
2 cups flour	

Cream margarine. Gradually add sugar and beat until fluffy. Add eggs. Combine banana and lemon juice. Stir into creamed mixture. Combine flour, baking powder, and salt. Add to creamed mixture, stirring until moistened. Stir in jam, nuts, and raisins. Pour into greased 9x5-inch loaf pan. Bake at 350° for 50 minutes. Cool 10 minutes. Remove from pan. Cool on wire rack.

Trinity Catholic School Cookbook (New York)

Pineapple Spice Scones

3 cups flour
⅓ cup plus 1 tablespoon
  sugar, divided
2½ teaspoons baking powder
½ teaspoon salt
¾ cup margarine or butter,
  softened

1 (18-ounce) can crushed
  pineapple (juice pack)
Light cream or milk
3 tablespoons macadamia nuts
  or walnuts, chopped
½ teaspoon cinnamon

Preheat oven to 425°. In a mixing bowl, stir together flour, ⅓ cup sugar, baking powder, salt, and butter. Make a well in center. Stir in undrained pineapple until dry ingredients are just moistened (dough will be sticky). On lightly floured surface, knead gently 10–12 times. Roll dough to ¼-inch thickness. Cut with floured 2½-inch biscuit cutter. Place dough in circle on ungreased baking sheet. Brush tops with cream or milk. Combine nuts, 1 tablespoon sugar, and cinnamon. Sprinkle teaspoon of mixture over each scone. Bake for 15 minutes. Makes 21 scones.

Recipe from Gansevoort House Bed and Breakfast, Little Falls
**Bed & Breakfast Leatherstocking Welcome Home Recipe
Collection (New York)**

Sour Cream Corn Muffins

1 cup yellow cornmeal
1 cup flour
¼ cup sugar
2 teaspoons baking powder
1 teaspoon salt

½ teaspoon baking soda
1 cup sour cream
2 eggs, slightly beaten
¼ cup butter, melted

Butter 12 muffin tins. In a medium bowl, combine cornmeal, flour, sugar, baking powder, salt, and soda. In a small bowl, combine sour cream, beaten eggs, and melted butter; blend well. Add to dry ingredients and stir until evenly blended; do not overmix. Drop batter into prepared muffin tins and bake at 425°, 25–30 minutes. Cool in pans for 5 minutes before removing. Serve hot.

Memories from Brownie's Kitchen (Maine)

Berry Patch Coffee Cake

1 (8-ounce) package cream
  cheese
1 cup sugar
½ cup vegetable shortening
  or margarine
2 eggs
1 teaspoon vanilla
1¾ cups all-purpose flour
  (not self-rising)

1 teaspoon baking powder
½ teaspoon baking soda
¼ teaspoon salt
¾–1 teaspoon cinnamon
¼ cup milk
½ cup chopped pecans
½ cup raspberry or
  blackberry preserves

Soften cream cheese at room temperature. Combine with sugar and shortening, mixing until well blended. Add eggs one at a time, mixing well after each addition. Blend in vanilla. Sift dry ingredients together and add alternately with the milk. Blend thoroughly. Stir in pecans.

Pour into a greased and floured 9x13-inch pan. Dot with preserves and cut through batter several times for a marbled effect. Bake at 350° for 35 minutes until done.

Heritage Fan-Fare (Massachusetts)

The Freedom Trail is a 2.5 mile red-brick walking trail in Boston, Massachusetts, comprised of 16 nationally significant historic sites that tell the story of the American Revolution.

The Freedom Trail includes: The Boston Common, The State House, Park Street Church, Granary Burying Ground, King's Chapel, King's Chapel Burying Ground, Benjamin Franklin Statue/Boston Latin School, Old Corner Book Store, Old South Meeting House, Old State House, Site of the Boston Massacre, Faneuil Hall, Paul Revere House, The Old North Church, Copp's Hill Burying Ground, Bunker Hill Monument, and the USS Constitution.

Morning Cake Delight with Topping

CAKE:

1 pound butter
2 cups sugar
6 eggs
½ cup sour cream
½ cup milk
1 banana, mashed

1½ teaspoons almond
   extract
4 cups flour
1 tablespoon baking powder
1 cup berries (raspberries,
   blueberries, or blackberries)

Preheat oven to 350°. In a large bowl cream together the butter and sugar. Beat in eggs. Then add sour cream, milk, banana, and almond extract. Mix well. In a separate bowl combine flour and baking powder. Add to creamed mixture and blend well but do not overbeat.

Pour half the batter into a greased and floured 12-inch Bundt pan, sprinkle with berries, and cover with remaining batter. Bake at 350° for 50–60 minutes. This is a big cake, so be sure to test with a toothpick to be certain it's done.

Cool in pan for a few minutes, and then turn out of pan to cool completely on a rack.

TOPPING:

½ cup whipping cream
½ cup yogurt with fruit

½ cup sour cream

Whip the cream. Fold in the yogurt and sour cream. Serve each portion of cake with a generous dollop of the topping.

A recipe from Hawthorne Inn, Concord
The Bed & Breakfast Cookbook (Massachusetts)

Apple Honey-Buns

½ cup butter
1 cup brown sugar
1 teaspoon cinnamon
1 tablespoon honey
⅓ cup milk
1 (16-ounce) package Hot
  Roll Mix

¾ cup very warm water
⅓ cup sugar
1 egg
½ cup chopped nuts
1¼ cups chopped apples

Combine butter, brown sugar, cinnamon, honey, and milk in a small saucepan. Stir over low heat until butter melts and mixture is smooth. Pour half of the mixture into an ungreased 13x9x2-inch baking pan; reserve the remaining mixture.

Dissolve the yeast from the Hot Roll Mix in warm water in a large bowl; stir in sugar, egg, and nuts. Add flour mixture from Hot Roll Mix and apples; blend well.

Drop dough by heaping tablespoonfuls on top of the brown sugar mixture in the pan, forming 15 rolls. Drizzle with remaining brown sugar mixture.

Cover; let rise in a warm place for 45–60 minutes or until light and doubled in bulk. Bake for 30–35 minutes or until golden. Let stand a few minutes; remove from pan. Yields 15 honey-buns.

Apple Orchard Cookbook (Massachusetts)

Ice Cream Strudel

½ pound butter, melted
½ pint vanilla ice cream,
  softened
2 cups flour

1 (16-ounce) jar apricot
  preserves
Chopped nuts
Raisins (optional)

Melt butter, mix with ice cream and flour, and form into soft ball. Refrigerate at least 1 hour (overnight if possible).

Divide into 4 parts. Roll each into rectangular sheet on floured surface. Fill with apricot preserves, nuts, and raisins, if desired, and roll like jellyroll.

Place on greased cookie sheet. Slit each roll halfway-down in 10 places. Brush with milk. Bake 45 minutes at 350°. Makes 40 pieces.

The Way to a Man's Heart (Pennsylvania)

Apple Danish Bars

2½ cups all-purpose flour
1 teaspoon salt
1 cup shortening
1 egg, separated
1 cup cornflakes
8 cups sliced peeled apples

1 teaspoon lemon juice
¾ cup sugar
1 teaspoon cinnamon
1 cup powdered sugar
4–5 teaspoons milk

Mix flour and salt in bowl. Cut in shortening until crumbly. Combine egg yolk with water to measure ⅔ cup. Add to flour mixture; mix well. Roll half the dough to fit a 10x15-inch baking pan. Fit over bottom and sides of pan. Sprinkle with cornflakes. Layer apples over cornflakes. Sprinkle with lemon juice and mixture of sugar and cinnamon. Top with remaining pastry. Seal edges; slash top. Brush with slightly beaten egg white. Bake at 350° for 50 minutes. Mix powdered sugar and milk in bowl. Drizzle over top while warm. Cool. Cut into bars. Yields 36 bars. Can do ahead; easy; can freeze.

Laurels to the Cook (Pennsylvania)

Cheese Blintzes

¾ cup flour
1 tablespoon baking powder
½ teaspoon salt
2 tablespoons sugar

2 large eggs
⅔ cup milk
⅓ cup water
½ teaspoon vanilla

In medium bowl, sift flour, baking powder, salt, and sugar. In a small mixing bowl, beat eggs slightly. Add milk, water, and vanilla. Beat until combined. Gradually beat liquid mixture into sifted dry ingredients. Continue beating until smooth. Make sure all tiny lumps disappear. Over moderate heat, place an 8-inch skillet, brushed with salad oil. Pour 2 level tablespoons batter into skillet. Swirl and spread batter. Turn pancakes over and cook just slightly on other side. You must be very careful to maintain a proper temperature.

FILLING:

1 large egg
1 carton (1½ cups) dry
   cottage cheese

⅛ teaspoon cinnamon
1 teaspoon sugar
⅛ teaspoon salt

Beat egg; add cottage cheese, cinnamon, sugar, and salt. Gently beat to blend. Pour spoonful of filling into blintze. Roll up and put in a greased frying pan and brown, or bake in a large Pyrex casserole dish in a moderate oven for 20 minutes. Serve with sour cream and assorted jams and jellies.

Bobbie's Kitchen (New York)

The New York State Barge Canal System is the longest internal waterway system in any state. The development of the Erie Canal had great impact on the rest of the state. Prior to construction of the canal, New York City was the nation's fifth largest seaport, behind Boston, Baltimore, Philadelphia and New Orleans. Within 15 years of its opening, New York was the busiest port in America, moving tonnages greater than Boston, Baltimore and New Orleans combined.

Saratoga Rose Grand Marnier French Toast

3 eggs
¼ cup cream
1 teaspoon cinnamon
1 teaspoon sugar (optional)
½ teaspoon vanilla
2 jiggers Grand Marnier, divided

2 tablespoons butter or margarine
6 slices French bread
Garnish: Whipped cream, warm maple syrup, fresh strawberries, powdered sugar, and orange slices

Combine and mix eggs, cream, cinnamon, sugar, vanilla, and 1 jigger Grand Marnier. In a large sauté pan, melt butter over medium heat. Dip bread into mixture and cook in pan until golden on one side. Turn bread over and increase heat. Then either add a jigger of Grand Marnier directly and flambe, or remove pan from heat and add Grand Marnier, letting it simmer into the French toast for about 30 seconds. Garnish with fresh strawberries and orange slices and whipped cream. Sprinkle with powdered sugar and serve with warm syrup. Serves 2.

Recipes from the Children's Museum at Saratoga (New York)

Rum Raisin French Toast

¾ cup rum raisin ice cream, melted
3 large eggs, beaten
1 tablespoon dark rum
¼ teaspoon cinnamon
5 tablespoons finely ground walnuts

5 tablespoons sweet butter
6 (or more) slices raisin bread
Vermont maple syrup
Scoops of rum raisin ice cream

Combine melted ice cream, eggs, rum, cinnamon, and nuts in a bowl. Beat with a wire whisk until well mixed. Dip raisin bread into egg mixture, coating well on both sides. Sauté in butter over medium-low heat until "toasted." Serve with a scoop of rum raisin ice cream napped with Vermont maple syrup. Serves 3–4.

From the Inn's Kitchen (Vermont)

Blender Apple Pancakes

1 egg
1 tablespoon sugar
1 tablespoon soft butter
1 cup evaporated milk
1 medium apple, peeled, sliced
1 cup pancake mix

Place egg, sugar, butter, milk, and apple in blender. Blend. Add pancake mix and blend. Fry as for ordinary pancakes.

Three Rivers Cookbook I (Pennsylvania)

Rhode Island Johnnycakes

Made with white cornmeal and cooked on a hot griddle. Some Rhode Island cooks would omit the sugar, others the eggs.

3 eggs
2 cups stone-ground white
 cornmeal
2 teaspoons baking powder
2 tablespoons flour
1 teaspoon salt
2 tablespoons sugar (optional)
1 tablespoon melted butter
 or shortening
Milk (1–2 cups)

In medium bowl, beat eggs well. Add remaining ingredients, stirring in enough milk to make thin batter. Pour batter onto hot griddle (use ¼-cup measure to dip batter). Cook until brown on one side; flip and brown on other side. Serve with butter and maple syrup. Yields about 12 (4-inch) cakes.

Variation: Break completely with tradition! Try serving johnnycakes topped with smoked salmon and Crème Fraîche or sour cream; sprinkle with plenty of fresh snipped dill.

All Seasons Cookbook (Rhode Island)

 Native Americans probably taught the Pilgrims at Plymouth how to make a type of griddle cake from stone-ground cornmeal which the Indians called "jonakin." New Englanders still make this regional specialty more than 350 years later—johnny cakes! And the unequivocal ingredient in any variation is still stone-ground cornmeal.

Blueberry Hill Wild Blueberry Pancakes

This has been the most-requested breakfast entrée, as attested to by the many a "blue" smiles of guests leaving the dining room. Serve them up with Country Apple Sausage (next page) for a truly Vermont-style breakfast.

1¼ cups unbleached
   white flour
1 tablespoon sugar
1 tablespoon baking powder
½ teaspoon salt
4 eggs, separated

2 cups milk
¼ cup sweet butter, melted
1 cup wild blueberries, rinsed
   and picked over
Butter
Maple syrup

In a large mixing bowl, mix together all the dry ingredients. Set aside. Lightly beat the egg yolks, then add the milk and melted butter and mix well. Set aside.

Beat the egg whites until they form stiff—but not dry—peaks. Set aside. Make a hollow in the center of the dry ingredients. Pour in the milk mixture and blend batter well. Don't worry about a few lumps—they will work themselves out. Carefully fold in the egg whites until well incorporated. Gently stir in the blueberries.

Ladle the batter onto a lightly greased hot skillet or griddle to form 3-inch circles. Cook till bubbles form, flip, and cook until golden brown, about 1 minute. Serve with butter and heated Vermont syrup. Serves 4.

Tony Clark's New Blueberry Hill Cookbook (Vermont)

Blueberry Hill in Goshen, Vermont, is nestled at the foot of Romance Mountain in the Green Mountain National Forest. The inn, a restored 1813 farmhouse boasts spectacular panoramic views. When in season, you can pick all the sun-ripened blueberries you can eat.

Buttery Waffles

4 eggs
2 cups all-purpose flour
1 teaspoon salt
1 teaspoon baking soda

1 teaspoon baking powder
1 cup milk
1 cup sour cream
1 cup butter, melted

Preheat waffle iron. Beat eggs until light. Sift together flour, salt, soda, and baking powder. Mix milk and sour cream. Add flour mixture and milk mixture alternately to beaten eggs, beginning and ending with flour mixture. Add melted butter; blend thoroughly.

For each waffle, pour batter into center of lower half of waffle iron until it spreads to 1 inch from edge—about ½ cup. Lower iron cover on batter; cook as manufacturer directs, or until waffle iron stops steaming. Carefully loosen edge of waffle with fork; remove.

Cool. Place waxed paper between waffles. Freeze in airtight container. To serve, remove from freezer and toast until heated through.

Dining on Deck (Vermont)

Country Apple Sausage

Make a special breakfast even more special by presenting these sausages baked with apples. They're easy to serve to a crowd, as you can prepare them ahead of time just to the point when you'd put them in the oven. Another bonus is the drippings—they're delicious, and can be used to baste other meats.

4 large sweet Italian pork
  sausages
3 Cortland apples, cored and
  cut into wedges

⅓ cup Vermont made syrup

Preheat the oven to 400°. In a heavy skillet, with no fat added, sauté the sausages over medium to high heat until brown. Transfer the sausages to a small baking dish, cover them with the apple wedges, and drizzle with the maple syrup. Cover and bake for 10 minutes. Decrease the temperature to 350° and continue baking until done, about 15–20 minutes. (The apples should not fall apart.) Serves 4.

Tony Clark's New Blueberry Hill Cookbook (Vermont)

Sausage Whirls

1 pound hot bulk sausage
½ cup chopped onion
1 tablespoon oil
2 cups flour

½ teaspoon salt
3 teaspoons baking powder
5 tablespoons butter
⅔ cup milk

In a large fry pan, sauté sausage and onion in 1 tablespoon oil until browned. Set aside. In a large bowl, combine flour, salt, and baking powder. Cut in butter with pastry blender until mixture resembles coarse crumbs. Stir in milk to make soft dough. Divide dough in half. Roll out each half on a floured surface making 2 (10x15-inch) rectangles ½-inch thick. Spread evenly with sausage and onion. Roll up as for jellyroll. Seal edges.

Wrap in plastic wrap and freeze until ready to use. Thaw bread and preheat oven to 400°. Bake "loaves" on greased baking sheet 10 minutes until golden. Cool 10 minutes before slicing. Serve warm. Makes 40 pieces.

Moveable Feasts Cookbook (Connecticut)

Eggs Kennett Square

1½ cups hash brown
  potatoes, frozen
½ cup diced onions
½ pound fresh mushrooms
½ cup shredded Cheddar

4 eggs, beaten
½ cup half-and-half
Salsa for garnish

In a skillet, brown hash brown potatoes and onions in hot oil. Slice and sauté mushrooms. Grease 2 (8-ounce) casserole dishes. Arrange potatoes and onions evenly in dishes. Top with mushrooms. Sprinkle with cheese. In a small mixing bowl, beat eggs and half-and-half. Pour egg mixture over potato/mushroom/cheese mixture. Bake, uncovered, at 350° for about 25 minutes or until centers appear set. Let stand 5 minutes. Garnish with salsa. Makes 2 servings.

Note: This recipe is very flexible—can be made with bacon, sausage, peppers, artichoke hearts, or tomatoes.

Submitted by Kennett House Bed & Breakfast, Kennett Square
Inncredible Edibles (Pennsylvania)

Swiss Baked Eggs

Baked eggs with a fondue-like flavor make an appealing breakfast for 6 with French bread toast and café au lait or hot chocolate.

¼ pound Swiss cheese,
  thinly sliced
1 green onion, thinly sliced
1 tablespoon chopped parsley
6 eggs
Salt

Ground nutmeg
Freshly ground pepper
¼ cup whipping cream
2 tablespoons dry white wine
French bread slices, hot,
  buttered, toasted

Preheat oven to 325°. Line sides and bottom of a generously buttered, shallow 1½-quart baking dish (about 8x12-inches) with cheese. Sprinkle evenly with onion and parsley. Break eggs carefully into dish and sprinkle lightly with salt, nutmeg, and pepper.

In medium bowl, beat cream with wine just until well blended; pour around and between eggs. Bake, uncovered, until eggs are set to your liking (12–18 minutes). Place eggs on hot, buttered, toasted French bread slices. Stir any melted cheese and cream remaining in baking dish until smooth; spoon over eggs. Makes 6 servings.

Recipe from Adam Bowman Manor Bed & Breakfast, Utica
Bed & Breakfast Leatherstocking Welcome Home Recipe Collection (New York)

Fruit and Nut Granola

½ cup canola oil
½ cup honey
6 cups oatmeal, not
  quick-cooking
1 cup raw wheat germ

1 cup raw sunflower seeds
1 cup chopped or sliced nuts
Chopped dried fruits
  (optional)

In a very large pot, heat oil and honey just until blended. Stir in remaining ingredients except for dried fruits. Spread out on 2 cookie sheets and bake in preheated 250° oven until golden brown, about 50–60 minutes. Remove from oven and separate grains by pressing with back of a wooden spoon. Cool. Dried fruits can be added at this point. Place in jars with tight-fitting lids and keep refrigerated. Can be frozen. Yields 24–30 servings.

Specialties of the House (New York)

Apple Butter

The wonderful aroma while making this Apple Butter will bring back memories of years gone by. The flavor is the same, with much less work.

12 pounds tart cooking apples, peeled, cored, and quartered (in the fall, use Winesap apples)

2 cups water
3½ cups granulated sugar
1 cup cider vinegar
1 teaspoon cinnamon

Cook the apples and water in a pan over low heat until soft, about 20 minutes. Rub through a food mill.

Add the sugar, cider vinegar, and cinnamon, mixing well. Put mixture in a heavy roaster pan, uncovered, and cook in a preheated 375° oven for approximately 2½ hours, stirring every 15 minutes with a wooden spoon. The Apple Butter is thick enough when you can put 2 tablespoons of the mixture on a saucer and turn it upside down without it dropping off. Ladle into hot sterilized pint or quart jars and seal. Makes about 3½ quarts, or 7 pints.

Betty Groff's Up-Home Down-Home Cookbook (Pennsylvania)

Vermont Blueberry Sauce

A simple but delicious sauce with many uses; on vanilla ice cream, orange sherbet, pound cake or angel food, pancakes or johnnycakes, sliced fresh peaches or nectarines, or frozen lemon mousse.

1½ cups blueberries,   **¾ teaspoon cinnamon**
  fresh or frozen   **¼ teaspoon nutmeg**
¼ cup sugar

Combine all ingredients in saucepan over low heat; cook, stirring frequently, for about 10 minutes. Serve warm or cold. Yields about 2 cups.

All Seasons Cookbook (Connecticut)

Soft Pretzels

Take the dough to children's worship and let them create their own shapes (letters, animals, braids). The "pretzels" can bake during the fellowship meal and be ready for dessert.

PRETZELS:
2 tablespoons yeast   **¼ cup margarine**
2 cups warm water   **1 egg**
½ cup sugar   **6½ cups flour, divided**

Dissolve yeast in warm water. Beat sugar, margarine, egg, and yeast mixture with several cups flour. Knead in the remaining flour. Cover dough with aluminum foil and refrigerate from 2–24 hours. Divide dough into 16 pieces. Roll into 20-inch-long strips and shape into Pretzels. Place on greased cookie sheet.

TOPPING:
1 egg yolk   **Coarse salt**
2 tablespoons water

Combine egg yolk and water and brush each Pretzel. Sprinkle with coarse salt. Let rise 20 minutes. Bake at 350° for 20 minutes. Makes 16 servings.

The Best of Mennonite Fellowship Meals (Pennsylvania)

Westside Bruschetta

1 baguette with sesame seeds
4–6 tablespoons extra virgin olive oil
1 tablespoon minced garlic
1 tablespoon Romano cheese
¼ teaspoon ground black pepper
1 red bell pepper, cut into ¼-inch pieces
1 yellow bell pepper, cut into ¼-inch pieces
2 plum tomatoes, cut into ¼-inch slices

3 green onions, cut into ¼-inch slices
½ cup shredded mozzarella, asiago or gorgonzola cheese
4 ounces mushrooms, cut into ⅛-inch slices
4 ounces prosciutto or smoked ham, cut into ½-inch strips
Freshly grated Pecorino Romano cheese

Slice the baguette lengthwise into halves. Place cut-side-up on a baking sheet. Combine the olive oil, garlic, 1 tablespoon Romano cheese and pepper in a bowl and mix well. Spread over the cut sides of the bread halves. Arrange the bell peppers, tomatoes and green onions on each bread half. Sprinkle with the mozzarella cheese. Top with the mushrooms and prosciutto. Bake at 350° for 5–10 minutes or until the cheese melts. Broil for 2–3 minutes or just until the cheese begins to brown. Cut into 2-inch slices. Sprinkle with freshly grated Romano cheese. Serves 4–6.

Great Lake Effects (New York)

The Society Hill's Philadelphia Phenomenon Cheese Steak

1 (8-inch) round Italian roll
2 tablespoons vegetable oil
6 ounces thinly sliced steak
2 slices cheese (American, mozzarella, or provolone)
2 tablespoons or more water
1 tablespoon chopped, sautéed onion (optional)
1 tablespoon chopped, sautéed green pepper (optional)
1 tablespoon chopped, sautéed mushrooms (optional)
1 slice bacon, fried and crumbled (optional)
1 tablespoon chopped artichoke heart (optional)
1–2 tablespoons commercial pizza sauce (optional)

Cut roll in half and hollow out. Heat roll in a 250° oven until warm, approximately 4–5 minutes. Heat oil on grill or in frying pan. When oil is hot, sizzle steak. (Break steak apart for faster cooking.) When steak has cooked for 10–15 seconds, place cheese on top; add water to grill or frying pan to aid cheese in melting. Remove from grill or pan; stuff roll with steak and cheese and any or all of the optional toppings. Serves 1.

Pennsylvania's Historic Restaurants and Their Recipes (Pennsylvania)

Pennsylvanians Pat and Harry Olivieri are often credited with inventing the Philly Cheesesteak sandwich by serving chopped steak on hoagie rolls in the early 1930s. They began selling this variation of steak sandwiches at their hot dog stand near south Philadelphia's Italian Market. They became so popular that Pat opened up his own restaurant which still operates today as Pat's King of Steaks. Variations of cheesesteaks are now common in several fast food chains. Versions of the sandwich can also be found in locations ranging from bars to high-end restaurants.

Short-Cut Pepperoni Bread

1 loaf frozen bread dough	1 egg
½ pound Swiss cheese, sliced	Grated Parmesan cheese
½ pound pepperoni, thinly sliced	

Thaw dough according to package directions and let rise. After dough has risen, cut in half; roll out each half as thin as possible. Layer with Swiss cheese and pepperoni. Beat egg and spread thinly over pepperoni and cheese. Sprinkle with Parmesan cheese. Roll into loaves. Bake at 350° for 30 minutes or until golden brown. Yields 15 slices.

Philadelphia Homestyle Cookbook (Pennsylvania)

Stromboli

Hungry teenagers will make this disappear.

1 loaf frozen bread dough	1 small onion, sliced thin
¼ pound provolone cheese, grated	1 teaspoon oregano
¼ pound American cheese, grated	½ teaspoon pepper
½ pound pepperoni or salami, sliced thin	½ teaspoon garlic powder
1 large tomato, cut in chunks (optional)	½ cup grated Parmesan cheese
	2 tablespoons olive oil

Defrost and raise bread dough according to package directions. Roll out dough to ½-inch thickness. Spread provolone and American cheese over dough, keeping ½ inch from edge. Spread pepperoni next. Top with tomato, onion rings, seasonings, and Parmesan cheese. Sprinkle olive oil over all. Roll as you would a jellyroll and seal the edges. Rub with olive oil, puncture with fork, and place on oiled cookie sheet. Bake at 350° for 30–40 minutes. Yields 4–6 servings.

Hint: Add other sliced meats if you enjoy a meatier sandwich.

The Eater's Digest (Pennsylvania)

Soups, Chilis, and Stews

HISTORICBUILDINGSCT.COM

The New London Harbor Lighthouse was built in 1801 and is the oldest surviving lighthouse in Connecticut. With its octagonal, brick-lined brownstone tower rising to 89 feet, it is also the state's tallest lighthouse. New London Harbor Light is still an active aid to navigation.

Potato Rivel Soup

This is another dish great for those cold winter evenings.

1 medium onion, chopped	2 eggs, beaten
5 medium potatoes, peeled, diced	1 teaspoon salt
	½ cup butter
Salt and pepper to taste	⅛ teaspoon celery seed
Water	1–1½ quarts milk
Flour	Chopped parsley

Cook first 3 ingredients in water to cover until potatoes are soft. To make rivels, add flour to eggs and salt, and toss and stir until mixture is lumpy and almost dry. Sift out excess flour, then dump rivels into potato mixture and boil 15 minutes. Add butter, celery seed, milk, and a pinch of parsley. Heat soup and serve it.

Amish Cooking (Pennsylvania)

Cream of Potato and Ham Soup

5 tablespoons butter	4 chicken bouillon cubes
1 medium onion, chopped	4 cups water
5 large carrots, peeled and sliced	2 cups milk
10 large potatoes, peeled, cut in cubes	3 cups ham, cubed

Melt butter in pot and add onion and carrots and cook until softened. Add potatoes, bouillon, and water. Cook covered until bubbly, then simmer for 1 hour. Take about half of soup mixture and blend in processor or blender until puréed and smooth. Return to pot; add milk slowly, stirring. Add ham and heat thoroughly. Serves 10 or more.

Our Daily Bread, and then some... (New York)

Savory Mushroom Soup

12 ounces mushrooms, thinly
  sliced
2 tablespoons garlic, minced
1 leek with green portion,
  chopped
1 medium onion, chopped
2 ribs celery, chopped
1 bay leaf

2 tablespoons butter
2 tablespoons flour
2 (14-ounce) cans chicken
  broth
1 teaspoon lemon juice
2 cups half-and-half
Pepper and salt to taste

Sauté mushrooms, garlic, leek, onion, celery, and bay leaf in butter until soft. Stir in flour; when hot, slowly add the broth and lemon juice. Simmer 30 minutes. Remove bay leaf, stir in cream, reheat, adjust the seasonings, and serve. Serves 4.

More Than Delicious (Pennsylvania)

Brie Soup

2½ pounds Brie cheese
  (about ½ of large wheel)
1 quart hot chicken stock
  or broth
2 tablespoons butter
1 cup julienned carrots

1¼ cups fresh sliced
  mushrooms
1 cup sliced green onions
¼ cup dry sherry
2 cups heavy cream

After removing the crust from Brie, dissolve in hot chicken stock in large saucepan. Strain. Melt butter in Dutch oven over low heat. Add carrots, mushrooms, and green onions, and sauté until tender. Add cheese mixture. Stir in sherry and cream. Serve hot. Serves 6.

Three Rivers Cookbook III (Pennsylvania)

Spicy Carrot Peanut Soup

This thick soup when served with a crisp salad makes an interesting meal. Rich and aromatic, the flavor combination was inspired by African and Southeast Asian cuisines. It's one of our favorites at Moosewood.

1 tablespoon canola or other vegetable oil	1 teaspoon Chinese chili paste*
1 large onion, thinly sliced (about 2 cups)	6 cups water
2 pounds carrots, peeled and thinly sliced (about 6 cups)	2 tablespoons peanut butter
1 celery stalk, thinly sliced	3 tablespoons soy sauce
1 teaspoon salt	2 tablespoons fresh lime juice
	A few fresh lime wedges

In a soup pot on medium heat, warm the oil and add the onions, carrots, celery, salt, and chili paste (*or use 1 fresh chile stemmed and chopped and 2 minced garlic cloves). Sauté on high heat for 5 minutes, stirring often. Add the water, cover, and bring to a boil. Lower the heat and simmer until the carrots are soft, about 25 minutes. Stir in the peanut butter, soy sauce, and lime juice. In a blender, purée the soup in batches. Reheat, if necessary. Serve with lime wedges. Serves 6–8.

Note: If you wish, replace the peanut butter with freshly ground peanuts. Grind ½ cup unsalted roasted peanuts in a blender or small food processor and add them to the soup just before puréeing it.

Variation: Try serving the soup cold. It's not your usual chilled soup candidate, but we like it!

Moosewood Restaurant Daily Special (New York)

New York City is nearly four centuries old, older than most American cities. And more than half of all people living in America today are descended from immigrants who entered this country through New York harbor.

Cream of Broccoli Soup

10 ounces chopped broccoli, fresh or frozen
1 cup milk
½ teaspoon salt

1 (10¾-ounce) can Cheddar cheese soup
1 cup milk or cream

Cook broccoli in boiling water until tender. Drain. Put broccoli with the milk, salt, and soup in a blender. Add milk or cream and heat, but do not boil.

Society of Farm Women of Pennsylvania Cookbook (Pennsylvania)

Tomato Cognac Soup

No doubt, this is one of our most popular soups and an honored classic.

1 large Spanish onion
3 ounces butter
3 pounds canned, peeled plum tomatoes
1 tablespoon dried basil
1 pint heavy or all-purpose cream

1–2 tablespoons dark brown sugar
5 tablespoons cognac
Salt and pepper to taste
Minced parsley for garnish

Chop the onion and sauté in butter for 20 minutes until soft and translucent but not brown. With your fingers, squash the tomatoes; add them and all the liquid in the can to the onion. Add the basil and stir. Bring the soup to a boil, then simmer, covered, for 30 minutes. Set aside and cool slightly, then purée the soup in a food processor.

In a small saucepan heat the cream with the sugar, whisking often. Pour this mixture into the soup. Reheat, but do not boil. Just before serving, add the cognac and season with salt and pepper. Garnish with parsley and serve. Just great! Serves 6.

Recipes from a New England Inn (Maine)

Champagne Onion Soup

Serve with French bread and a glass of Swedish Hill Blanc de Blanc Champagne.

3 cups finely chopped white onions
4 tablespoons butter
5 cups beef stock

2 cups Swedish Hill Blanc de Blanc Champagne
Salt and pepper to taste

Quick and easy. In a large sauté pan, cook the onions in the butter until they are soft. Put the onions in a large pot, add the stock, champagne and salt and pepper. Bring to a boil, lower the heat and simmer, covered for 3 minutes. Serves 6.

Uncork New York! Wine Country Cookbook (New York)

Italian Vegetable Soup

1 pound ground beef
1 cup diced onion
1 cup sliced celery
1 cup sliced carrots
2 cloves garlic, minced
1 (16-ounce) can tomatoes, undrained
1 (15-ounce) can tomato sauce
1 (15-ounce) can kidney beans
2 cups water

5 teaspoons beef bouillon granules
1 tablespoon dried parsley
1 teaspoon salt
½ teaspoon oregano
½ teaspoon basil
¼ teaspoon black pepper
2 cups shredded cabbage
1 cup frozen or fresh green beans, cut into 1-inch pieces
½ cup elbow macaroni
Parmesan cheese

Brown beef in large kettle; drain. Add all ingredients except cabbage, green beans, macaroni, and Parmesan. Bring to boil. Lower heat and simmer 20 minutes. Add cabbage, green beans, and macaroni; bring to boil and simmer until vegetables are tender. Sprinkle with Parmesan cheese before serving. Serves 12.

Great Taste of Parkminster (New York)

Potage de Vermont

This smooth and creamy soup does justice to our wonderful Vermont Cheddar cheese. Although I always served it as a first course, it would make a delicious dinner of its own, accompanied by a loaf of crusty bread and a simple salad.

2 tablespoons sweet butter
½ cup chopped carrots
½ cup chopped onion
½ cup chopped fresh dill weed
½ cup chopped celery
5 tablespoons unbleached white flour

5 cups chicken stock
3 cups grated Vermont Cheddar cheese
2 cups half-and-half
Salt and freshly ground white pepper to taste
Toasted sesame seeds for garnish

Sauté the carrots, onion, dill, and celery in the butter in a large saucepan. Sprinkle in the flour 1 tablespoon at a time, stirring after each addition.

Add the stock. Bring to a boil over medium heat, and cook for about 5 minutes. Strain out the vegetables, purée them in a food processor fitted with a steel blade, then return the puréed vegetables to the stock. Continue to cook over medium heat until the soup boils, then reduce the heat and let it simmer slowly for 15 minutes. Add the grated cheese, stirring constantly with a large wire whisk until it is melted. Slowly add the half-and-half and stir until well blended. Add the salt and pepper to taste. Serve at once garnished with the toasted sesame seeds. Serves 8.

Tony Clark's New Blueberry Hill Cookbook (Vermont)

White Bean with Roasted Garlic Soup

2 cups navy or white beans (cleaned well)	1 large onion (diced)
4–5 cups water or stock	1 bay leaf
1 bulb fresh garlic	1 tablespoon dried thyme leaves
2 tablespoons oil	Salt and pepper to taste
2 carrots (peeled and diced)	

Soak beans overnight in water. Drain and rinse well in colander. Place in a soup pot with water or stock. Bring to a boil, then simmer for 1–1½ hours, skimming the surface from time to time. Separate the bulb of garlic into individual cloves, keeping skin on. Toss garlic in oil and wrap loosely in aluminum foil. Roast in a 450° oven for 10–15 minutes or until cloves become soft. Cool. Add prepared vegetables, bay leaf, thyme, and salt and pepper, to the beans. Squeeze the cloves out of their skins and mash with a fork. Stir into the soup. Simmer until vegetables are tender. Add more liquid if too thick. Serve with unseasoned croutons. Yields 6–8 servings.

Washington Street Eatery Cook Book (New Hampshire)

New Hampshire has held a presidential primary since 1916, as part of the process of choosing the Democratic and Republican nominees for the presidential elections to be held the subsequent November. Since 1920, the New Hampshire primary has been the first in a series of nationwide political party primary elections held every four years. The primary has been considered an early measurement of the national attitude toward the candidates for nomination. Unlike a caucus, the primary measures the number of votes each candidate received directly, rather than through precinct delegates. The popular vote gives lesser-known candidates a chance to demonstrate their appeal to the electorate at large.   Until the 1992 elections, no candidate had ever won the presidency without first winning in New Hampshire. Bill Clinton broke the pattern in 1992, as did George W. Bush in 2000, and Barack Obama in 2008.

Hearty French Market Bean Soup

1 pound assorted beans
2 quarts water
1 quart chicken stock
1 tablespoon salt
1 ham hock
2 bay leaves
½ teaspoon dried thyme
1 (28-ounce) can tomatoes, chopped

2 cups chopped onions
2 cups chopped celery
1 clove garlic, mashed
8 ounces smoked sausage, sliced
8 ounces chicken breast, diced

Wash and soak beans at least 2 hours, preferably overnight.

In a large soup kettle, combine beans, water, stock, salt, ham hock, bay leaves, and thyme. Cover and simmer for 2½–3 hours. Add tomatoes, onions, and celery. Cover and simmer 1½ hours. Add garlic, sausage, and chicken. Cover and simmer 40 minutes. Serve. Makes 10–12 servings.

Favorite Recipes from Quilters (Pennsylvania)

Corn Chowder

3 large potatoes, peeled and cut into chunks
1 large onion, cut into chunks
1 large can whole kernel corn

1 can creamed corn
1–2 cans whole milk
2–3 tablespoons butter
Salt and pepper to taste

Cut potatoes into small chunks and boil until tender, not mushy, and drain. Sauté onion. Add onion to drained potatoes. Add corn, milk, butter, salt and pepper. Stir and heat thoroughly; do not allow it to boil. Serve with warm crusty bread and crisp tossed salad for a hearty lunch.

Note: Cream of potato soup can be added for additional body. More corn can be added, if desired. Some people like to add leftover ham or crumbled bacon.

Fabulous Feasts from First United (New York)

Fresh Corn and She-Crab Chowder

10 ears fresh corn, husked and shucked (reserve cobs)
4 cups milk
2 bay leaves
¼ cup diced salt pork
¼ cup diced hickory-smoked bacon
½ pound butter
¼ cup diced onions
¼ cup diced carrots
¼ cup diced celery
¼ cup each: diced red, green, and, yellow bell peppers
½ cup flour

1 quart fresh or bottled clam juice
3 pounds fresh or frozen crabmeat
½ cup white potato, blanched, peeled, and diced
1 (12- to 14-ounce) can creamed corn
2 tablespoons chopped parsley
1 teaspoon fresh basil
1 teaspoon fresh thyme
Pinch of dried oregano
Salt and white pepper to taste

Place the shucked corn cobs in a large pan and cover them with the milk. Add the bay leaves, bring to a boil, and reduce the heat to a simmer. Cook for 15 minutes, strain, and reserve the liquid.

In a large soup pot, render the diced salt pork and bacon over low heat until just crisp. Add the butter and diced onions, carrots, and celery. Sweat the vegetables over low heat for 5 minutes. Add the diced peppers and continue to sweat the mixture over low heat for 3 minutes. With the heat still low, dust the vegetables with the flour, stirring constantly, making a roux; cook for 15 minutes, stirring occasionally. Add clam juice, increase heat to medium, and continue to cook for 5–10 minutes.

Add the fresh corn kernels, cooked diced potatoes, and creamed corn, and continue to cook over moderate heat for 15 minutes, stirring occasionally. Add the strained reserved milk and the chopped crabmeat. Cook the chowder for 5 minutes, adding the herbs, spices, salt and pepper to taste. Garnish with shreds of lobster meat. Serves 8–10.

The Regatta of Cotuit recipe, Cotuit
A Taste of Cape Cod (Massachusetts)

Clam Chowder

I think our clam chowder is the best in the business—and the public certainly agrees. We sell about 700 gallons of clam chowder each week at our restaurants and take-out counters. The reason for its popularity is simple. We use only the best ingredients and plenty of them. Don't try and economize by cutting back on the amount of clams or cream because the chowder will never taste as flavorful as ours.

**4 quarts littleneck clams
    (about 1⅔ cups, cooked
    and chopped)**
1 clove garlic, chopped
1 cup water
**2 ounces salt pork, finely
    chopped**
2 cups chopped onions

3 tablespoons flour
4½ cups clam broth
3 cups fish stock
**1½ pounds potatoes, peeled
    and diced into ½-inch cubes**
2 cups light cream
Oyster crackers (optional)

Clean the clams and place them in a large pot along with the garlic and water. Steam the clams just until opened, about 6–10 minutes, depending upon their size. Drain and shell the clams, reserving the broth. Mince the clam flesh and set aside. Filter the clam broth either through coffee filters or cheesecloth and set aside.

In a large, heavy pot slowly render the salt pork. Remove the cracklings and set them aside. Slowly cook the onions in the fat for about 6 minutes, stirring frequently, or until cooked through but not browned. Stir in the flour and cook, stirring, for 3 minutes. Add the reserved clam broth and fish stock, and whisk to remove any flour lumps. Bring the liquid to a boil, add the potatoes, lower the heat, and simmer until the potatoes are cooked through, about 15 minutes.

Stir in the reserved clams, salt-pork cracklings, and light cream. Heat the chowder until it is the temperature you prefer. Serve in large soup bowls with oyster crackers on the side. Serves 8.

The Legal Sea Foods Cookbook (Massachusetts)

Connecticut Coastline Seafood Chowder

You can't beat the powerful aroma of this chowder simmering on the stove on a chilly afternoon.

CHOWDER BASE:

¼ pound diced salt pork
2 large onions, peeled and chopped
2 leeks, cleaned and sliced
1 rib celery, sliced
1 cup water
2 cups Doxie clam juice or fish stock

3 cups peeled and diced potatoes
1 tablespoon chopped parsley
½ teaspoon oregano
½ teaspoon thyme
1 bay leaf, broken in half
Freshly ground pepper

Cook the salt pork in a large soup kettle over medium heat until fat is rendered and pork is crisp. Add onions and leeks and sauté for 4 minutes. Add remaining chowder base ingredients to the pot, bring to the boil, reduce heat and simmer, covered, for about 15 minutes or until potatoes are tender. Cool base and chill overnight if possible.

INGREDIENTS TO FINISH CHOWDER:

½ pound bay scallops
½ pound firm white fish, cubed
3 dozen quahogs (or any kind of clams), coarsely chopped

4 cups light cream
Few drops Tabasco
2 tablespoons unsalted butter

Return pot to stove and bring base to a simmer. Add seafood, including any clam liquor, and simmer for 3 minutes. Add remaining ingredients and cook over low heat until just heated through. Serve chowder immediately. Yields 8 servings.

Off the Hook (Connecticut)

Broccoli and Crab Bisque

Good for weight-watchers and cholesterol-counters. Tastes creamy and elegant—but good for you!

1 head broccoli
4 potatoes
1½ cups diced carrots
1 pound crabmeat
  (imitation) or sea legs
1½ cups chopped onion
2 teaspoons margarine or oil
5 cups broth (fish, chicken,
  or vegetable)

¾ cup chopped celery
½ teaspoon black pepper
1 teaspoon lemon juice
¼ teaspoon thyme
1 bay leaf
¾ teaspoon or less salt
2 cups skim milk

Slice broccoli stems crosswise and reserve flowerets. Peel and dice potatoes and carrots. Slice crabmeat into ½-inch pieces.

Sauté onion in margarine until soft. Add broth (fish bouillon cubes best), broccoli stems, half of potatoes and carrots, celery, pepper, lemon juice, thyme, bay leaf, and salt. Bring to boil, reduce heat, simmer for 15 minutes or until vegetables are tender.

Remove bay leaf. Purée vegetables and broth in blender. Return purée to pot. Add remaining half of diced potatoes and carrots; cook soup over low heat about 10 minutes or until vegetables are tender.

Add broccoli flowerets and cook for 5–10 minutes until broccoli is tender-crisp. Add milk and crabmeat; heat but do not boil. Serve with favorite croutons, if desired.

The Marborough Meetinghouse Cookbook (Connecticut)

On October 9, 1701 the Collegiate School of Connecticut was chartered in Old Saybrook. It moved to New Haven in 1716, and was later renamed Yale University.

Turkey, Vegetable, and Bean Chili

3 tablespoons olive oil, divided
2 pounds ground turkey, preferably breast meat
2 large yellow onions, chopped
8 cloves garlic, minced
2 (28-ounce) cans peeled tomatoes, chopped
½ can beer
1 (10-ounce) can pinto beans
1 (10-ounce) can kidney beans
1 (10-ounce) can chick-peas
2 tablespoons ketchup
½ cup chopped green pepper
1 cup chopped carrots
1 cup chopped squash
1 cup chopped zucchini
1 tablespoon cumin, or to taste
2 tablespoons chili powder, or to taste
1 teaspoon salt, or to taste
¼ teaspoon cayenne pepper, or to taste

In a large skillet, heat 1 tablespoon olive oil, and brown ground turkey until it is cooked through. Pour off fat and place turkey on paper towel to absorb additional fat. Heat remaining 2 tablespoons olive oil in a large pot over medium heat. Add onions and garlic and cook for 1 minute. Add turkey and tomatoes, and stir to combine. Add beer, pinto beans, kidney beans, chick-peas, ketchup, green pepper, carrots, squash, and zucchini. Add cumin, chili powder, salt, and cayenne. Partially cover and simmer for 45 minutes, stirring frequently. Serves 8–10.

Note: If you don't have all the ingredients on hand, feel free to make substitutions. You can use all of one kind of beans; and leave out a vegetable, if you like—just add more of another vegetable to compensate.

La Cocina de la Familia (New York)

New York City Transit: How many stations? From the original 28 stations built in Manhattan and opened on October 27, 1904, the subway system has grown to 468 stations, most of which were built by 1930. How much track? Laid end to end, tracks would stretch from New York City to Chicago (more than 800, counting subway yards). Riders? In 2009, average weekday subway riders totaled 5.1 million, the second highest daily number since 1952. Subway cars? There are roughly 6,380 subway cars making an average of 8,279 trips daily. Miles traveled? The average number of miles traveled by an average subway car in 1982 was 7,145 miles; in 2009, it was 153,201.

Peter's Red Hot Chili

3 tablespoons oil
2 pounds stew beef
5 cups water
1 diced green pepper
1 diced onion
1 diced tomato
1½ tablespoons salt
2 teaspoons cayenne pepper

1 tablespoon granulated
  garlic
¼ cup chili powder
2 tablespoons cumin
1½ cups water
⅓ cup cornmeal
1 (6-ounce) can tomato paste

Brown beef in oil. Add next 9 ingredients and simmer for 2 hours. In a small bowl mix the water, cornmeal, and tomato paste. Stir cornmeal mixture into chili to thicken. Simmer another 20 minutes. Garnish with sliced raw onions and grated Monterey Jack cheese. Serves 4.

Peter Christian's Recipes (Maine)

Lobster Stew

The lobster feed is enjoyed by inlanders as well as those on the coast. One of the delicious aftermaths of a lobster feed is a lobster stew. The coral (eggs in some lobsters) and tomalley (lobster liver) add good flavor, plus the meat from claws and body of the crustacean, picked by patient lobster "pickers." We find that it takes about 5 (¼-pound) lobsters to make 1 pound or 3 cups of clear meat.

¼–½ cup butter or
  margarine
2–3 cups lobster meat

2 quarts milk
Salt and pepper to season
Coral and tomalley

In a kettle, melt butter over low heat and sauté the lobster meat, stirring until meat is pink in color. Add milk and continue cooking, stirring frequently. Reduce heat; do not boil. A double boiler at this stage is recommended. The stew will have blossomed to a rosy color. Add tomalley and coral. Heat to serve hot. Many cooks prepare the stew early in the day, refrigerate and reheat when needed.

Memories from Brownie's Kitchen (Maine)

Cape Cod Oyster Stew

1 quart oysters with their liquor
½ cup butter
3 cups hot milk
1 cup hot cream
Seasoned salt and pepper to taste
Paprika

Heat the oysters in a heavy kettle just until the edges begin to curl, adding the butter as they begin to heat. Add milk and cream and seasonings. Turn the heat off as the milk and cream are added. When the oysters begin to rise in the stew, serve at once in heated bowls with paprika on top. Serves 4.

My Own Cook Book (Massachusetts)

Holiday Beef Stew

Serve with Brotherhood Merlot.

2½ pounds beef cubes (shoulder or chuck)
Vegetable oil
1 can Campbell's Tomato Soup (condensed)
1 envelope Lipton Dry Onion Soup Mix
2 cups boiling water
1 empty soup can filled with Brotherhood Holiday Spiced Wine
Fresh string beans (optional)
4 quartered potatoes and/or yams
4 carrots, cut in chunks
Frozen green peas (optional)

Brown cubed beef in oil. Add soups, boiling water and 1 soup can filled with wine. Add fresh string beans, if desired. Cover and simmer 1½ hours. Add potatoes and carrots. Cook approximately 45 minutes until vegetables are soft. Add frozen peas and heat through. Serves 4–6.

Uncork New York! Wine Country Cookbook (New York)

Salads

PHOTO BY GWEN McKEE

An Amish horse and buggy travel along a Pennsylvania country road that twists among acres of picture-perfect farmland. The Amish are known for their plain dress and avoidance of modern conveniences such as cars and electricity. They came to the area in the 18th and 19th centuries for the freedom of religion offered by William Penn, and were attracted by the rich soil and mild climate.

Strawberry Spinach Salad with Poppy Seed Dressing

DRESSING:

½ cup mayonnaise
½ cup sour cream
1 tablespoon poppy seed
1 tablespoon honey

1 tablespoon orange juice
1 teaspoon grated orange rind
¼ teaspoon ground ginger

Thoroughly mix all Dressing ingredients. Chill several hours to blend flavors.

SALAD:

10–12 ounces fresh spinach
2 small oranges, peeled,
  sliced

2 cups halved strawberries
⅓ cup sliced, toasted almonds

Wash and drain spinach and tear it into bite-sized pieces. Arrange in large bowl. Top with orange slices, strawberries, and almonds. Drizzle Dressing over Salad. Makes 6–8 servings.

VARIATION FOR POPPY SEED DRESSING:

½ cup sugar
2 tablespoons sesame seeds
1 tablespoon poppy seeds
1½ teaspoons minced
  green onion

¼ teaspoon Worcestershire
¼ teaspoon paprika
½ cup cooking oil
¼ cup cider vinegar

Thoroughly mix all ingredients. Chill and drizzle over salad.

The Best of Mennonite Fellowship Meals (Pennsylvania)

Of all the ethnic groups and religions that came to Pennsylvania for freedom—Anabaptists, Quakers, Mennonites, Dunkards, Moravians, Schwenkfelders—only the Amish (Anabaptists) and Mennonites of the Pennsylvania Dutch country in the east-central section have kept their individual identity.

Splendid Raspberry Spinach Salad

An outstanding salad that delights the palate and excites the eye. Equally splendid with strawberries, strawberry jam, and strawberry vinegar.

2 tablespoons raspberry
    vinegar
2 tablespoons raspberry jam
⅓ cup vegetable oil
8 cups spinach, rinsed,
    stemmed, torn into pieces

¾ cup coarsely chopped
    almonds or macadamia nuts,
    divided
1 cup fresh raspberries,
    divided
3 kiwis, peeled, sliced, divided

Combine vinegar and jam in blender or small bowl. Add oil in a thin stream, blending well.

Toss spinach, half of nuts, half of raspberries, and half of kiwis with dressing on a platter or in a flat salad bowl. Top with remaining nuts, raspberries, and kiwis. Serve immediately. Serves 8.

Birthright Sampler (Pennsylvania)

Spinach Couscous Salad

A close friend and excellent cook shared this recipe with me when I was searching for no- and low-cholesterol dishes. It is particularly good served on a warm summer day.

1 cup chicken broth
¾ cup couscous
½ cup Italian salad
    dressing
2 cups shredded fresh
    spinach

12 cherry tomatoes
1 (6-ounce) can sliced water
    chestnuts

In a saucepan, bring the broth to a boil and stir in the couscous. Remove from the heat, cover, and let stand for 5 minutes. Transfer the couscous to a bowl and add the salad dressing. Cover and chill for 2–4 hours, or overnight. Before serving, toss the couscous mixture with the spinach, tomatoes, and water chestnuts. Serves 4.

As You Like It (Massachusetts)

German Cabbage Salad

1 small head cabbage,
  shredded
4–6 slices bacon
3 or 4 green onions, sliced
2 tablespoons mild vinegar

2 tablespoons water
1 tablespoon sugar
Pepper and salt
2 hard-cooked eggs, sliced

Shred cabbage and soak in ice water ½ hour or longer. Drain thoroughly. Dice bacon and fry until crisp. Remove bacon with slotted spoon and add onions, vinegar, water, sugar, salt, and pepper to drippings. Bring to boil and pour over cabbage. Sprinkle bacon over top and garnish with slices of hard-cooked egg.

Cooking with the Groundhog (Pennsylvania)

Red Cabbage Slaw
with Poppy Seed Dressing

This is an excellent, colorful slaw. It keeps well as it does not wilt or get watery.

1 medium red cabbage
1 avocado, peeled and thinly
  sliced

1–2 teaspoons lemon juice
¼ pound green seedless
  grapes, cut in half lengthwise

Finely shred or grate red cabbage. A food processor is great for this. Dip avocado slices in lemon juice to prevent discoloration. Combine cabbage with avocado slices and grapes.

DRESSING:
⅓ cup vinegar
¾ cup sugar
1½ tablespoons freshly
  grated onion

1 teaspoon dry mustard
1 cup salad oil
1½ tablespoons poppy seeds

In a blender or food processor, mix together vinegar, sugar, onion, and mustard. Slowly incorporate oil. Stir in poppy seeds by hand. Combine dressing with slaw mixture. Chill until ready to serve.

The East Hampton L.V.I.S. Centennial Cookbook (New York)

Mixed Broccoli and Cauliflower Salad

2 cups cauliflower flowerets
  (raw)
4 cups broccoli flowerets
(raw)
½ cup chopped mixed red
  and white onions
¼ cup raisins

8 slices crispy bacon,
  crumbled
¼ cup slivered almonds
2 tablespoons chopped fresh
  red bell pepper
2 tablespoons chopped fresh
  green bell pepper

Combine all ingredients; set aside while making Dressing.

DRESSING:
¾ cup mayonnaise
2 tablespoons vinegar

½ cup French dressing

Mix and pour over vegetables. Marinate one hour before serving.

My Italian Heritage (New York)

Better Than Potato Salad

4 cups cooked long grain rice
8 sliced radishes
4 hard-boiled eggs, chopped
1 medium cucumber, seeded
  and chopped
2 cups thinly chopped celery

½ cup chopped onion
  (optional)
1½ cups mayonnaise
3 tablespoons mustard
¾ teaspoon salt

In large bowl, combine rice, radishes, eggs, cucumber, celery, and onion. Combine mayonnaise, mustard and salt and mix well. Pour over rice and refrigerate for at least an hour. (May also season with parsley flakes and celery salt, if desired.)

Sharing Our Bounty Through 40 Years (New York)

Groff's Potato Salad

Guests at Groff's Farm have asked for this recipe for years. Charlie has finally consented to printing his specialty. Bravo! It's definitely his claim to fame!

**10 pounds potatoes,
  preferably new, if possible**
4 cups heavy mayonnaise
2 cups sour cream
½ cup apple cider vinegar
1 cup granulated sugar
½ tablespoon white pepper
2 tablespoons dry mustard

¼ cup celery seed
2 tablespoons lemon juice
½ cup chopped fresh parsley
2 tablespoons chopped chives
1 cup minced onion
1 cup minced celery
2 tablespoons Worcestershire
¼ cup salt

Peel and cook the potatoes until medium soft, then drain, slice, and cool. Mix the mayonnaise and sour cream together, then add the rest of the ingredients. Let the salad stand for at least 3 hours, overnight if possible. This recipe can be cut in half for a smaller number of servings.

Betty Groff's Up-Home Down-Home Cookbook (Pennsylvania)

WIKIPEDIA.ORG

Every year on February 2nd (Groundhog Day), the town of Punxsutawney, Pennsylvania, celebrates their beloved resident groundhog Punxsutawney Phil with a festive celebration. During the ceremony, Phil emerges from his temporary home on Gobbler's Knob; if Phil sees his shadow and returns to his hole, there will be six more weeks of winter. If Phil does not see his shadow, spring will arrive early.

Bildner's Famous Red Potato Salad

The quintessential picnic food, and our top-selling item at Bildner's. Since there's no mayonnaise in the dressing, it's a perfect outdoor food— no chance of spoiling in the sun.

1½ pounds medium new red potatoes
1 shallot
2 tablespoons Dijon mustard
1 tablespoon coarse mustard (with seeds), such as Pommery

¼ cup virgin olive oil
2 tablespoons red wine vinegar
2 tablespoons chopped fresh Italian parsley
Salt and freshly ground pepper to taste

Wash and boil the unpeeled potatoes until just tender (about 20 minutes). Drain and cool them completely. Cut into ½-inch slices. Place in a large serving bowl and set aside. Mince the shallot finely. In a small bowl, combine the mustards and olive oil. Add the red wine vinegar, minced shallot, chopped parsley, and salt and pepper. Mix to blend.

Pour the mustard mixture over the sliced potatoes and toss to coat. Serve or keep covered in the refrigerator. Return to room temperature before serving. Yields 6 servings.

J. Bildner & Sons Cookbook (Massachusetts)

German Potato Salad

Shirley A. Kopp of Glen Ellyn, Illinois, shares this recipe handed down from her great-grandmother Raum of Thueringen, Germany.

5 or 6 medium potatoes, boiled and peeled (white or red, not Idaho)
½ pound bacon, cut into small pieces
1 tablespoon all-purpose flour
¾ cup vinegar
¼ cup water
¼–½ cup sugar, to taste
Salt and pepper, to taste
3 or 4 green onions, sliced, with stems or 1 small sweet onion, chopped

Boil potatoes with jackets on, drain, cool slightly and then peel and slice. While potatoes are boiling, make sauce as follows: fry cut up bacon until almost crisp. Drain off most of grease. Add flour, tanning slightly. Add vinegar, water, sugar, salt and pepper. After this is all mixed, add onion. Keep cooking and stirring until sauce is thickened (taste for seasoning). Pour hot mixture over sliced, boiled potatoes. Can garnish above with hard boiled eggs and then, if preferred, sprinkle a little paprika on sliced eggs. By making and experimenting a couple of times, you'll find just exactly how you most prefer seasonings. Be sure there's plenty of sauce. Serves approximately 4.

The Ellis Island Immigrant Cookbook (New York)

Swiss Green Bean Salad

A great salad to bring to a picnic!

1½ pounds fresh, whole
  green beans
⅓ pound premium Swiss
  cheese, cut into thin strips

½ cup chopped ripe olives
½ cup thinly sliced red pepper
½–¾ cup chopped,
  toasted almonds

Wash and string green beans. Steam beans until just tender. Remove from heat; immediately rinse in cold water. Drain well; set aside.

DRESSING:

5 tablespoons fresh lemon
  juice
2 large cloves garlic, crushed
½ cup olive oil
1 tablespoon red wine vinegar
½ teaspoon crushed tarragon
½ teaspoon dried dill weed

½ teaspoon salt, or to taste
Freshly ground black pepper
  to taste
2 teaspoons prepared dark or
  Dijon mustard
½ cup packed minced fresh
  parsley

In large bowl, whisk together all ingredients for Dressing. Add beans and cheese; toss until Dressing is well distributed. Cover tightly and marinate 2–3 hours, stirring once an hour, at room temperature.

Add olives and sliced pepper. Mix well; re-cover and marinate another 5 hours or overnight in refrigerator. Serve topped with almonds. Yields 4 servings.

The Heart of Pittsburgh (Pennsylvania)

The borough and the region of Indiana, Pennsylvania, as a whole promotes itself as the "Christmas Tree Capital of the World" because the national Christmas Tree Grower's Association was founded there. Actor Jimmy Stewart was born and raised in Indiana, so the town annually holds a Jimmy Stewart film festival as part of the town's "It's a Wonderful Life" holiday celebration.

Broccoli and Raisin Salad

Very good, very crunchy, with a highly agreeable, sweet, and pungent flavor.

2 bunches broccoli	2 tablespoons vinegar
⅓ cup sugar	1 cup mayonnaise
⅔ cup raisins	4 bacon slices, cooked and
½ cup chopped onions	crumbled

Blanch broccoli for 2 minutes if you wish. Cut off florets and cut into serving pieces, discard stems. Freshen florets in ice water for 5 minutes, drain, and dry. Put florets in a salad bowl. Mix together sugar, raisins, onions, vinegar, and mayonnaise. Pour dressing over broccoli and toss lightly. (Can be prepared an hour or so in advance; cover and refrigerate.) Just before serving, add crumbled bacon on top. Serves 8–10.

The Lymes' Heritage Cookbook (Connecticut)

Peas and Cheese Stuffed Tomatoes

2 cups cooked peas	⅓ cup mayonnaise
1 cup cubed Cheddar cheese	½ teaspoon salt
2 hard boiled eggs, chopped	⅛ teaspoon pepper
¼ cup chopped celery	¼–½ teaspoon Tabasco sauce
2 tablespoons chopped onions	12 medium tomatoes
2 tablespoons chopped pimento	12 large lettuce leaves

In a large bowl, combine peas, cheese, eggs, celery, onions, and pimento. In another bowl, combine mayonnaise, salt, pepper, and Tabasco sauce. Add to pea mixture and toss to coat. Cover and chill several hours or overnight. Cut each tomato into wedges, being careful not to cut all the way through. Spoon mixture on top and serve on lettuce leaves. Serves 12.

It's Our Serve (New York)

Zesty Shrimp Pasta Salad

Perfect for those watching their fat intake!

6 ounces uncooked pasta
9 ounces cooked, peeled and deveined shrimp
1 cup quartered cherry tomatoes
½ pound low-fat mozzarella cut into ½-inch cubes

1 cup pitted black olives
½ cup green bell pepper strips
½ cup nonfat plain yogurt
3 tablespoons Dijon mustard
2 tablespoons chopped chives
1 teaspoon lemon juice
Pinch of cayenne pepper

Cook pasta and drain well. Toss with shrimp, tomatoes, cheese, olives, and bell pepper strips.

In a small bowl, combine yogurt, mustard, chives, lemon juice, and cayenne. Pour over pasta mixture and toss gently to combine. Refrigerate, covered, at least two hours to allow flavors to develop. Serves 8.

Friend's Favorites (New York)

Crevettes et Avocats

The most delicious salad I've ever eaten! Served at one of our first gourmet dinners.

1 pound cooked shrimp
3 avocados
¼ teaspoon dry mustard
½ teaspoon salt
¼ teaspoon black pepper

⅓ cup olive oil
3 tablespoons wine vinegar
1 onion, chopped
1 clove garlic, minced

Shell shrimp and cut into small pieces. Cut the avocados in half and carefully scrape out meat, reserving shells. Cube the avocado meat and combine with shrimp.

Mix mustard, salt, and pepper in a bowl. Gradually add the oil, mixing carefully until the spices are dissolved. Add the vinegar, onion, and garlic and beat well. Pour over shrimp and avocado mixture and mix carefully. Fill shells with mixture. Serves 6.

The Fine Arts Cookbook II (Massachusetts)

Turkey Salad with Strawberries

1 pound asparagus
2 cups fresh strawberries, sliced
6 cups assorted salad greens
3 cups cooked turkey, cut into ½-inch cubes
¼ cup pecan halves for garnish

Cut asparagus into 1-inch pieces. Discard woody ends. Cover with water and cook until crisp tender, about 5 minutes. Drain and rinse with cold water. Combine asparagus, berries, greens, and turkey.

DRESSING:
¾ cup sugar
1 teaspoon dry mustard
1 teaspoon salt
⅓ cup cider vinegar
2 tablespoons minced onion
1 cup oil
1 tablespoon orange juice
1 teaspoon grated orange zest
1½ tablespoons poppy seeds

In a food processor, combine sugar, mustard, salt, vinegar, and onion. Gradually add oil, orange juice, orange zest, and poppy seeds. Toss the dressing with salad ingredients. Top with pecans. Serves 6–8.

Beyond Chicken Soup (New York)

Curried Turkey Salad

This salad is standard fare at Falmouth Academy faculty luncheons. Do adjust ingredients according to supplies in your larder.

1½ pounds cooked turkey, cut up
½ cup raisins
½ cup toasted almonds, chopped
½ cup sliced celery
½ cup mayonnaise
1–2 tablespoons curry powder, or to taste
3 large Granny Smith apples, peeled and coarsely diced

Combine all ingredients, except apples, in a large bowl 1 day before serving. Stir once or twice. Just before serving, fold in apples. Serves 4 as salad, 6 as sandwiches.

The MBL Centennial Cookbook (Massachusetts)

Festive Chicken and Fruit Salad

DRESSING:

½ cup mayonnaise
½ cup sour cream
2 tablespoons finely chopped
  parsley

2 tablespoons lemon juice
½ tablespoon salt
½ tablespoon pepper

Combine all ingredients and blend.

SALAD:

1 (5-pound) roasting chicken
  or chicken breasts
¾ cup diced celery
1 cup seedless white grapes,
  halved

1 cup Mandarin orange
  sections, drained
¼ cup toasted, slivered
  almonds
Lettuce

Steam chicken for 1 hour or until tender, being careful not to let it boil. Cool. Remove skin. Bone and cut into large bite-sized pieces. Place in a medium-size mixing bowl and add celery, grapes, and orange sections. Chill. Pour Dressing over chicken and fruit; toss to coat. Cover. Chill for several hours to allow flavors to blend.

Serve on lettuce cups. Sprinkle with almonds. Can be garnished with extra grapes and orange sections. Serves 6.

Philadelphia Homestyle Cookbook (Pennsylvania)

Drafting the Declaration of Independence in 1776 became the defining event in Thomas Jefferson's life. The Continental Congress appointed him the task of producing a draft document for its consideration. Jefferson wrote a stunning statement of the colonists' right to rebel against the British government and establish their own government based on the premise that all men are created equal and have the inalienable rights of life, liberty, and the pursuit of happiness.

Avocado and Grapefruit Salad with Celery Seed Dressing

2 (16-ounce) cans grapefruit sections
1 ripe avocado, peeled, sliced

Watercress for garnish
1 cup pomegranate seeds or cranberries for garnish

Drain grapefruit; reserve juice. Brush avocado slices with juice. Arrange grapefruit sections and avocado slices on small plates. Add watercress trim; sprinkle with pomegranate seeds or sweetened halved cranberries. Pass Celery Seed Dressing. Yields 8 servings.

CELERY SEED DRESSING:

⅔ cup sugar
1 teaspoon dry mustard
1 teaspoon paprika
1 teaspoon celery seed
¼ teaspoon salt

⅓ cup honey
⅓ cup vinegar
1 tablespoon lemon juice
1 teaspoon grated onion
1 cup vegetable oil

Mix dry ingredients; blend in honey, vinegar, lemon juice, and onion. Add oil in slow stream, beating constantly with electric or rotary beater.

Philadelphia Main Line Classics (Pennsylvania)

Baked Apples, Extraordinary

These apples are great when served with pork dishes.

1 cup flour
1 cup light brown sugar
1 teaspoon cinnamon
¼ teaspoon nutmeg
½ cup butter or margarine
6 baking apples

¼ cup granulated sugar
⅓ cup chopped cashews or
  pecans
¼ cup currant jam or
  cranberry jelly
Whipped cream

Blend flour, brown sugar, cinnamon, nutmeg, and butter in food processor until crumbly. Core and peel apples. With a fork, scratch the sides of the apples on all sides and roll in the crumb mixture, packing as much as possible on the sides. Place the apples in a greased baking dish. Combine the granulated sugar, nuts, and jam. Spoon into the cavities of apples. Bake in preheated 350° oven for 45 minutes or until apples are tender and crisp. Serve warm with whipped cream.

Betty Groff's Up-Home Down-Home Cookbook (Pennsylvania)

Jellied Beet Salad

1 package lemon gelatin
  (low-calorie is fine)
1 cup boiling water
1 teaspoon salt
2 tablespoons horseradish

2 tablespoons vinegar
1 tablespoon chopped onion
½ cup beet liquid
1½ cups diced (cooked or
  canned) beets

Mix gelatin and boiling water and stir until gelatin is dissolved. Add all other ingredients except beets and chill until slightly thickened. Fold in beets and spoon mixture into a well-rinsed and lightly oiled mold. Chill thoroughly. At serving time, turn out on chilled plate and serve with a sauce of equal parts mayonnaise and sour cream or plain yogurt. Serves 4.

Vermont Kitchens Revisited (Vermont)

Creamsicle Salad

1 small package orange Jell-O
1 small package cook and
  serve vanilla tapioca
3 cups boiling water
1 (8-ounce) carton Cool Whip
1 (11-ounce) can mandarin
  oranges, drained

Add Jell-O and tapioca to boiling water and allow to return to a boil. Remove mixture from heat and allow to cool slightly. Stir in Cool Whip and mandarin oranges. Refrigerate.

Our Best Home Cooking (New York)

Frosted Apricot Salad

3 cups water
1 cup pineapple-apricot juice
2 (3-ounce) packages orange-
  flavored gelatin
1 (20-ounce) can apricots,
  drained
1 (20-ounce) can crushed
  pineapple, drained

Combine water and fruit juice and bring to a boil. Remove from heat. Stir in gelatin until dissolved. Chill until syrupy. Add fruit and chill until set. Spread with Topping.

TOPPING:
½ cup sugar
3 tablespoons flour
1 cup pineapple-apricot juice
1 egg, slightly beaten
2 tablespoons butter
1 cup cream, whipped
½ cup chopped nuts

Combine sugar, flour, juice, and egg in saucepan and cook until thick. Remove from heat and stir in butter. Chill. When thoroughly chilled, fold in whipped cream. Spread over apricot salad and sprinkle with chopped nuts. Serves 8–10.

Cooking with the Groundhog (Pennsylvania)

I & J's Basil Cream Dressing

Whenever possible, use fresh basil for this dressing. Dried basil works well, but is not nearly as pungent and aromatic.

1 clove garlic, minced
2 tablespoons chopped
   parsley
¼ cup white wine vinegar
2 tablespoons Dijon mustard
1 egg
⅔ cup vegetable oil

4–6 tablespoons fresh-minced
   basil or 3–4 tablespoons
   dried
Dash of sugar
Salt and freshly ground
   pepper to taste

Place garlic, parsley, vinegar, mustard, and the egg into the bowl of a food processor. Mix well. With the processor running, add the vegetable oil in a slow, steady stream and process until smooth and thickened.

Stop the machine for a minute to add the basil, sugar, salt, and pepper. Process briefly until blended. Taste and correct the seasoning as needed. To serve, spoon over a mixed garden salad and enjoy! Makes 1 cup.

Recipes from a New England Inn (New Hampshire)

Boothbay Harbor French Dressing

A zippy, easy dressing from Down East.

1½ cups oil
⅔ cup vinegar
½ cup sugar
1 teaspoon dry mustard
1 teaspoon horseradish

1 teaspoon grated onion
½ teaspoon pepper
1 can tomato soup
   (undiluted)
Juice of 1 lemon

Mix well first 7 ingredients. Add can of soup and lemon juice. Mix well with egg beater. I make this in the blender. Store in refrigerator and it will keep very well. It yields 1 quart.

Cooking with H.E.L.P. (Maine)

Honey Mustard

¾–1 cup oil
⅓ cup cider vinegar
1 teaspoon cayenne pepper,
  scant level
2 teaspoons salt

1⅛ cups honey
1 cup mustard, cheap brand
2 cups mayonnaise (not salad
  dressing)

Combine all ingredients and beat with electric mixer or blender and store, covered, in refrigerator. Makes about 1½ quarts.

Celebrating 200 Years of Survival & Perseverance (New York)

Pennsylvania Dutch Dressing

The dressing is also good on dandelion and romaine salad.

2 strips bacon
1 tablespoon sugar
1 tablespoon flour

1 tablespoon vinegar
½ cup cold water
Salt and pepper

ENDIVE SALAD:
1 head endive

Onion to taste

Cut bacon in small pieces and render until crisp. Add sugar and flour and brown, stirring constantly. Add vinegar and water; continue to stir until thickened; add salt and pepper to taste.

Bucks Cooks (Pennsylvania)

Vegetables

The quiet beauty of a leaf-strewn country road in South Peacham, Vermont. Many travelers come from afar and plan months in advance to see the spectacular autumn color in Vermont and New England. Many nightly newscasters include foliage conditions in their reports during the peak months of September and October.

Pennsylvania Dutch Green Beans

3 strips bacon, cooked, crumbled
1 small onion, sliced
1 (8-ounce) can water chestnuts, sliced
1 (1-pound) can cut green beans

2 teaspoons cornstarch
¼ teaspoon salt
¼ teaspoon dry mustard
1 tablespoon brown sugar
1 tablespoon vinegar

Brown onion and water chestnuts slightly in hot bacon fat. Drain beans, saving ½ cup liquid. Mix liquid with remaining ingredients and add to onion in skillet. Cook, stirring until mixture boils. Add beans and heat thoroughly. Serve garnished with crumbled bacon. Yields 4 (1-cup) servings.

Bountiful Harvest Cookbook (Pennsylvania)

Festive Green Beans

1 pound fresh green beans, trimmed
8 scallions with long green stems
1 red bell pepper, cut into ¼-inch strips

1 clove garlic, minced
4 tablespoons margarine
½ teaspoon fresh thyme
¼ teaspoon salt
¼ teaspoon white pepper

Cook beans in salted water to cover for 3 minutes. Plunge into ice water to stop cooking process. Drain. Cook scallions in boiling water for 15 seconds. Pat dry and cut off the white onion bulb. Set aside. Divide beans into 8 portions. Make bundles by tying a scallion stem around each bundle, placing several red pepper strips under each knot. Place the bundles in greased 8x8-inch casserole.

Slice onion bulbs and sauté with garlic for 3 minutes in margarine. Add thyme, salt, and pepper. Pour over beans. Bake in 375° oven until heated through. Serves 8.

Note: Can be prepared one day ahead before baking. Cover and refrigerate. Bring to room temperature and bake as directed.

Beyond Chicken Soup (New York)

Boston Baked Beans

1 (2-quart) bean pot
2 pounds beans; pea beans, navy beans, or small white
1 pound salt pork
1 medium onion
8 tablespoons dark brown sugar

⅔ cup dark molasses
2 teaspoons dry mustard
⅔ teaspoon salt
½ teaspoon pepper

Soak beans overnight. In morning, parboil them for 10 minutes with a teaspoon of baking soda. Run cold water through beans in a colander or strainer.

Dice salt pork and onion in small pieces. Put half of each on bottom of pot. Put in half of beans. Add rest of pork and onion, then rest of beans. Mix other ingredients with hot water (about 2 cups). Pour over beans to cover. Put in 300° oven for 6 hours.

Add water as necessary to keep beans moist—a little at a time. Don't flood the beans. Serves 10.

Come Savor Swansea (Massachusetts)

 Beans slow-baked in molasses have been a favorite Boston dish since colonial days. Boston Baked Beans continue to be one of New England's most-loved traditional dishes. The beans are so popular, Boston has been nicknamed "Beantown."

Hearty Baked Beans

1 pound bacon, chopped
1 pound ground beef
1 cup brown sugar
1 (28-ounce) can Bush's
  Baked Beans (use liquid)
1 (16-ounce) can butter beans
  (use liquid)
1 (16-ounce) can kidney beans
  (use liquid)
1 cup ketchup
1 onion, chopped

Fry chopped bacon. Drain and set aside. Brown ground beef and pour off fat. Add to ground beef the brown sugar, all beans, ketchup, onion, and bacon. Pour into lightly greased casserole dish and bake at 375° for 1 hour. Serves 12–14.

Sharing Our Bounty Through 40 Years (New York)

Mushroom and Onion Gratins

These stuffed onions are wonderful with roast chicken or beef.

3 very large onions, peeled
  and cut in half crosswise
6 tablespoons unsalted
  butter, divided
¾ pound mushrooms,
  chopped coarsely
1 tablespoon fresh thyme
  leaves
Coarse salt and freshly ground
  pepper
¾ cup fresh white bread
  crumbs

Preheat oven to 400°. Scoop out as much of the center of each onion half as you can and still leave a firm shell. Chop the centers coarsely. In a sauté pan, melt half the butter and sauté chopped onions and mushrooms with thyme until vegetables are limp and lightly browned. Season insides of onion shells with salt and pepper and fill each half with mushroom mixture. Melt remaining butter and combine with bread crumbs. Pat 2 tablespoons of crumb mixture over each onion half. Put onions in small baking pan and roast for about 1 hour, or until they are tender and the tops are well browned. Serves 6.

The Hudson River Valley Cookbook (New York)

Onion Shortcake Casserole

¼ cup butter
1 pound sliced Bermuda
  onion
1 (15½-ounce) can creamed
  corn
1 egg, beaten
⅓ cup milk

1½ cups corn muffin mix
2 drops Tabasco
1 cup sour cream
¼ teaspoon salt
¼ cup dill
1 cup shredded Cheddar
  cheese, divided

Sauté onions in butter. In bowl, mix together creamed corn, egg, milk, corn muffin mix, and Tabasco. Add sour cream, salt, and dill to onions. Add ½ cup shredded cheese to onion mixture. Pour corn mixture in bottom of an 8-inch square pan. Pour sour cream mixture over corn mixture. Sprinkle on remaining cheese. Bake at 425° for 30–40 minutes. Serves 8.

Friend's Favorites (New York)

Harvest Dinner Onion Pie

1 cup finely crushed saltine
  crackers
¼ cup melted butter
2 cups thinly sliced onions
2 tablespoons butter

¾ cup milk
2 eggs, slightly beaten
Salt and pepper
¼ cup shredded sharp cheese
Paprika

Press crackers and melted butter into bottom of 9-inch pan. Sauté onion in butter until tender. Add to crackers. Pour milk and egg mixture over all. Add salt and pepper. Top with cheese and sprinkle with paprika. Bake at 350° for 25–30 minutes till brown and bubbly. Doubling recipe will make 9x13-inch oblong pan.

200 Years of Favorite Recipes from Delaware County (New York)

Tomato-Basil-Onion Frittata

We wait anxiously until the first tomatoes from our garden ripen and we have fresh basil before we make this frittata. It is well worth the wait. Our guests love this for breakfast, but it is also a wonderful lunch or light summer supper dish.

2 tablespoons olive oil
2 medium-ripe tomatoes,
  cut in medium dice
½ medium onion, finely
  chopped

Salt and pepper
½ cup fresh basil leaves,
  chopped
6 eggs, divided
4 tablespoons milk, divided

In a medium skillet, heat the oil and sauté the tomatoes and onion. Add salt and pepper to taste. Turn off the heat and mix in the basil. (If there is a lot of liquid in the pan, drain off before making frittata). Lightly coat an 8-inch non-stick omelette pan with oil spray. Add ½ of the tomato-basil mixture and cook it over medium heat.

In a small bowl, whisk together 3 eggs with 2 tablespoons milk. Pour egg mixture into omelette pan, distributing evenly over the tomato-basil mixture, stir gently with a rubber spatula to combine. Allow the eggs to cook 1–2 minutes to set the bottom. Then using a rubber spatula, gently lift an edge of the eggs, and tipping the pan, allow uncooked egg mixture to run underneath building up the height of the frittata. Continue this gentle cooking process until the eggs are nearly cooked through, about 5 minutes.

To finish cooking the top of the frittata, slide the pan into a preheated broiler for 1–2 minutes. Repeat this procedure for the second frittata. Yields 2 servings.

Tasting the Hamptons (New York)

L. Frank Baum, author of *The Wizard of Oz*, was born in Chittenango, New York. The town features a yellow brick road leading to Auntie Em's and other Oz-themed places like the Emerald City Grill, Over the Rainbow Crafts, and Tin Man Construction Company. You can also buy Oz Cream, and shop at the Land of Oz and Ends. Chittenango has an annual Munchkins parade.

Tomatoes with Spinach Mornay

3 (10-ounce) packages frozen chopped spinach
Salt and pepper
4 tablespoons butter
3 tablespoons flour
Dash of salt
Dash of cayenne pepper
1 teaspoon Dijon mustard
1 teaspoon dry mustard
1 cup milk
4 tablespoons shredded Swiss cheese
4 tablespoons grated Parmesan cheese
4 tablespoons half-and-half
8–10 medium tomatoes
Grated Parmesan cheese

Cook spinach slowly, without any additional water. Drain thoroughly. Season with salt and pepper. Melt butter in separate pan. Remove from heat and add flour. Season with salt, cayenne, mustards, and blend in milk. Stir over heat until it boils, then add cheeses and light cream. Simmer 5 minutes, then combine with spinach mixture. Cut tops off tomatoes and remove seeds and center membranes. Pile spinach into tomato cases and sprinkle with Parmesan cheese. Bake at 350° for 20 minutes. Serves 8–10.

RSVP (Maine)

Crock-Pot Cabbage Rolls

12 large cabbage leaves
1 beaten egg
¼ cup milk
¼ cup finely chopped onion
1 teaspoon salt
¼ teaspoon pepper
1 pound lean ground beef
1 cup cooked rice
1 (8-ounce) can tomato sauce
1 tablespoon brown sugar
1 tablespoon lemon juice
1 teaspoon Worcestershire sauce

Immerse cabbage leaves in large kettle of boiling water for about 3 minutes or until limp; drain. Combine egg, milk, onion, salt, pepper, beef, and cooked rice. Place about ¼ cup meat mixture in center of each leaf; fold in sides and roll ends over meat. Place in crockpot. Combine tomato sauce with brown sugar, lemon juice, and Worcestershire. Pour over cabbage rolls. Cover and cook on low 7–9 hours. Serves 6.

Sharing Our Best (New York)

Spanacopita
(Spinach Pie)

4 (4-ounce) packages frozen
   chopped spinach, drained
1 bunch scallions, chopped
1 onion, chopped
1 cup oil
1 pound feta cheese
4 (8-ounce) packages cream
   cheese, softened

6 eggs
Dill to taste
Salt to taste
1 pound filo dough
1 cup melted butter

In a pan cook spinach, scallions, onion, and oil until onion and scallions are transparent. Remove from heat, let stand.

In a bowl, mix feta cheese, cream cheese, and eggs till smooth. Add the spinach mixture, mix together, add dill and salt to taste.

Lay out filo dough in 13x15-inch pan; brush the entire sheet with melted butter. Repeat this until half the dough has been used. Add mixture, smooth it out so that it covers the pan.

Add remaining filo dough, remembering to butter every sheet when finished. Score the top into 2-inch pieces; sprinkle with water. Bake at 325° for 45 minutes or until golden brown on top. Cool and serve.

The Bronx Cookbook (New York)

MWANNER, WIKIPEDIA.ORG

The Adirondack Park in northeast New York is the largest park and the largest state-level protected area in the contiguous United States, and the largest National Historic Landmark. The park covers some 6.1 million acres, a land area greater than Vermont, or of Yellowstone, Yosemite, Grand Canyon, Glacier, and Great Smoky Mountains National Parks combined.

Pennsylvania-Dutch Potato Pancakes

2 medium-size potatoes
  (about 12 ounces), peeled
1 tablespoon lemon juice
¼ cup butter or margarine,
  melted
2 tablespoons all-purpose
  flour
1 tablespoon thinly sliced
  scallions

¼ cup finely chopped onion
1 large egg, beaten
½ teaspoon salt
¼ teaspoon black pepper
¼ teaspoon baking powder
1 tablespoon vegetable oil
1 tablespoon butter or
  margarine

Using coarse side of grater, grate potatoes into large bowl. Toss with lemon juice to coat well. Let stand 5 minutes; drain well. Add ¼ cup melted butter, flour, onion, scallions, egg, salt, pepper, and baking powder to potatoes. Stir to mix well.

In 8-inch skillet over medium-high heat, heat oil and remaining butter. Working in batches of 3–4 pancakes, add potato mix in heaping tablespoons to skillet. Using tines of fork, flatten each portion into very thin round pancakes, about 2½ inches thick. Cook 3–4 minutes on each side until golden brown. Drain on paper towels. Makes 16 pancakes.

Birthright Sampler (Pennsylvania)

New Peas and Potatoes

This is a good way to stretch the first peas from the garden.

3 cups shelled fresh peas
12 small new potatoes,
  washed well
1½ teaspoons salt

1½ cups milk
1½ teaspoons flour
2 tablespoons butter, melted

Cook peas and potatoes separately in salted water until soft and almost dry. Add peas to potatoes and pour milk over them. Bring milk to boiling point, then add paste of butter and flour. Cook until slightly thickened, and serve.

An Amish Kitchen (Pennsylvania)

Hash Brown Casserole

2 pounds frozen hash brown
potatoes
1 (10¾-ounce) can cream of
chicken soup
½ cup chopped onion
Salt to taste

1 (8-ounce) package shredded
sharp Cheddar cheese
1 pint sour cream
1 stick margarine, melted,
divided
2 cups cornflakes

Mix first 6 ingredients with ¾ cup margarine and place in buttered
9x13-inch baking dish. Top with remaining ¼ cup melted margarine
mixed with cornflakes. Cover with foil. Bake 1½ hours at 350°.

Society of Farm Women of Pennsylvania Cookbook
(Pennsylvania)

Reuben Baked Potatoes

4 large baking potatoes
2 cups finely diced cooked
corned beef
1 (14-ounce) can sauerkraut,
rinsed, well drained and
finely chopped
½ cup shredded Swiss
cheese
3 tablespoons sliced green
onions

1 garlic clove, minced
1 tablespoon prepared
horseradish
1 teaspoon caraway seed
1 (3-ounce) package cream
cheese, softened
3 tablespoons grated
Parmesan cheese
Paprika

Bake the potatoes at 425° for 45 minutes or until tender. Cool. In
a bowl, combine the corned beef, sauerkraut, Swiss cheese, onions,
garlic, horseradish, and caraway seed. Cut potatoes in half, lengthwise. Carefully scoop out potato, leaving shell intact. Mash potatoes with cream cheese; stir into the corned beef mixture. Mound
potato mixture into the shells. Sprinkle with Parmesan cheese and
paprika. Return to oven for 25 minutes or until heated through.
Makes 8 servings.

Recipes from the Children's Museum at Saratoga (New York)

Block Island Potatoes

3 pounds small new or red
  potatoes
6 tablespoons unsalted
  butter
3 tablespoons olive oil
3 large garlic cloves,
  crushed (I prefer to mince)
1 tablespoon crushed fresh
  thyme, or ½ teaspoon
  dried

1½ teaspoons crushed fresh
  or dried rosemary
1½ teaspoons paprika
Dash of cayenne pepper
½ teaspoon salt
¼ teaspoon fresh ground
  pepper
½ cup chopped fresh
  parsley

Preheat oven to 375°. Scrub and dry potatoes. Melt butter in oil over moderate heat in roasting pan or casserole. Add the next 8 ingredients. Stir to mix. Add potatoes and roll them in butter mix to coat well. Bake, basting potatoes occasionally, for about 40 minutes or until tender.

A Taste of Salt Air & Island Kitchens (Rhode Island)

Red Lion Inn Home Fries

Chef Mongeon uses this seasoning mix for a variety of dishes. He sprinkles it over roasted potatoes, or rubs it into the skin of a chicken before roasting it, as well as using it as a seasoning for Red Lion Inn Home Fries.

2 pounds potatoes, peeled and diced into ¼-inch cubes
1 cup butter

¾ cup diced onions
2 tablespoons Home Fries Seasoning Mix
Butter, for serving (optional)

Cook the potatoes in a vegetable steamer over simmering water for 20–30 minutes, until just tender.

Melt the butter in a heavy skillet, and add the onions and 1 tablespoon of the seasoning mix. Sauté over medium heat until the onions are limp and translucent, about 10 minutes. Do not let them brown. Add the potatoes, and sprinkle with the remaining 1 tablespoon seasoning mix. Sauté over medium heat until golden brown and crisp, about 15 minutes. Dot with more butter for added flavor. Serves 8.

HOME FRIES SEASONING MIX:

1 cup salt
½ cup paprika
¼ cup ground black pepper

¼ cup ground white pepper
½ cup onion powder
½ cup garlic salt

Combine all the ingredients in a large jar or other covered container. Shake to mix well. This will last up to 6 months. Yields 3 cups.

The Red Lion Inn Cookbook (Massachusetts)

Since 1773, the Red Lion Inn has been welcoming travelers to the beauty of the Berkshires with traditional New England hospitality. The inn has hosted five presidents and numerous other notable figures, including Nathaniel Hawthorne, William Cullen Bryant, and Henry Wadsworth Longfellow. An outstanding collection of early American furnishings and china adorn the guest rooms and common areas. Located at the center of the historic village of Stockbridge, Massachusetts, the inn was immortalized in Norman Rockwell's painting, "Stockbridge Main Street at Christmas." The inn epitomizes New England charm.

Potatoes au Gratin Kaleel

The best scalloped potatoes you'll ever make!

6–8 cloves garlic
1½ teaspoons salt
1 tablespoon butter
6 small shallots, finely
   minced
5–6 large potatoes, peeled
   and thinly sliced

¾ teaspoon pepper
¾ pound freshly grated
   Parmesan cheese, divided
2 cups heavy cream, divided
½ pound Swiss cheese,
   grated

Chop garlic; add salt and pulverize using a mortar and pestle until no garlic is visible. Generously grease a 2-quart casserole with 1 tablespoon butter. Sprinkle ⅓ shallots and ⅓ garlic-salt mixture into the bottom of the casserole. Add a layer of potato slices ½- to ¾-inch thick. Sprinkle with ½ teaspoon pepper and ⅓ of Parmesan cheese and cover with ⅓ cup cream. Sprinkle with shallots and garlic-salt mixture. Continue 2 more layers in same order until pan is nearly full. Add remaining Parmesan cheese, gently mixing throughout casserole. Top with grated Swiss cheese. Cover with foil and bake at 350° for 45 minutes or until potatoes are tender.

Connecticut Cooks III (Connecticut)

Red Lion Inn

Dale's Pineapple-Filled Sweet Potatoes

3 large sweet potatoes
1 tablespoon margarine
½ teaspoon salt
½ teaspoon cinnamon
½ cup crushed pineapple,
  drained (reserve juice)

1 tablespoon milk
½ cup pecan pieces (optional)
½ cup mini marshmallows
2 tablespoons reserved
  pineapple juice, heated

Bake sweet potatoes at 450° for 40 minutes till soft. Split potatoes in half lengthwise; scrape out meat. Take care not to break shells. In bowl, mash potatoes, adding margarine, seasonings, pineapple, milk, and nuts, if desired. Refill the shells. Place in 1-quart casserole. Top with marshmallows. Baste with hot pineapple juice. Bake at 325° for 20 minutes, till marshmallows are lightly brown. Serves 6.

The Best of the Sweet Potato Recipes Cookbook (Pennsylvania)

Caramelized Garlic

6 heads fresh garlic
2 tablespoons olive oil

1 (12-inch) square of
  aluminum foil

Lay each garlic head on its side and cut off ¼-inch from the bottom or root end, exposing the garlic cloves. Brush with olive oil. Place the heads, exposed end down, in a single layer in an ovenproof dish or directly on the grill. Roast in a 325° oven or on a very low grill, uncovered, until light brown. Cover with aluminum foil and cook 8–10 minutes longer, or until creamy.

Allow the garlic to cool. Remove the clove from the head as needed. Garlic may be stored in a tightly covered container in the refrigerator for several days.

To purée, crush garlic cloves with the flat of a knife.

George Hirsch Living It Up! (New York)

Asparagus Strudel

1 pound thin asparagus, trimmed and cut into 1-inch pieces
1 onion, chopped
2 tablespoons butter or margarine
2 teaspoons dried dill (save a little for topping)
1 cup Swiss cheese, shredded
1 cup dry bread crumbs
1 tablespoon lemon juice
1 teaspoon country-style Dijon mustard
½ teaspoon salt
½ teaspoon pepper
2 eggs, lightly beaten
½ (17¼-ounce) package puff pastry sheets (1 sheet), thawed

Preheat oven to 350°. In large skillet, sauté asparagus and onion in butter for 2–3 minutes; cool for 10 minutes. Stir in next 7 ingredients and ½ the eggs. On floured surface, roll out pastry to 10½x11½-inch rectangle. Place asparagus mixture lengthwise along center of pastry. Brush ½ remaining egg along empty edges. Overlap sides to cover filling; seal. Place seam-side-down on baking sheet. Brush with remaining egg. Sprinkle top with dill. Bake for 45–50 minutes until golden. Makes 10 servings.

Recipe from Pratt Smith House Bed & Breakfast, Deerfield
Bed & Breakfast Leatherstocking Welcome Home Recipe Collection (New York)

 The first capital of the United States was New York City. In 1789 George Washington took his oath as president on the balcony at Federal Hall.

Scalloped Asparagus

1½–2 pounds asparagus
6 tablespoons butter
6 tablespoons flour
1 teaspoon salt
⅛ teaspoon pepper
2 cups milk

¾ cup grated mild or sharp cheese
2 tablespoons chopped onion
5 hard-boiled eggs, sliced
½ cup buttered bread crumbs

Steam asparagus until just tender. Drain and set aside.

Make a white sauce by melting butter. Stir in flour and add salt and pepper. Add milk, stirring constantly, and cook over low heat until smooth. Blend in ½ cup grated cheese, stirring until smooth. Combine white sauce with asparagus, onion, and eggs. Pour mixture into a 1½-quart greased casserole. Top with crumbs and remaining ¼ cup cheese. Bake at 350° for 15–20 minutes or until casserole is bubbly and cheese melts. Makes 8 servings.

The Central Market Cookbook (Pennsylvania)

Sour Cream Party Broccoli

4 cups broccoli, fresh or frozen, cut into florets
2 tablespoons minced onion
2 tablespoons butter
1½ cups commercial sour cream

2 teaspoons sugar
1 teaspoon white vinegar
¼ teaspoon paprika
½ teaspoon salt
Dash of black pepper
½ cup broken cashew nuts

Cook broccoli in boiling water until tender, about 10 minutes; drain well. Sauté onion in butter in saucepan. Add remaining ingredients, except nuts, stirring well. Pour sauce over broccoli in heated serving dish. Sprinkle nuts over top. Yields 4–6 servings.

Mennonite Country-Style Recipes & Kitchen Secrets
(Pennsylvania)

Roasted Broccoli with Sesame Dressing

1 pound large broccoli
flowerets, including 3
inches of stem
3 tablespoons olive oil
4 tablespoons fresh lemon
juice
2 teaspoons oriental sesame
oil

4 teaspoons soy sauce
3 tablespoons vegetable oil
4 teaspoons sesame seeds,
toasted
1 teaspoon ground ginger
½ teaspoon minced garlic
Pinch of sugar

In a bowl, toss the broccoli with the olive oil until it is coated well, and roast in a jellyroll pan in a preheated 500° oven, turning it occasionally with tongs, for 10–12 minutes, or until crisp-tender.

While the broccoli is roasting, in a blender or food processor, blend the lemon juice, the sesame oil, the soy sauce, the vegetable oil, the sesame seeds, the ginger, the garlic, and the sugar until the dressing is smooth. Transfer the broccoli to a serving dish and pour the dressing over it. Serves 4.

Hasbro Children's Hospital Cookbook (Rhode Island)

DANIEL CASE, WIKIPEDIA.ORG

The International Tennis Hall of Fame at the Newport Casino opened in Newport, Rhode Island, in 1880. Features include changing exhibits on tennis, and the history of the game and its players. Major professional tennis tournaments are played there during the summer months.

Eggplant Parmigiana

2 firm eggplants
½ cup flour
2 eggs, slightly beaten
½ teaspoon salt
½ teaspoon ground pepper
1 cup olive oil
3–4 cups tomato sauce

1 pound ricotta cheese
¼ cup dried parsley
2 eggs, lightly beaten
1 cup grated Parmesan
8 ounces mozzarella, thinly
  sliced

Pare and cut eggplant into thin rounds. Flour and dip slices into beaten eggs, seasoned with salt and pepper. Sauté slices in hot olive oil until golden brown on both sides. Drain on absorbent paper. Arrange a layer of eggplant in the bottom of an ovenproof 2-quart baking dish and cover with ⅓ tomato sauce. Combine ricotta, parsley, eggs, and Parmesan and mix thoroughly. Spread half ricotta mixture over tomato sauce in casserole. Repeat layers until eggplant is used. Cover with tomato sauce and top with mozzarella. Bake, uncovered, in a 350° oven 30 minutes until cheese is lightly browned and filling is hot. Makes 8 servings.

Birthright Sampler (Pennsylvania)

Sautéed Zucchini Patties

5 medium zucchini
3 eggs
1 tablespoon grated cheese
1 tablespoon grated onion
2 tablespoons flour

½ cup chopped parsley
1 teaspoon salt
1 teaspoon pepper
½ cup oil

Clean and remove ends, but leave zucchini unpeeled. Shred coarsely. Sprinkle with salt. Let stand 1 hour; drain, pressing out all possible liquid. Mix zucchini with unbeaten eggs, cheese, onion, flour, parsley, salt and pepper. Shape into patties and sauté in small amount of heated oil. Add more oil as needed. Serves 6–8. If frozen, reheat in oven before serving.

Savor the Flavor (New York)

Spinach-Stuffed Zucchini Boats

4 medium zucchini
Salt to taste
1 pound fresh spinach,
  rinsed, trimmed
1 egg
½ cup crumbled feta cheese

Garlic powder, nutmeg, and
  freshly ground pepper to
  taste
½ cup grated Parmesan
  cheese

Cut zucchini into halves lengthwise. Cook in salted water in saucepan for 5 minutes. Drain, reserving cooking liquid; remove and discard seeds. Steam spinach in saucepan until wilted. Drain and chop spinach, pressing out excess moisture. Combine spinach with egg, feta cheese, garlic powder, nutmeg, and pepper in bowl; mix well. Spoon into squash. Arrange in nonstick baking pan. Sprinkle with Parmesan cheese. Pour reserved cooking liquid into pan. Bake, covered with foil, at 350° for 10 minutes. Bake, uncovered, until tops are brown. Yields 8 servings.

Rhode Island Cooks (Rhode Island)

Italian Zucchini Casserole

2–2½ pounds zucchini
½ cup chopped onion
½ cup chopped green pepper
4 tablespoons margarine
1 package spaghetti sauce
 mix

½ cup shredded Cheddar
 cheese
1 (4-ounce) can mushrooms
1 (6-ounce) can tomato paste
1 cup water
Grated Parmesan cheese

Slice zucchini into ½-inch pieces and drop into boiling water. Cook 4–5 minutes and drain. Place zucchini in casserole dish. Sauté onion and green pepper in margarine. Add sauce mix, Cheddar cheese, mushrooms, tomato paste, and water. Mix well and pour over zucchini. Sprinkle top with Parmesan cheese. Bake 25–30 minutes at 350°, or microwave 13 minutes on HIGH; turn once. Let stand 5–10 minutes before serving.

What's Cooking at Moody's Diner (Maine)

Fried Zucchini Rounds

⅓ cup biscuit mix
¼ cup grated Parmesan
 cheese
⅛ teaspoon pepper
2 eggs, slightly beaten

2 cups shredded, unpeeled
 zucchini (2 medium)
2 tablespoons butter or
 margarine

Combine biscuit mix, cheese, and pepper. Stir in eggs just till mixture is moistened. Fold in zucchini. In 10-inch skillet, melt margarine over medium heat. Using 2 tablespoons for each round, cook 2–3 minutes on each side or until brown. Makes 12 rounds.

The Dinner Bell Rings Again! (Pennsylvania)

Vegetable-Cheese Casserole
(Microwave)

2 zucchini squash, ¼-inch slices
1 yellow summer squash, ¼-inch slices
1 green sweet pepper, strips
1 stalk celery, 1-inch slices
1 carrot, sliced
1 cup fresh mushrooms or canned
¼ cup water
1 tablespoon olive oil
2 cloves of garlic
1 large onion, cut in thin slices
½ teaspoon thyme
⅛ teaspoon oregano
Salt
Freshly ground pepper
1 cup shredded mozzarella cheese

Place zucchini, squash, green pepper, celery, carrot, and fresh mushrooms in a casserole dish with ¼ cup cold water and cook in the microwave for 2 minutes. Stir. Cook for 2 minutes longer. Drain water and set aside.

In a frying pan, heat oil and sauté garlic and onion slices. Add microwave vegetables and spices. Stir gently and simmer for 5–7 minutes. Remove from heat and place vegetables in casserole dish. Top with shredded mozzarella cheese and place under broiler until cheese melts. Serves 4.

Heritage Cooking (Massachusetts)

BC.JORDAN, WIKIPEDIA.ORG

The Naismith Memorial Basketball Hall of Fame, located in Springfield, Massachusetts, was established in 1959 to honor exceptional basketball players, coaches, referees, executives, and other major contributors to the game. Named after James Naismith, the inventor of basketball, the Basketball Hall of Fame is dedicated to preserve and promote basketball at all levels and serve as the ultimate library of the sport's history.

New England Autumn Casserole

2½ cups sliced pumpkin or
    winter squash, peeled and
    seeded
1½ cups sliced apples
¼ cup butter, melted
3–4 tablespoons brown sugar

1 teaspoon cinnamon
½ cup walnuts or almonds,
    broken up
Salt to taste
Butter

Place a layer of pumpkin, then a layer of apples, in a 2-quart casserole. (The pumpkin or squash will not cook as quickly, so slice it more thinly than the apples.)

Combine ¼ cup melted butter, sugar, cinnamon, nuts, and salt; drizzle some over apples and pumpkin. Continue alternating layers and drizzling with butter-and-sugar mixture until all ingredients have been used. Dot with a bit more butter.

Cover casserole and bake at 350° for 45–60 minutes or until pumpkin and apples are tender. Yields 4 servings.

Apple Orchard Cookbook (Massachusetts)

Stuffed Acorn Squash

4 medium acorn squashes
1 pound mushrooms, chopped
2 cups chopped onions
2 garlic cloves, mashed
½ cup minced fresh parsley

1 teaspoon dried basil
4 tablespoons dry white wine
1½ cups wild/brown rice
    blend, cooked

Cut squashes in half lengthwise. Remove seeds and bake for 30–35 minutes at 350°. Meanwhile, sauté mushrooms, onion, and garlic in a lightly oiled skillet until ingredients are lightly browned. Combine with herbs, wine, and cooked rice. Set aside.

Remove pulp from cooked squash and transfer to a large mixing bowl. Blend in the vegetable-rice mixture and spoon into each squash shell. Sprinkle with freshly ground pepper, paprika, and a little more parsley. Bake at 350° for 25–30 minutes, or until heated through. Makes 8 servings.

The Chef's Palate Cookbook (Vermont)

Fiddleheads

(Microwave)

My first introduction to fiddleheads was in the early 1980s, when they suddenly became a "gourmet" treat, yet these fern sprouts have been eaten as a vegetable since Colonial times. They have a delicate flavor, similar to asparagus, and should be cooked as soon as possible after picking.

1 pound fresh or frozen fiddleheads
¼ cup water
2 tablespoons butter or margarine

1 tablespoon cider vinegar
1 teaspoon salt
⅛ teaspoon ground black pepper

If the fiddleheads are frozen, unwrap and put in a 1-quart casserole. Heat at DEFROST or LOW (30%) power for 3–4 minutes or just until almost completely thawed. Stir once while heating. Let stand for 5 minutes. Drain off any liquid.

If the fiddleheads are fresh, rinse well and drain. Remove any bruised parts and veils (thin covering over the curl). Put in a 1-quart casserole. Add ¼ cup water to the thawed or fresh fiddleheads. Cover with vented plastic wrap. Heat at HIGH (100%) power for 3–5 minutes, or until just tender. Stir once while heating. Drain.
Add the butter, vinegar, salt, and pepper. Stir gently to melt the butter. Serve hot. Makes 6 servings.

Classic New England Dishes from Your Microwave (Maine)

STEVEN WALLING, WIKIPEDIA.ORG

Fiddleheads are the fronds of ostrich ferns. In the spring they are available fresh in many food stores. The young shoots of cinnamon and bracken ferns are also sometimes eaten as "fiddleheads." If you pick your own, gather them in very early spring before the veil covering the frond turns yellow. Snap off fronds that are about 6 inches high. Pick fronds from several plants, if possible, so that the ferns remain in good health and can be picked next season.

Copper Pennies
(Marinated Carrots)

2 pounds carrots, scraped and sliced (or use canned carrots)

1 teaspoon salt

1 medium onion, sliced into rings

1 bell pepper, sliced into thin rings

Boil carrots in salted water for 5 minutes. (Don't use salt if using canned carrots.) Place carrots in casserole dish along with onion and pepper. Layer onions and bell pepper rings with carrots.

MARINADE:

¾ cup vinegar

½ cup oil

1 cup sugar

1 teaspoon mustard

1 teaspoon Worcestershire

1 can tomato soup

Salt and pepper to taste

Combine ingredients for marinade together and simmer for 15 minutes. Pour marinade while hot over carrots. Best if refrigerated overnight, but serve at room temperature or slightly warmed.

The Proulx/Chartrand 1997 Reunion Cookbook (New York)

Sister Mary's Zesty Carrots

6 carrots

Salt

Water to cover

2 tablespoons grated onion

2 tablespoons horseradish

½ cup mayonnaise

1 teaspoon salt

¼ teaspoon pepper

¼ cup water

¼ cup buttered bread crumbs

Preheat the oven to 375°.

Clean and cut the carrots into thin strips. Cook until tender in salted water. Drain the carrots and place them into a 6x10-inch baking dish.

Mix together the onion, horseradish, mayonnaise, salt, pepper, and water. Pour this over the carrots. Sprinkle the buttered bread crumbs over the top. Bake at 375° for about 15 minutes. Serves 4–6.

A recipe from Hancock Shaker Village, Pittsfield
Best Recipes of Berkshire Chefs (Massachusetts)

Baked Corn

2 cups creamed corn
2 tablespoons butter
1½ tablespoons flour
1 cup milk

1 tablespoon sugar
1 teaspoon salt
⅛ teaspoon pepper
2 eggs

Mix all ingredients together. Bake in moderate oven (325°–350°) until corn is firm, about 1 hour.

Society of Farm Women of Pennsylvania Cookbook (Pennsylvania)

Baked Corn on the Cob

So simple—so good!

6 ears fresh corn
1 (4-ounce) package whipped
cream cheese with chives

4 tablespoons butter, softened
¼ teaspoon salt
Dash of pepper

Remove husks and silk from ears. Stir cream cheese into butter, add salt and pepper, and blend. Place ears of corn on individual large squares of foil. Spread each ear with mixture. Fold up foil and seal. Bake in a 350°–400° oven for 30–45 minutes until corn is tender. Carefully open each ear and spoon hot chive butter over ears to serve. Serves 6.

Note: May be done on an outdoor grill. Cooking time is approximately the same.

Three Rivers Cookbook (Pennsylvania)

Pittsburgh lost the "h" in its spelling in 1891, but after twenty years of much public protest, the U.S. Board on Geographic Names relented and the "h" was restored. Pittsburgh is one of the few American cities to be spelled with an "h" at the end of a burg suffix; for this reason, it is the most commonly misspelled city in America.

Oven Roasted Vegetables

1 pound red skin potatoes,
  cut into 1-inch pieces
1 (16-ounce) bag peeled baby
  carrots
1 medium onion, sliced
3 garlic cloves, minced
2 tablespoons dried oregano
2 tablespoons finely chopped
  fresh basil
1 teaspoon salt
1 teaspoon pepper
½ cup olive oil
3 tablespoons fresh lemon
  juice
1 zucchini, cut into ½-inch
  wide strips
1 large red bell pepper, cut
  into ½-inch strips
1 large green bell pepper, cut
  into ½-inch strips

Preheat oven to 450°. In a 9x13-inch pan, combine potatoes, carrots, and onion. Mix all spices, oil, and lemon juice, and drizzle over vegetables. Toss to coat. Bake, uncovered, 30 minutes, turning occasionally.

Remove from oven and add remaining vegetables. Return to oven and bake an additional 15–20 minutes. If vegetables are too dry, add more olive oil and toss. Serves 6–8.

Three Rivers Renaissance Cookbook IV (Pennsylvania)

Harvard Beets

1 tablespoon cornstarch
⅓ cup sugar
¼ cup vinegar
¼ cup water
½ teaspoon salt
2 cups diced boiled beets
2 tablespoons melted butter

Mix cornstarch and sugar, add the water, vinegar, and salt, and bring to a boil, stirring until thick and smooth. Add beets, and cook over slow fire 15 minutes. When ready to serve, add butter and bring to a boil. Serves 4.

Good Maine Food (Maine)

Pasta, Rice, Etc.

PHOTO COURTESY OF NIAGARA FALLS CONVENTION AND VISITORS BUREAU

Straddling the Canadian-United States International Border, and both in the province of Ontario and the state of New York, Niagara Falls attracts some 12 million tourists to her majestic awesome beauty each year. Niagara Falls is one of the world's largest waterfalls, second only to Zimbabwe's Victoria Falls in Africa.

Seafood Lasagna

This dish was created for seafood, and is an especially good choice for a festive buffet. But it also works with cooked turkey or chicken—a great addition to your basic repertoire of reliable recipes.

1 pound lasagna noodles	6 tablespoons butter
¾ pound peeled, deveined shrimp	½ cup flour
	Salt, pepper
¾ pound scallops	Paprika
2 cups white wine	Sherry, to taste
2 cups stock (fish or chicken depending on what you're making)	2 pounds sharp Cheddar cheese, grated

Cook lasagna noodles al dente according to package directions and cool on sheets of aluminum foil.

In a large saucepan, cook seafood in wine and stock for 3–5 minutes. Save the stock for the sauce. Remove seafood to food processor and chop coarsely. In saucepan, melt butter, add flour and seasonings, and cook, stirring, for a few minutes. Stir in 2 cups of the wine-stock mixture and cook until thickened. Add seafood mixture and set aside.

Layer noodles, cheese, and seafood mixture, in that order, in a greased lasagna pan, finishing with a layer of cheese. Bake at 375° for 45 minutes, or until bubbly. Let stand 10 minutes before serving. Serves 10–12 and freezes well.

Vermont Kitchens Revisited (Vermont)

The Hood Milk Bottle is an ice cream stand and snack bar located on the Hood Milk Bottle Plaza in front of Boston Children's Museum. It has been located on this spot since April 20, 1977, when Hood shipped the bottle by ferry to Boston on a voyage it called the "Great Bottle Sail." The structure is 40 feet tall, 18 feet in diameter and weighs 15,000 pounds. If it were a real milk bottle, it would hold 58,620 gallons of milk.

Short Cut Spinach Lasagna

This is a wonderful low cholesterol, lowfat pasta dish that appeals to people of all ages. It is especially appealing to the cook, because it is so quick and easy to make! You don't even have to cook the lasagna first, which saves both time and mess.

1 (10-ounce) package frozen chopped spinach
2 cups (1 pound) low-fat or nonfat cottage cheese
2 cups (¼ pound) part-skim shredded mozzarella cheese, divided
1 egg or egg substitute
1 teaspoon oregano
Salt and pepper, to taste
1 (29- to 32-ounce) jar spaghetti sauce
9 lasagna noodles (¼ pound), uncooked
1 cup water

Thaw and drain spinach. In large bowl combine cottage cheese, 1 cup of mozzarella, egg, spinach, oregano, salt, and pepper. In greased 9x13-inch baking dish, layer 1 cup sauce, ⅓ of noodles and half the cheese mixture. Repeat. Top with remaining noodles, then remaining sauce. Sprinkle with remaining 1 cup mozzarella. Pour water around edges. Cover tightly with foil. Bake at 350° for 1 hour and 15 minutes or until bubbly. Let stand 15 minutes before serving.

Hint: This may be made up to 2 days in advance. It also freezes very well.

From Ellie's Kitchen to Yours (Massachusetts)

PHOTO BY GWEN McKEE

Boston Children's Museum

Reuben Lasagna

1 (27-ounce) can sauerkraut, rinsed and drained
1 pound sliced deli corned beef, coarsely chopped
1 (10¾-ounce) can cream of mushroom soup
1 (8-ounce) bottle Thousand Island Dressing
1¼ cups milk
1 medium onion, chopped
1 teaspoon dry mustard
9 oven-ready (no boil) lasagna noodles
1 cup (4 ounces) shredded Swiss cheese
½ cup plain bread crumbs
1 tablespoon butter, melted

Preheat oven to 350°. Coat 9x13-inch baking dish with Pam. In medium bowl, combine sauerkraut and corned beef. Mix well. In another medium bowl, combine well soup, dressing, milk, onion, and mustard. Spread ½ mixture in baking dish. Place 3 lasagna noodles on top. Top with ½ the corned beef mixture, then ½ of remaining soup mixture. Layer with 3 more noodles, then remaining corned beef mixture. Add the last 3 noodles and cover with remaining soup mixture. Sprinkle Swiss cheese, then bread crumbs over top. Drizzle butter over top. Cover with aluminum foil. Bake 45–50 minutes, or until bubbly. Uncover and bake 5–10 minutes or until golden. Let set for 5–10 minutes. Cut and serve.

Note: Oven-ready lasagna noodles are thinner, so they don't need to be boiled before using. You can find them near the regular lasagna noodles.

The Cookbook AAUW (New York)

Chicken with Fine Herbs and Sun-Dried Tomatoes

10 sun-dried tomatoes, cut julienne

2 tablespoons chopped shallots

2 (8-ounce) boneless chicken breasts, cut into julienne strips

¼ cup white wine

½ teaspoon each: freshly chopped basil, thyme, and tarragon

¼ cup heavy cream

½ pound fettuccine, cooked al dente

Salt and white pepper to taste

¼ cup Parmesan cheese

Sauté sundried tomatoes and shallots in olive oil in a skillet for a few minutes. Add chicken, cook on both sides until almost done, then deglaze the pan with white wine. Add the fresh herbs, heavy cream and pasta. Reduce the heavy cream over medium heat while tossing the pasta gently. Season with salt and white pepper. Garnish with chopped parsley and Parmesan cheese. Serves 2.

A recipe from Café Zelda, Newport
A Taste of Newport (Rhode Island)

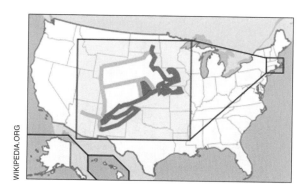

WIKIPEDIA.ORG

Rhode Island was the first of the thirteen original colonies to declare independence from British rule and the last to ratify the United States Constitution. It is the smallest state in size in the United States. It covers an area of 1,214 square miles. Its distances north to south are 48 miles and east to west, 37 miles.

Spinach Pasta with Scallops

The boursin cheese adds a savory flavor to the tender scallops in this recipe.

2 tablespoons butter
2 tablespoons olive oil
¾ pound bay or sea
  scallops
½ green bell pepper,
  seeded and diced
1 large tomato, seeded and
  diced
4 green onions, chopped
10 mushrooms, sliced

2 cups heavy cream
½ cup freshly grated
  Parmesan cheese
1 (5-ounce) package boursin
  garlic cheese
9 ounces spinach fettuccine,
  cooked al dente and drained
Salt and freshly ground
  black pepper to taste

In a large skillet over moderate heat, melt butter with olive oil. Add scallops and sauté 1–2 minutes. Stir in green pepper, tomato, green onions, and mushrooms. Sauté for 4 minutes. Add cream and Parmesan cheese and stir until well blended. Reduce heat and simmer until sauce thickens, about 8 minutes. Add boursin cheese and stir until blended. In heated serving dish, toss warm fettuccine with scallop mixture. Add salt and pepper to taste. Serve immediately. Makes 4–6 main dish servings or 8–10 side dish servings.

More Than Sandwiches (Massachusetts)

WIKIPEDIA.ORG

Sketch of the Old North Church c. 1882,

Angel Hair Pasta Primavera

1 (16-ounce) package angel
   hair pasta or vermicelli
¼ cup vegetable oil
1 medium-sized yellow
   squash, sliced (about 1 cup)
1 medium-sized onion, diced
1 cup sliced fresh mushrooms
4 ounces fresh or 6 ounces
   frozen Chinese pea pods,
   thawed

1 large clove garlic
2 large ripe tomatoes,
   chopped
1½ teaspoons salt (optional)
1 teaspoon dried basil
¼ cup grated Parmesan
   cheese

In a deep 4-quart saucepan bring 2 quarts of water to a boil. Cook angel hair pasta according to package directions. In a 12-inch skillet over medium heat, heat oil, adding squash, onion, mushrooms, pea pods, and garlic. Cook 5 minutes, stirring occasionally until vegetables are crisp-tender. Add tomatoes, salt, and basil to vegetables; cook 2 minutes until heated through. Drain pasta. Add vegetables to pasta in saucepan along with ¼ cup Parmesan cheese. Stir to mix. Serve with additional cheese. Serves 6.

The Parkview Way to Vegetarian Cooking (Maine)

It was at Old North Church in Boston that lanterns were hung to signal Paul Revere to begin his ride to Lexington and Concord. Actually two riders, Revere and his North Street neighbor William Dawes both set off to sound the alarm to be sure the message got through if one was captured. Revere was in fact captured, and Dawes got through, but it was Revere that Longfellow immortalized in his famous poem, "Paul Revere's Ride."

Andrea's Spaghetti Pie

¾ pound spaghetti
¼ cup butter
2 eggs, beaten separately
2 deep dish pie pans
1 (16-ounce) container
  ricotta cheese
1 (10-ounce) package
  chopped spinach, thawed
  and drained
Parsley

⅛ teaspoon garlic powder
8 ounces mozzarella cheese,
  shredded
4 links Italian sausage, cooked
  and sliced
1 (28-ounce) jar spaghetti
  sauce, or an equal amount
  homemade
Grated cheese

Cook spaghetti a little less than normal. Drain; add butter and one of the beaten eggs. Mix. Divide in two; put in 2 greased pie pans, lining the pan, coming up the sides. Mix ricotta, spinach, parsley, garlic powder, mozzarella, and the other egg. Mix sausage and spaghetti sauce. Spread a layer of cheese/spinach mixture, then sausage, topping with grated cheese. Bake at 350° for about 25–30 minutes. Let set 10–15 minutes before slicing. Serves 6–8 people.

What's Cooking at Stony Brook (New York)

Benjamin Franklin (center) at work on a printing press.

CHARLES E. MILLS, LIBRARY OF CONGRESS

116

Eggplant Sauce for Spaghetti

This thick sauce is a good way to introduce eggplant to skeptics.

1 medium onion, finely
  chopped
1 clove garlic, crushed
2 teaspoons dried parsley, or
  ¼ cup fresh, snipped
1 tablespoon olive oil
1 cup water
2 large eggplants, cut in
  ½-inch cubes

1 (28-ounce) can whole
  tomatoes, or 8–10 fresh
  Italian tomatoes, chopped
2 (6-ounce) cans tomato paste
2 teaspoons dried oregano
1 teaspoon salt
1 teaspoon sugar
Dash of pepper

In saucepan, sauté onion, garlic, and parsley in oil until onion is tender. Add water and eggplant cubes; bring to a boil, reduce heat, and simmer 5 minutes. Add tomatoes, tomato paste, oregano, salt, sugar, and pepper. Heat mixture to boiling; reduce heat. Cover and simmer 15 minutes, stirring occasionally. Serve over hot spaghetti; sprinkle with Parmesan cheese. Serves 6.

Note: May add fresh or canned mushrooms. May substitute zucchini squash for 1 eggplant.

Extending the Table (Pennsylvania)

In 1723 at the age of seventeen, Benjamin Franklin left his hometown of Boston, Massachusetts, for Philadelphia, seeking a new start in a new city. By age twenty-four, Franklin owned his own printing business and a newspaper, *The Pennsylvania Gazette.* He launched the first firefighting company in America, the first fire insurance company, street lighting and paving, reorganization of the town watch, a local militia, and Philadelphia's first hospital. Franklin was the only person to sign all four of the key documents that led to the formation of the United States of America. The documents are: the Declaration of Independence, the Treaty of Alliance with France, the Treaty of Paris, and the Constitution of the United States.

Pasta Godjabuda

(Sicilian Pasta with Onions and Olive Oil)

2 medium onions, cut in half
  vertically and then cut
  each half into ½-inch
  slivers
⅓ cup olive oil
2 cloves garlic, sliced fine
1 tablespoon oregano
Sprinkle of thyme
1 teaspoon basil
2 shakes of cayenne pepper
2 shakes of crushed red
  pepper
Salt to taste
Parmesan cheese
1 pound linguine, cooked

While the water is boiling for the pasta, sauté the onions in olive oil over medium heat until transparent. Add the garlic and sauté. Add spices; cover and simmer while pasta is cooking. When pasta is ready, strain pasta, but leave some water. Mix ⅓ of onions and garlic with pasta. Put pasta in bowls and add onion mixture to top. Season with Parmesan cheese. Serves 3–4.

In Good Taste (New York)

Bow Ties with Gorgonzola

1 pound cooked bow tie pasta
1 pound fresh spinach
3 large cloves garlic, minced
1 tablespoon olive oil
8 large plum tomatoes, cut
  into wedges
1 cup wine or chicken broth
Salt and pepper to taste
2–3 fresh basil leaves, chopped
8 ounces Gorgonzola cheese
  (broken into chunks)

Cook pasta according to package directions (al dente). Wash and take stems off spinach. Sauté garlic in olive oil. Add tomato wedges; simmer for 20 minutes. Add spinach, wine, salt, pepper, and basil. Simmer for 5 minutes. Add Gorgonzola and stir. When cheese melts, mix with pasta and serve. Serves 4.

Savor the Flavor (New York)

Linguine with Tomatoes and Basil

Perfect for those hot, lazy days of summer when ripe tomatoes and basil are abundant. The heat of the pasta warms and brings out the flavors of the sauce in a wonderfully subtle way. Delicious and easy.

4 large ripe tomatoes (1 pound) cut into ½-inch cubes
1 pound Brie cheese, rind removed, torn into irregular pieces
1 cup cleaned fresh basil leaves, cut into strips
3 garlic cloves, peeled and finely minced

1 cup plus 1 tablespoon best quality olive oil
2½ teaspoons salt
½ teaspoon freshly ground black pepper
1½ pounds linguine
Freshly grated imported Parmesan cheese (optional)

Combine tomatoes, Brie, basil, garlic, 1 cup olive oil, ½ teaspoon salt, and pepper in a large serving bowl. Prepare at least 2 hours before serving and set aside, covered, at room temperature.

Bring 6 quarts water to boil in large pot. Add 1 tablespoon olive oil and remaining salt. Add the linguine and boil until tender, but still firm, 8–10 minutes. Drain pasta and immediately toss with tomato sauce. Serve at once, passing the pepper mill and grated Parmesan cheese. Serves 4–6.

Tasty Temptations from the Village by the Sea (Massachusetts)

NASA

Nantucket is an island 30 miles south of Cape Cod, Massachusetts. It is a tourist destination and summer colony. The population of the island soars from approximately 10,000 to 50,000 during the summer months, due to tourists and summer residents. According to *Forbes Magazine*, in 2006, Nantucket had the highest median property value of any Massachusetts zip code. The island features one of the highest concentrations of pre-Civil War structures in the United States.

Pasta with Black Olives and Tomato Sauce

2 or 3 cloves garlic, finely
  chopped
Olive oil
1 (28-ounce) can Italian
  peeled tomatoes
1 (16-ounce) can black pitted
  olives, drained and sliced
1 (8-ounce) can tomato sauce

1 pound small pasta shells
1 pound mozzarella cheese,
  diced
5 slices bacon, cooked and
  crumbled
Grated Parmesan cheese
Parsley, finely chopped

Sauté garlic in pan coated with olive oil. Add Italian peeled tomatoes (break big tomato chunks apart with wooden spoon) and simmer for 30 minutes. Stir in olives and tomato sauce. Simmer about 1–1½ hours or until sauce thickens.

Cook small shells according to directions on package and drain. On a serving platter or bowl, layer sauce, shells, and mozzarella cheese. Top with remaining sauce and sprinkle with bacon and Parmesan cheese. Top with parsley. Serves 4–6.

It's Our Serve (New York)

Rigatoni with Thick Mushroom Sauce

1 tablespoon butter
¼ cup olive oil
1 pound brown mushrooms,
   preferably portobello or
   cremini
2 cloves garlic, minced
⅛ teaspoon crushed red
   pepper (optional)
1½ cups chicken broth

½ chicken bouillon cube
1½ tablespoons chopped
   Italian parsley
1 pound short tubular pasta,
   such as rigatoni, mezze or
   maniche
¼ cup freshly grated
   Parmesan cheese

Put butter and oil in a large non-stick skillet. Using the largest holes on a grater, shred mushrooms and add to skillet. Add garlic and red pepper. Sauté over medium heat until liquid from mushrooms evaporates, about 10 minutes. Add broth and bouillon cube, increase heat to HIGH and cook 10–12 minutes for flavors to blend and liquid to partially reduce. Remove from heat; stir in parsley and set aside.

While sauce cooks, prepare pasta according to package directions. When pasta is cooked, drain and return to pot. Add mushroom sauce and stir over medium heat one minute. Remove from heat; add cheese and toss to mix. Serve immediately. Serves 4–6.

Asbury Cooks 1799-1999 (New York)

Linguini with Broccoli and Bay Scallops

This recipe was featured on our first Commissary recipe calendar in 1979, and judging from the feedback we received, it was the most frequently tried and enjoyed recipe on the calendar that year.

4 cups broccoli florets and
  stems
¾ pound fresh linguini or
  ½ pound dried
¾ cup butter, divided
2 teaspoons minced garlic

1 pound bay scallops
2 teaspoons salt
1 teaspoon pepper
⅔ cup grated Parmesan
  cheese or more, to taste

Peel broccoli stems and cut into ¼-inch slices. Blanch broccoli in boiling salted water, drain, refresh under cold water, drain, and set aside. Cook linguini until al dente in a large pot of boiling salted water. Drain well and toss with ¼ cup butter. Heat remaining ½ cup butter in a large skillet. Add garlic and sauté until softened. Add scallops, salt, and pepper. Sauté 3 minutes or until scallops are just opaque. Add broccoli and heat 1 minute. Add pasta and heat through. Add cheese and serve at once. Serves 4.

The Frog Commissary Cookbook (Pennsylvania)

Lemon Asparagus Pasta

1 (8-ounce) package angel
  hair pasta
2½ cups cut fresh asparagus
  (1-inch pieces)
1 tablespoon butter
½ cup chopped green onions
1½ teaspoons grated lemon
  peel

3 tablespoons lemon juice
¾ cup milk
2 eggs
1 tablespoon chopped fresh
  dill
¼ teaspoon salt
⅛ teaspoon ground nutmeg

Cook pasta in boiling water 4 minutes. Add asparagus and cook 2 minutes longer or until tender. Drain.

While pasta cooks, melt butter in large frying pan over medium heat. Add green onions and lemon peel and sauté 1 minute. Add lemon juice and cook until liquid is almost evaporated.

Beat together milk and eggs. Add milk mixture, pasta, and asparagus to pan with green onions. Cook over low heat until milk mixture is slightly thick, about 4 minutes. Do not boil. Stir in dill, salt, and nutmeg. Serve immediately. Serves 4–6.

Simply in Season (Pennsylvania)

PENNSYLVANIA TURNPIKE

Construction of the Pennsylvania Turnpike began in 1937 and was completed from Ohio to New Jersey in 1956. It was the first roadway in the United States that had no cross streets, no railroad crossings, and no traffic lights over its entire length. A trip through the mountains of Pennsylvania with grades of no more than 3% was unheard of prior to this time. A four-lane superhighway through the Allegheny Mountains with unrestricted passing (except through tunnels), the Pennsylvania Turnpike even made the pages of *Scientific American* due to its state-of-the-art design and construction. One of the hallmarks of the original turnpike was the seven tunnels bored through the mountains of Pennsylvania.

Basic Pesto

Although originally made with mortar and pestle, pesto now can be made without sacrificing quality by blending all the ingredients in a blender. Recipes vary from locale to locale, restaurant to restaurant.

2 cups fresh basil leaves
½ cup fresh parsley leaves
½ cup olive oil
¼ cup pinoli (pine nuts), sweet walnuts, or shelled almonds (pine nuts are preferable, but they are very expensive and not readily available)

2 cloves fresh garlic, chopped
¼ cup grated Parmesan cheese
¼ cup grated Romano cheese
Pinch of salt
Freshly ground pepper to taste

Blend all ingredients until a paste-like consistency is achieved. If fresh basil is unattainable, use 2 cups fresh parsley, plus 2 tablespoons dried basil. The condiment can be stored by covering with olive oil and refrigerating for future use.

Pesto is best over pasta, as a sauce for shrimp, most seafood, as a base for soups, and on some meats.

Variations: Use of different types of grated cheeses or combinations thereof: orange or lemon rind; 1–2 tablespoons heavy cream; eliminating garlic; including ricotta; adding a few anchovies.

Recollections and Collections (Pennsylvania)

The Liberty Bell weighs 2,080 pounds and is 12 feet in circumference at the lip. It bears the following inscription: "Proclaim Liberty Throughout All the Land Unto All the Inhabitants Thereof."

Spring Vegetable Risotto

3 tablespoons butter
3 tablespoons olive oil
½ cup chopped scallions, white part only (reserve green part)
2 stalks celery, coarsely chopped
½ cup coarsely chopped fresh parsley
2 cups rice (preferably arborio)

4 cups chicken broth
¼ pound asparagus, trimmed and cut into 1-inch lengths
¾ cup shelled fresh peas
½ teaspoon pepper
¼ cup minced scallions, green part only
Parmesan cheese

Combine butter and oil in 11x14-inch glass dish. Cover and place in microwave oven, cooking on high power for 3 minutes. Add white scallions, celery, parsley, and rice, stirring to coat. Cook uncovered for 4 minutes on high power. Stir in broth and cook uncovered for 12 minutes on high. Stir in asparagus and peas and cook uncovered for another 12 minutes on high. Remove dish from microwave oven. Stir in pepper and green scallions. Cover loosely and allow to sit for 8–10 minutes. Serve with Parmesan cheese at table. Serves 6.

Note: Risotto, a classic Italian rice dish, is usually made with arborio rice, but will work with long and short-grain rice as well. The rice should be creamy, while still being "al dente," or having an inner bite.

Delicious Developments (New York)

Nutty Brown Rice

1 pound mushrooms, sliced
4 green onions, cut into
   ½-inch pieces, including
   green parts
1 garlic clove, minced
4 tablespoons unsalted butter
2 cups uncooked brown rice
½ teaspoon dried thyme
¼ teaspoon ground turmeric
Freshly ground pepper
6 cups beef broth
1½ cups chopped pecans
Whole pecans and chopped
   green onion tops for garnish

In an ovenproof casserole, sauté mushrooms, onions, and garlic in butter for 5–7 minutes. Stir in rice and cook for 3 minutes. Add seasonings and broth, heat to boiling and bake, uncovered, in preheated 400° oven for 45 minutes. Stir in pecans and bake another 15 minutes. Test rice and cook a little longer if not done. To serve, garnish with whole pecans and green onion tops. Yields 8 servings.

Specialties of the House (New York)

Three Cheese Baked Rice

1 small onion, chopped
1 small red pepper, diced
1 small green pepper, diced
1 rib celery, diced
3 tablespoons butter
1 cup uncooked rice
1¾ cups chicken broth
¾ cup white wine
1 small green chile pepper,
   diced
¾ teaspoon salt
1½ cups sour cream
2½ ounces Gruyère cheese,
   cubed
2½ ounces grated Cheddar
   cheese
2½ ounces grated mozzarella
   cheese

Preheat oven to 350°. In Dutch oven or oven-safe pan sauté onion, peppers, and celery in butter for 3 minutes. Add rice, chicken broth, wine, chile pepper, and salt. Bring to boil, cover and place in oven. Bake 15–20 minutes or until all liquid has been absorbed. Remove from oven and transfer to large bowl. Let cool slightly.

Stir sour cream and cheeses into cooled rice mixture and transfer to a buttered 9x13-inch pan. Bake at 400° for 20 minutes or until lightly browned. Serves 6–10.

It's Our Serve (New York)

Eggplant and Rice Provençale

This is really special!

Large eggplants, about 2
  pounds
4 tablespoons olive oil
3 cups finely chopped onions
1 green bell pepper, cored,
  seeded, cut into 1-inch
  cubes
2 cloves garlic, finely minced
1 teaspoon chopped fresh
  thyme or ½ teaspoon dried

1 bay leaf
3 tomatoes, peeled, cored,
  chopped
1 cup raw rice
3¾ cups chicken broth
Salt and freshly ground black
  pepper
½ cup grated Parmesan
  cheese
2 tablespoons butter

Preheat oven to 400°. Trim off ends of eggplants and cut into 1-inch
cubes. Heat oil in a large skillet and add eggplant cubes. Cook over
high heat, shaking skillet occasionally. Add the onions, green pepper, garlic, thyme, and bay leaf, stirring. Stir in the tomatoes and
lower the heat. Simmer 5 minutes or until most of the liquid in the
skillet has evaporated. This is important—the ingredients must be
stewed until fairly thickened. Stir in rice and chicken broth. Season
with salt and pepper. Spoon mixture into a greased baking dish, and
sprinkle with cheese. Dot with butter and bake, uncovered, 30 minutes. Serves 8.

Three Rivers Cookbook I (Pennsylvania)

Oriental Rice

(Indonesia)

1 tablespoon vegetable oil
2 cups cooked rice, chilled
½ cup raisins

½ cup water chestnuts
¼ cup soy sauce

Heat oil in a wok or skillet; add rice, stirring and tossing until grains
are coated with oil. Add raisins and water chestnuts; stir until mixture is heated through. Add soy sauce and blend. Yields 4 servings.

Variation: Cooked, diced beef or chicken may be added.

The Art of Asian Cooking (Massachusetts)

Beans and Rice Casserole

1 cup brown rice
1 tablespoon olive oil
1 medium onion, chopped
3 cloves garlic, minced
1 (28-ounce) can seasoned
  diced tomatoes
1 (15½-ounce) can dark red
  kidney beans, drained

1 (15½-ounce) can white
  beans, drained
Parsley, celery seed, basil,
  white pepper, ground cumin
  to taste
1 bay leaf

Bring 2½ cups water to boil. Add 1 cup brown rice. Cover; reduce to simmer for 45 minutes. Sauté onion and garlic cloves in olive oil in large skillet. Add seasoned tomatoes in juice and drained beans to onion and garlic. Add parsley, celery seed, basil, white pepper, and ground cumin to taste. Add 1 bay leaf. Let simmer for 20 minutes. Add cooked brown rice. Simmer 10–15 additional minutes. Serve with a fresh green salad and corn bread.

Gather Around Our Table (New York)

Broccoli Rice Bake

1 cup brown rice
½ teaspoon salt
2 tablespoons oil
1 large onion, chopped
2 cloves garlic, minced
1 teaspoon each: dill,
  thyme, oregano
4 tablespoons chopped
  parsley

½ pound mushrooms, sliced
1 green pepper, diced
2 pounds broccoli, stalks
  peeled and all thinly sliced
½ cup cashews, broken
1 cup grated Gruyère cheese
¼ cup grated Parmesan
  cheese
1 cup sour cream

Cook rice in salted water until barely done; sauté onion, garlic, seasonings, parsley, mushrooms, and green pepper in oil briefly. Add broccoli; cook and stir until crisp-tender; add nuts. Spread cooked rice in a greased 9x13-inch baking dish; cover with vegetable mixture, sprinkle with cheeses, and put sour cream on top. Bake in a 350° oven for 20 minutes or until bubbling. Serves 8.

The MBL Centennial Cookbook (Massachusetts)

Pierogi
(Dumplings)

SOFT DOUGH:

1 cup sour cream
12 eggs
1 tablespoon oil

1 teaspoon salt
2½ cups flour

Beat the first 4 ingredients. Mix in the flour, adding more flour, if necessary, until the dough forms a soft ball. Divide dough in half. On a floured board, roll each half of the dough into a thin sheet. Cut circles in the dough with a cutter 3½–4 inches in diameter.

CHEESE FILLING:

2 egg yolks
1 tablespoon soft butter
1 pound farmers cheese (solid
  cottage cheese), mashed

¼ teaspoon salt
1 tablespoon sugar

Cream yolks and butter. Combine with other ingredients and mix. Put 1 teaspoon of filling on each dough circle, being careful to place it off center. Moisten the rim of the circle with water. Fold the unfilled side of the circle over the filling and press the edges of the resulting crescent firmly to seal them. Drop Pierogi into boiling salted water. Cook gently for 5 minutes. Remove with perforated spoon. Serve with melted butter and sautéed onions. Serves 6.

Note: Never crowd or pile Pierogi: uncooked Pierogi stick to each other; when crowded or piled, cooked Pierogi become misshapen and heavy.

The Whole Valley Cookbook (Pennsylvania)

Mock Pierogi

3 small onions, chopped
¼ pound margarine (1 stick)
1 medium can sauerkraut,
   drained
1 (12-ounce) package wide
   noodles, cooked

1 can cream of mushroom
   soup
¼ cup sour cream
1 (4-ounce) can mushroom
   pieces

Sauté onions until golden brown in margarine. Add rinsed sauer-kraut. Pour over cooked noodles. Add soup and sour cream; stir. Add drained mushrooms; reserve liquid (add if you need more liquid). Place in casserole and bake at 350° for 20 minutes until bubbly.

Our Best Home Cooking (New York)

Two-and-a-Half-Minute Skillet Pizza

No one should have to wait to eat a pizza like you do when you call up for one to go—"That'll be twenty minutes, please." This one's gone by then.

Start with a low, round loaf of bread. Its diameter should closely match the frying pan you'll use. Cut the bread in half so that you have two round loaves (you'll love this pizza so much that you'll want to make another right away). Heat ¼ inch of olive oil in the frying pan until it just begins to smoke. Quickly sprinkle in a healthy mixture of herbs—I use 2 tablespoons each of basil, black pepper, garlic, marjoram, oregano, and rosemary; also 1 tablespoon of beef bouillon. Add 1 cup of tomato sauce; stir a few times as it begins to bubble. Then sprinkle 2 cups of mixed grated provolone and Jarlsberg cheese and ½ cup of grated Parmesan evenly across the sauce. Lay the bread, cut-side-down, into the sauce. Let it simmer for about 30 seconds. Turn it upside down onto a plate and cut into wedges to serve. It goes without saying that you can add whatever you want to that sauce—mushrooms, pepperoni, and so on.

Another Blue Strawbery (New Hampshire)

Crabmeat Quiche

1 (9-inch) unbaked pie shell
½ pound Swiss cheese, cut
  in strips
1 cup crabmeat
½ cup small shrimp
2 cups light cream
4 eggs, beaten

1 tablespoon flour
½ teaspoon salt
Dash of pepper
Dash of cayenne
¼ teaspoon nutmeg
2 tablespoons melted butter
2 tablespoons sherry wine

Line pie shell with cheese. Cover with a layer of crabmeat and shrimp. Combine cream, eggs, flour, salt, pepper, cayenne, and nutmeg. Stir in melted butter and sherry. Beat well and pour over seafood. Refrigerate or freeze. When ready to serve, bake at 375° for 40 minutes or until golden brown. Let stand 20 minutes before serving.

Sandy Hook Volunteer Fire Co. Ladies Aux. Cookbook
(Connecticut)

Zucchini Quiche

French

Here is a simple, tasty crustless quiche that is good for lunch or a light supper.

4 eggs, beaten
1 medium onion, finely
  chopped
4 slices bacon, chopped, or
  ¼ pound ham, diced

2 zucchini, finely chopped
1 cup grated Cheddar cheese
2 rounded tablespoons
  self-rising flour

Preheat oven to 375°. In a bowl, combine all ingredients. The mixture will be fairly thick. Grease a 9-inch quiche or pie dish. Pour the mixture into the dish and smooth over. Bake in oven for 30 minutes. Serves 4.

Serving suggestion: Serve with a green salad.

The Original Philadelphia Neighborhood Cookbook
(Pennsylvania)

Lobster Quiche

CRUST:

1½ cups flour
1 teaspoon salt
6 tablespoons butter or
  shortening

3–5 tablespoons ice water

Mix together the flour and salt. Using a pastry fork or food processor, cut in the shortening until the mixture resembles coarse sand. Mix in just enough ice water to form a ball. Wrap the pastry in plastic wrap and refrigerate for 1 hour. Roll out the chilled dough on a lightly floured board to ⅛-inch to ¼-inch thickness. Line a 9-inch quiche pan with the pastry, cover with plastic wrap, and refrigerate until ready to use.

FILLING:

3 eggs
1½ cups half-and-half
1 tablespoon butter, melted
1½ cups coarsely chopped
  cooked lobster meat
¾ cup grated Swiss cheese
¾ cup grated Cheddar
  cheese

1 small onion
1 clove garlic
¼ teaspoon dry mustard
½ teaspoon tarragon
1 teaspoon parsley
Salt and pepper to taste

Preheat oven to 350°. In a large bowl, beat the eggs well. Add the half-and-half and beat again. Stir in the lobster meat and cheeses. Set aside. Chop the onion fine and sauté in a little butter. When the onion is almost done, crush the garlic and stir in; remove from heat. Add the onion and garlic, dry mustard, herbs, salt, and pepper to the lobster mixture and combine well. Pour into the quiche crust and bake at 350° for 45 minutes. Cool on a rack for 5 minutes before slicing.

A recipe from Murphy's Bed & Breakfast, Narragansett
The Bed & Breakfast Cookbook (Rhode Island)

Spring Vegetable Tart

1 sheet frozen puff pastry
2 pounds ricotta cheese
½ cup grated Parmesan
  cheese
½ cup sour cream
½ teaspoon oregano
½ teaspoon garlic salt

Salt to taste
½ teaspoon pepper
2 tomatoes, sliced
1 zucchini, sliced
1 yellow squash, sliced
16 asparagus spears
8 mushrooms, sliced

Thaw pastry at room temperature for 10–15 minutes. Press into greased and floured 10-inch tart pan with removable side. Combine ricotta cheese, Parmesan cheese, sour cream, oregano, garlic salt, salt, and pepper in bowl; mix well. Spread evenly in prepared tart pan. Arrange vegetables over top. Bake at 350° for 30 minutes or until pastry is golden brown. Place on serving plate; remove side of pan. Yields 8 servings.

Rhode Island Cooks (Rhode Island)

Chipped Beef Pot Pie

1 cup chopped onion
4 ounces dried beef, cut up
¼ cup hot fat
2 tablespoons flour
¼–½ teaspoon salt
¼ teaspoon pepper

2 cups thinly sliced carrots
2 cups thinly sliced potatoes
2 cups water
1 beef bouillon cube
Pastry, to cover casserole
  (optional)

Sauté onions and beef in hot fat. Stir in flour and seasonings. Add remaining ingredients and bring to a boil. Cover and simmer 5 minutes. Place in greased baking dish and top with pastry. Bake at 425° for 25–30 minutes. Makes 6 servings.

Note: In order to never have to make a pastry top especially for this recipe, I always save the leftovers whenever I bake pies. I either freeze the leftovers in the shape of a small circle, or else I cut every little scrap of leftovers into geometric shapes. When arranged on top of the casserole, it makes an attractive design.

The Festival Cookbook (Pennsylvania)

Vermont Turkey and Broccoli Puff

SHERRY CHEDDAR SAUCE:

¼ cup butter
¼ cup flour
1 cup light cream
½ cup sherry

1 teaspoon salt
½ teaspoon basil
1 cup shredded Vermont sharp
   Cheddar cheese

Melt butter in saucepan, add flour, and stir to combine. Stir in the cream, sherry, salt, and basil and cook over low heat, stirring, until thick. Stir in 1 cup Cheddar cheese until melted.

1 head broccoli
6 baked puff pastry squares
Fresh spinach leaves

Sliced turkey
Vermont sharp Cheddar
   cheese, sliced

Steam broccoli flowerets and stems; cut into diagonal slices ¼-inch thick, until tender. Mix the broccoli into the sauce and keep warm over low heat. Split baked puff pastry squares and layer on the bottom half of each, in order: fresh spinach leaves, sliced turkey, ½ cup broccoli in sauce, 2 slices Vermont sharp Cheddar cheese. Heat under a broiler or in a hot oven to melt cheese. Cover with top of puff and serve immediately. Serves 6.

Peter Christian's Favorites (Maine)

 Because of cold nights, Vermont turkeys have an extra layer of fat, which is good for natural basting. No Vermont turkey can be sold out of the state because there is no federal turkey inspection.

Cranberry Chutney

1 cup water
1 cup sugar
2 tablespoons vinegar
½ cup raisins
½ cup nuts (almonds or
    walnuts)

1 tablespoon brown sugar
¼ teaspoon cayenne pepper
¼ teaspoon ground ginger
¼ teaspoon garlic salt
2 cups cranberries

Combine all ingredients in a saucepan and cook on low heat for ½ hour or until thick. Pour into fancy jars and cover with wax to give as a gift. Great with poultry. Keep in the refrigerator. Will keep for several weeks.

More Than Sandwiches (Massachusetts)

Apricot Ginger Chutney

A wonderful accompaniment for freshly grilled fish, meat, or poultry.

2 cups dried apricots
1½ tablespoons chopped
    candied ginger
1 cup dark raisins
½ lime, thinly sliced
1 large onion, thinly sliced
1½ cups packed dark brown
    sugar

½–1 cup orange juice
½ cup wine vinegar
3 cloves garlic, minced
1 teaspoon dried mustard
½ cup tomato sauce
½ teaspoon cinnamon
½ teaspoon allspice
½ teaspoon cloves

Wash and chop apricots. Combine all ingredients in a medium saucepan and simmer 20 minutes, stirring often until slightly thickened. Pour cool chutney into a covered container and refrigerate. May be served cold or at room temperature. Serves 10–12 or more.

The Maine Collection (Maine)

Harvest Relish

Good with baked beans.

4 onions, ground	6 cups sugar
4 cups chopped cabbage	1 tablespoon celery seed
4 cups chopped green	2 tablespoons mustard seed
tomatoes	2 teaspoons turmeric
12 green peppers, chopped	4 cups vinegar
6 red peppers, chopped	2 cups water
½ cup salt	

Combine vegetables and salt and let sit overnight. In morning, rinse vegetables and drain. Combine remaining ingredients and pour over vegetables. Bring to a boil. Simmer 3 minutes, stirring frequently. Pack into hot sterilized pint jars and process in boiling water 10 minutes. Makes 8–10 pints.

Merrymeeting Merry Eating (Maine)

Meats

The Breakers was built in Newport, Rhode Island, as the summer home of the Vanderbilts. The 70-room mansion was completed in 1895. Although bought by the Preservation Society of Newport County in 1972, the family continues to live on the third floor of the Breakers, which is not open to the public. It is the most-visited attraction in Rhode Island.

Shrimp and Beef Filet Brochettes with Sesame Marinade

This is a delicious combination. The beef and shrimp marinate for only 5 minutes, long enough to give them a hint of Asian flavor, but not so long that the shrimp become tough.

1 cup peanut oil
½ cup soy sauce
3 tablespoons honey
3 tablespoons cider vinegar
2 tablespoons sesame seeds, toasted
2 cloves garlic, minced

1 teaspoon minced fresh ginger
3 pounds beef filet, cut into 1-inch cubes
45 medium shrimp, shelled and, if desired, deveined
16 bamboo skewers

In a bowl, whisk together the oil, soy sauce, honey, vinegar, sesame seeds, garlic, and ginger. Set aside. On each skewer, alternate 4 pieces of beef with 2 or 3 shrimp. Place in a roasting pan in one layer. Pour marinade over and let sit for 5 minutes. Grill over medium-hot coals for 4 minutes on each side or until the shrimp turn pink. Makes 6–8 servings.

The Long Island Holiday Cookbook (New York)

WIKIPEDIA.ORG

Kent Falls

Beef Burgundy

2 large onions
4 pounds beef sirloin tip,
    cut in cubes
Flour
Salt
Pepper
Celery salt

Garlic
A little nutmeg
1 (1-pint) box fresh
    mushrooms
Butter
1 cup beef stock
1 cup red wine

Chop onions and brown in a little fat in skillet. Remove to deep casserole or Dutch oven. Dust meat with flour and brown well in skillet with salt, pepper, celery salt, garlic, and a little nutmeg. Add to casserole.

Brown fresh mushrooms in butter and add. Pour beef stock and red wine over all. Cover tightly and cook in a slow oven (325°) for at least 2½ hours. Serve with rice or wild rice.

Note: I find 2 cans of sliced water chestnuts add much to this dish as well. Serves 6–10.

Berkshire Seasonings (Massachusetts)

The Berkshires, located in the western parts of Massachusetts and Connecticut, is both a specific highland geologic region and a broader associated cultural region. The Berkshires are a popular tourist attraction and vacation getaway. With numerous trails, including part of the Appalachian Trail, large tracts of wilderness, parks like Kent Falls, Berkshire Botanical Garden, and Hebert Arboretum, the Berkshires are very popular with nature lovers.

Braciole

2½ pounds round steak,
  ¼- to ½-inch thick
½ pound bulk Italian
  sausage
1 tablespoon parsley
1 teaspoon leaf oregano,
  divided

2 small cloves garlic,
  minced
1 large onion, finely chopped
1 teaspoon salt
1 (16-ounce) can Italian-
  style tomatoes
1 (6-ounce) can tomato paste

Trim all excess fat from steak. Cut into 8 evenly shaped pieces. Pound steak pieces between waxed paper until very thin and easy to roll.

In skillet, lightly brown sausage. Drain well and combine with parsley, ½ teaspoon oregano, garlic, onion, and ½ teaspoon salt; mix well. Spread each steak with 2–3 tablespoons sausage mixture. Roll up jellyroll fashion and tie.

Stack steak rolls in crockpot. Combine tomatoes, tomato paste, ½ teaspoon salt, and ½ teaspoon oregano; pour over rolls. Cover and cook on low setting for 7–10 hours. Serve steak rolls with sauce.

Cuisine à la Mode (Rhode Island)

Poor Man's Braciole

2 pounds ground beef
½ cup flour
1 cup Italian bread crumbs
1 tablespoon chopped fresh
  parsley
1 cup grated Parmesan cheese

¼ teaspoon garlic salt
Pepper to taste
2 hard-boiled eggs, sliced
4 very thin slices cooked
  salami

Roll out the ground beef between 2 pieces of parchment paper. Sprinkle a little flour on beef before placing top sheet. Roll out the beef to about ¾-inch. Spread bread crumbs, parsley, cheese, garlic salt, pepper, eggs, and salami over meat. Start rolling meat like a jellyroll, using bottom sheet to shape the roll. Place in a greased casserole dish. Bake at 350° for 1 hour and 15 minutes.

My Italian Heritage (New York)

Yankee Pot Roast

Really good. This recipe is for the pot roast famous at Clay Hill Farm.

4–6 pounds round roast or
   rump roast
2 cups red wine
2 cups tomato juice
1 large onion, minced
2 carrots, finely minced

1 clove garlic, minced
½ cup brown sugar
2 bay leaves
¼ teaspoon nutmeg
Salt and pepper to taste

Do not brown the pot roast. Place the meat in a heavy roasting pan that has a tight-fitting lid. Mix all the other ingredients together and pour over the meat. Cover and cook at 300° for about ¾ hour per pound. Turn roast over about halfway through cooking time. Let roast rest; thicken gravy and serve.

Visions of Home Cook Book (Maine)

Sauerbraten

If you have the time . . . it's worth the wait!

1 cup beef broth
½ cup red wine vinegar
1 teaspoon poultry seasoning
1 bay leaf
½ teaspoon pepper

1 teaspoon salt
1 tablespoon dry mustard
1 clove garlic, minced
3–4 pounds eye of round roast

Combine all ingredients except meat in saucepan. Place over medium temperature until thoroughly heated. Place meat in a bowl. Pour mixture over meat. Cover and refrigerate for 24–48 hours.

Roast the beef at 350° for 2½–3 hours or until desired doneness. Drippings can be used to make gravy and are tasty served with egg noodles. Serves 6–8.

There Once Was a Cook... (Pennsylvania)

New England Boiled Dinner

6 pounds brisket or rump of
  corned beef
½ clove garlic
6 peppercorns
6 carrots
3 large yellow turnips, cut
  in quarters

4 small parsnips
8 small peeled onions
6 medium-sized potatoes,
  pared and cut in quarters
1 head cabbage, quartered

Place corned beef in cold water with garlic and peppercorns and cook slowly until tender, skimming now and then. If you use very salty corned beef, drain when it comes to a boil and use fresh water for the rest of the cooking time. Allow from 4–5 hours for simmering, testing tenderness with a fork. When done, remove the meat, and cook the vegetables in the stock. When the vegetables are done, return the meat to the pot and reheat.

Serve with grated fresh horseradish beaten with sour cream, or use prepared horseradish with sour cream, adding a little lemon juice. Serves 4–8, depending on the size of the beef.

We like the beef sliced thin, not in chunks. We arrange the slices overlapping on an ironstone platter, arrange the vegetables around them with a slotted spoon, and serve the stock in an ironstone tureen (never thicken it).

We like to corn our own beef. We put it down in a crock for 36 hours, weighted down with a plate and a clean stone. The brine is 8 cups of water, 1 cup of salt, 3 tablespoons of sugar, 6 peppercorns, 1 clove of garlic, 2 bay leaves, and 2 teaspoons of mixed spices. Add ¼ teaspoon of saltpeter and ½ cup of warm water. All I can say is, oh, my . . . .

My Own Cookbook (Massachusetts)

The first product bottled by Henry J. Heinz, founder of the H.J. Heinz Company, in 1869 in the basement of his Sharpsburg, Pennsylvania, home was not ketchup—it was horseradish. Heinz now manufactures thousands of food products in plants on six continents. World headquarters are in Pittsburgh, Pennsylvania, where the company has been located since 1890.

Marinated Flank Steak

Get out the grill!

⅓ cup vinegar
¼ cup ketchup
1 tablespoon Worcestershire
2 tablespoons soy sauce

2 tablespoons oil
1 clove garlic, crushed
1 teaspoon dry mustard
1 flank steak, scored

Combine vinegar, ketchup, Worcestershire, soy sauce, oil, garlic, and mustard. Pour over steak and marinate at room temperature at least 1 hour. Grill over hot coals about 10 minutes. Brush with marinade while grilling. Serves 4.

Three Rivers Cookbook III (Pennsylvania)

True Ireland Corned Beef and Cabbage

Should be served with boiled potatoes, especially small red potatoes.

1 (3-pound) corned beef
1 teaspoon ground cloves,
  or to taste
1 tablespoon freshly ground
  pepper, or to taste

3 bay leaves
1 tablespoon dry mustard
1 (1½- to 2-pound) head
  white cabbage, cut in
  8 sections

Place corned beef and all seasonings in large pot. Cover with water. Bring slowly to boil. Cover and simmer gently for 1 hour. After 1 hour, add cabbage. Simmer for 30 minutes. Let stand for 30 minutes. Serves 4–8.

The Bronx Cookbook (New York)

Red Flannel Hash

2 tablespoons minced onion
3 cups finely diced cooked
   corned beef
2 cups finely diced boiled
   potatoes
1 cup finely diced cooked
   beets

1 teaspoon Worcestershire
Ground black pepper to taste
3 tablespoons bacon
   drippings (or butter or
   margarine)
2 tablespoons chopped
   parsley

Put the minced onion in a custard cup. Cover with vented plastic wrap. Heat at high (100%) power for 1 minute. Let stand, covered, for 2 minutes.

Mix the diced corned beef, potatoes, and beets together. Add the onion and its liquid, Worcestershire, and pepper to taste. The mixture should not need any added salt, as the beef is usually very salty. Preheat a 10-inch browning dish at high for 5 minutes, or as directed in manufacturer's instructions. Put the bacon drippings in the preheated dish, tilting to spread evenly. Spoon the corned beef mixture into the dish. Press down to cover bottom completely. Heat at high for 4 minutes. Carefully turn hash over with a spatula. Heat at high for another 2 minutes. Serve sprinkled with the chopped parsley. Makes 4–6 servings.

Classic New England Dishes from Your Microwave (Maine)

Goulash

2 pounds boneless beef
  chuck, cut in 1-inch cubes
3 tablespoons cooking oil
1 (14-ounce) can beef broth
1 cup chopped onion
1 small green pepper,
  chopped
2 tablespoons tomato paste

2 tablespoons paprika
2 teaspoons caraway seed
½ teaspoon salt
¼ teaspoon pepper
⅓ cup cold water
3 tablespoons flour
Broad noodles, cooked
Dairy sour cream (optional)

In large saucepan, brown beef cubes in hot oil. Add beef broth, onion, green pepper, tomato paste, paprika, caraway seed, salt and pepper. Blend cold water into flour. Stir into beef mixture. Simmer, covered, until meat is tender, about 1½ hours; stir occasionally. Serve over broad noodles. Sour cream as a garnish is optional. Serves 8.

The Bronx Cookbook (New York)

Patchwork Casserole

2 pounds ground beef
2 green peppers, chopped
1 large onion, chopped
2 pounds frozen hash brown
  potatoes
2 (8-ounce) cans tomato sauce
1 (6-ounce) can tomato paste

1 cup water
1 teaspoon salt
½ teaspoon basil
¼ teaspoon pepper
1 pound thinly sliced American
  cheese, divided

Brown meat; drain. Add green peppers and onion; cook until tender. Add remaining ingredients except cheese; mix well. Spoon half of meat and potato mixture into 13x9-inch baking dish, or two 1½-quart casserole dishes. Cover with half of cheese. Top with remaining meat and potato mixture. Cover dish with aluminum foil. Bake at 350° for 45 minutes. Uncover. Cut remaining cheese into decorative shapes; arrange in patchwork design on casserole. Let stand 5 minutes or until cheese shapes have melted. Makes 12 servings. Can be frozen.

Sharing Our Bounty Through 40 Years (New York)

Hamburger Pie

6–8 white potatoes
Milk (½ cup or more)
Butter (½ stick or more)
Salt to taste
1½ pounds hamburger

1 small onion, chopped
1 can French-style green
 beans, drained
1 can tomato soup

Peel, cut and boil potatoes. When cooked, drain. Mash, adding milk, butter, and salt to taste. Use electric beater to obtain creamy texture. Sauté hamburger and onion in frying pan using vegetable oil. Drain liquid when sautéed. Combine with drained beans and tomato soup. Place mixture in casserole and cover with mashed potatoes. Bake in 350° oven for 30–35 minutes.

Our Best Home Cooking (New York)

Hobo Beans

1 pound hamburger
1 medium onion
¾ pound bacon
2 cans pork and beans
2 cans kidney beans, drained

1 can butter beans, drained
3 tablespoons white vinegar
1 cup catsup
½ cup brown sugar

Brown hamburger and onion together. Crisp bacon and crumble. Add these ingredients to the pork and beans, kidney beans, and butter beans. Add vinegar, catsup, and brown sugar. Mix well. Place in crockpot on high for 4–5 hours. Yields 8–10 servings.

Fabulous Feasts from First United (New York)

Supper-in-a-Dish

1 pound hamburger or
  sausage, browned,
  drained
1 or 2 potatoes, sliced
1 carrot, sliced
1 cup peas
¼ cup chopped onion
¼ cup chopped celery

¼ cup chopped green bell
  pepper
Salt and pepper to taste
1 (10¾-ounce) can cream of
  chicken or cream of
  mushroom soup
¼ cup milk
⅔ cup grated cheese

In greased baking dish, layer meat, potatoes, carrot, peas, onion, celery, and pepper. Season to taste. In mixing bowl, combine soup and milk. Pour mixture over top of layered ingredients. Bake at 350° for 1¼ hours. Sprinkle grated cheese on top and return to oven until melted.

Mennonite Country-Style Recipes & Kitchen Secrets
(Pennsylvania)

Mock Stuffed Cabbage

1 small head cabbage,
  shredded
1½–2 pounds ground
  beef, turkey, or chicken
1 egg
¾ cup bread crumbs
½ teaspoon garlic powder

1 (15-ounce) can tomato
  sauce
8–12 ounces whole or
  "crushed berry" cranberry
  sauce
2 tablespoons brown sugar

Place shredded cabbage in a Dutch oven. Combine ground beef, egg, bread crumbs, and garlic. Shape into meatballs and place on top of cabbage. Combine tomato sauce, cranberry sauce, and brown sugar and pour over meatballs. Cover and cook on top of stove or in a 350° oven for 1 hour. Serve with noodles or rice.

Hint: This tastes almost like stuffed cabbage, but without all the work! To keep this recipe as low in cholesterol as possible, substitute ground chicken or turkey for the beef and use an egg substitute or 2 egg whites instead of the whole egg. This freezes well.

From Ellie's Kitchen to Yours (Massachusetts)

Individual Meat Loaves

1 egg
1 cup soft bread cubes
¼ cup milk
1½ teaspoons onion salt
1 teaspoon parsley flakes
Dash of pepper
1½ pounds ground beef or
  ground chuck
6 sticks cheese (2½x½x½)
3 tablespoons oil

2 (15-ounce) cans tomato sauce
½ cup chopped onion
3 teaspoons crumbled parsley
  flakes
½ teaspoon crumbled, dried
  oregano leaves
¼ teaspoon garlic salt
12 ounces elbow macaroni,
  rigatoni, or your choice

Beat egg in a large bowl; stir in bread cubes, milk, onion salt, 1 teaspoon parsley, and pepper. Mix into ground beef. Divide mixture into 6 equal parts and shape each into a loaf around a cheese stick. Brown on top and bottom in hot oil in skillet; remove from skillet and drain off fat. Add tomato sauce, onion, 3 teaspoons parsley, oregano, and ¼ teaspoon garlic salt to skillet. Heat and stir, loosening brown particles from bottom of skillet. Add meat loaves; spoon sauce over top. Cover and simmer 25 minutes.

Meanwhile, cook macaroni according to package directions. Drain. Serve meat loaves and sauce over hot macaroni.

The Best of Busy Bee #2 (Pennsylvania)

The first two bells cracked while being tested; the third casting of the Liberty Bell was hung in the tower of Independence Hall on June 7, 1753. It was hidden in a church basement in Allentown from 1777–1778 to protect it from the British. Rung every July 4th and on every state occasion until 1835, the bell cracked as it was being tolled for the death of Chief Justice John Marshall. In 1976, the Liberty Bell was moved to its present location in a glass pavilion near Independence Hall.

Old-Fashioned Meat Loaf

Old-Fashioned here means home-cooked, plain and simple, and so much in demand. I never had any leftovers when I made this meat loaf. Be sure to serve it with mashed potatoes and gravy. This is a no-frills food at its best. Some things are so obvious—a meat loaf dinner is clearly made for a crisp fall night.

THE SAUCE:

½ cup ketchup

3 tablespoons brown sugar, firmly packed

1 tablespoon Worcestershire

Place all ingredients in a small bowl and mix to combine. Set aside.

THE LOAF:

1 pound ground beef

½ pound ground veal

½ pound ground pork or lamb

1 medium onion, chopped or grated

1 large egg, beaten

½ cup plain dried bread crumbs

3–4 tablespoons cold water

2 tablespoons Worcestershire

Preheat oven to 350°. Combine the meats in a large mixing bowl. Add the remaining loaf ingredients and press into an 8½x4½-inch loaf pan, making a long indention in the center. Bake for 25 minutes. Pour the sauce over the top of the loaf and continue to bake until the meat loaf is caramelized and mahogany in color, another 20–30 minutes. Serve with Hot and Sweet Mustard.

Note: Use your hands to mix the meats together. It is easier. For weight-conscious people, you can substitute ground turkey for any of the meats, if you wish. The secret to this meat loaf is the water, because it makes the loaf light and airy. The combination of meats helps to this end as well.

Bridgehampton Weekends (New York)

Tailgaters' Loaf

A picnic special.

1 loaf day-old Italian or French bread

HERB BUTTER:

¼ cup melted butter
½ teaspoon thyme
½ teaspoon dill

½ teaspoon oregano
1 tablespoon minced parsley

STUFFING:

1¼ pounds ground round
  steak
1 teaspoon salt
½ teaspoon pepper
½ medium onion, diced
1 teaspoon prepared mustard
1 tablespoon ketchup

1 tablespoon Worcestershire
1 egg, beaten
1 teaspoon fresh ground
  pepper
½ cup bread crumbs
  (from loaf)

Remove 2-inch thick slice from each end of bread and scoop out inside of loaf, leaving ¾-inch crust on all sides. Brush inside and each end with Herb Butter. Mix Stuffing and pack into hollow loaf. Replace bread ends and wrap loaf loosely in foil. Bake at 350° for 1½ hours. Yields 6–8 servings.

Note: Tarragon mustard may be thinned with mayonnaise as an optional sauce to be spread over slices as they are served. Pack hot to serve at room temperature or serve cold.

The Albany Collection: Treasures & Treasured Recipes
(New York)

Albany, New York, is one of the oldest surviving European settlements from the original thirteen colonies and the longest continuously chartered city in the United States. The Dongan Charter legally established Albany as a city in 1686; it is the oldest United States city charter still in effect.

Meatballs in Sour Cream Gravy

Barb's grandmother, Mumsie, was known as an excellent cook in her home counties of Somerset and Huntingdon, Pennsylvania. This was one of her favorite ways to turn ground chuck into a "company" dinner.

4 cups cornflakes, crushed,
  or 1 cup cornflake crumbs
2 pounds ground chuck
1 cup milk
1¼ teaspoons salt, divided
½ teaspoon pepper
½ cup chopped onions

20 large green or ripe pitted
  olives
3 tablespoons shortening
3 tablespoons flour
½ cup water
2 cups sour cream
1 teaspoon dill seed

If using cornflakes, crush into fine crumbs and combine with the meat, milk, 1 teaspoon salt, pepper, and onions, and mix thoroughly. Shape into 2-inch balls around an olive. Melt the shortening in a skillet and put the meatballs in it, turning them to brown evenly. Remove to a platter and pour off all but 3 tablespoons of the brownings. Blend in the flour, then the water, and stir constantly until smooth and thickened. Stir in the sour cream, dill, and remaining ¼ teaspoon salt, and add the browned meatballs. Cover and cook slowly on low heat for 20–25 minutes. Serve over hot, buttered noodles. More salt may be desired by some cooks, but the addition of green olives makes it unnecessary. Makes 20–22 (2-inch) meatballs.

Betty Groff's Up-Home Down-Home Cookbook (Pennsylvania)

Beef and Pepper Roll

1 pound ground beef (lean)	4 tablespoons grated
1 cup bread crumbs	Parmesan cheese
1 egg, lightly beaten	¼ teaspoon garlic powder
1 (16-ounce) jar spaghetti	1 red and 1 green pepper,
sauce (meatless)	sliced
1 cup shredded Swiss cheese	6 large fresh mushrooms

Preheat oven to 350°. Combine ground beef, bread crumbs, egg, and ¼ cup spaghetti sauce. Combine in separate bowl, cheeses, and garlic; set aside. Place beef mixture between 2 pieces plastic wrap. With rolling pin, roll beef flat to approximately 12x12 inches, remove top plastic wrap, and spread cheese mixture over beef. Top with sliced peppers and mushrooms. Roll beef into long roll and tuck ends lightly; place seam-side-down. Sprinkle 2 tablespoons Swiss cheese over top and bake for 30 minutes on a cookie sheet. Remove and serve with remaining 1¾ cups sauce. Makes 8 servings.

Note: Beef rolls may be made ahead and chilled, or frozen to be cooked later. Joann O'Flaherty says you may substitute mozzarella for Swiss and marinara sauce for spaghetti sauce.

A Culinary Tour of the Gingerbread Cottages (Massachusetts)

Once Washington's headquarters (1775-76), the home and grounds of Henry Wadsworth Longfellow in Cambridge, Massachusetts, is open to the public. Longfellow (February 27, 1807–March 24, 1882) was an American poet and educator whose works include "Paul Revere's Ride." He became the most popular American poet of his day.

Pizza Cups

1 (6-ounce) can tomato paste
1 tablespoon instant minced
  onion
1 teaspoon Italian seasoning
½ teaspoon salt
¾ pound ground beef,
  browned and drained

1 (10-ounce) can refrigerated
  biscuits
¾ cup shredded mozzarella
  cheese

Add tomato paste, onion, and seasonings to meat. Cook over low heat 5 minutes, stirring frequently. Place biscuits in greased muffin cups, pressing to cover bottom and sides. Spoon about ¼ cup meat mixture into each muffin cup and sprinkle with cheese. Bake at 400° for 12 minutes.

Cooking Down the Road, and at home, too (New York)

Center Cut Pork Chops with Beer and Cabbage

4 center cut pork chops
  (about 1¼-inches thick)
Salt and pepper to taste
1 tablespoon vegetable oil
1 small onion, sliced
1 tablespoon mustard
1½ cups sliced mushrooms

½ head cabbage, cored and
  thinly sliced
1 large apple, peeled and
  thinly sliced
1 cup beer
½ cup chicken stock or
  canned broth

Season chops with salt and pepper. Heat oil in large heavy skillet until hot. Add chops for 4–5 minutes on each side, until well browned. Transfer chops to plate and set aside. Add onions to the pan and cook, stirring for 2–3 minutes, until light brown. Stir in mustard, mushrooms, and additional pepper to taste. Add cabbage and apple; season lightly with salt; cook, stirring for 1 minute. Add beer; bring to boil and cook 3–4 minutes. Return chops to skillet, burying them in the cabbage mixture. Pour broth over. Cover; simmer 40–50 minutes until chops are tender. Serves 4.

Hudson Valley German-American Society Cookbook (New York)

Stuffed Pork Chops

This recipe works with regular pork chops or smoked chops. Red onions are good. Sweet Vidalias are even better.

**4 double-cut pork chops
  with a pocket for stuffing
¼ cup Italian salad dressing
2 cups Pennsylvania Dutch
  Filling**

**½ teaspoon garlic salt
½ teaspoon black pepper
1 small red onion (or Vidalia),
  sliced into ¼-inch rings**

Preheat oven to 350°. Place chops in a small roasting pan or dish. Using a basting brush, coat chops inside and out with Italian dressing. Stuff chops firmly with filling and season them with garlic salt and black pepper. Lay onion rings on top of chops and add a little water to roasting pan. Cover with foil and bake 35 minutes. Uncover and bake 15 minutes longer. Makes 4 servings.

PENNSYLVANIA DUTCH FILLING:
What much of the rest of the world knows as stuffing or dressing is called filling in Pennsylvania Dutch country. Some recipes contain mashed potatoes in addition to the bread, but this one is more traditional. And it is filling.

**1 medium onion, chopped
1 stick butter
2 cups chopped celery
4 cups water**

**1 loaf bread, cubed
1 tablespoon dried parsley
1 teaspoon dried thyme**

In saucepan, sauté onion in butter. Add celery and cook until tender. Put water in large bowl. Add bread cubes, onion mixture, parsley, and thyme and mix well. Spoon filling into pork chops as directed above.

Famous Dutch Kitchen Restaurant Cookbook (Pennsylvania)

Grilled Pork Tenderloin with Fresh Peach and Ginger Sauce

1 tablespoon vegetable oil
1 cup chopped onion
5 tablespoons sugar
1½ cups dry red wine
¼ cup balsamic vinegar
2½ tablespoons, peeled, finely chopped fresh ginger
1½ teaspoons ground cinnamon

3 (14- to 16-ounce) pork tenderloins
3 medium peaches, blanched in boiling water, peeled, pitted, and chopped
2 tablespoons chopped fresh chives
½ teaspoon coarsely ground black pepper

Heat oil in heavy saucepan over medium-high heat. Add onion and sugar. Sauté until onion is golden brown, about 6 minutes. Mix in wine, vinegar, ginger, and cinnamon. Cook 1 minute longer. Remove from heat. Cool sauce completely. Place pork in large resealable plastic bag. Pour 1 cup sauce over pork. Seal and refrigerate at least 6 hours, or overnight (turning to coat). Cover remaining sauce separately and refrigerate.

Prepare barbecue (medium heat). Remove pork from marinade; discard marinade. Grill pork until meat thermometer inserted into center registers 155°, turning often, about 35 minutes. Meanwhile, boil remaining sauce in heavy medium saucepan until reduced by half. Add peaches, stir until heated through, about 1 minute. Slice pork and arrange on platter. Spoon sauce over top with chives. Season with pepper. Pass remaining sauce, separately.

The Cookbook AAUW (New York)

"The Big Apple" is a nickname for New York City. First popularized in the 1920s by John J. Fitz Gerald, a sports writer for the *New York Morning Telegraph*. By the late 1920s, New York writers other than Fitz Gerald were starting to use "Big Apple" and were using it outside of a horse-racing context. "The Big Apple" was a popular song and dance in the 1930s. Walter Winchell and other writers continued to use the name in the 1940s and 1950s. By the 1960s, "The Big Apple" was known only as an old name for New York. In the early 1970s, however, the New York Convention and Visitors Bureau began promoting "The Big Apple" for the city. It has remained popular since then. Mayor Rudolph W. Giuliani in 1997 signed legislation designating the southwest corner of West 54th Street and Broadway, the corner on which John J. Fitz Gerald lived from 1934 to 1963, as "Big Apple Corner."

Zesty and Sweet Spareribs

4 pounds pork spareribs, cut into serving-size pieces
¼ cup vinegar
¼ cup molasses
¼ cup chili sauce
2 tablespoons soy sauce
1 medium clove of garlic, crushed
1 (8-ounce) can crushed pineapple in juice, do not drain

Place ribs (meaty side up) on a rack in a shallow roasting pan. Roast in an oven for 1½ hours at 325°. Mix together remaining ingredients. Take ½ of mixture and brush over ribs while continuing to roast for an additional 45 minutes. Turn and brush frequently during this time. Heat remaining ½ of mixture to boiling, stirring occasionally. Serve as a sauce. Makes 6 servings.

In the Village (New York)

Sweet and Sour Ham Balls

2 pounds ground ham
2 cups soft bread crumbs, or 1½ cups dry crumbs
1 cup milk
2 eggs, lightly beaten
1 teaspoon salt
¼ teaspoon pepper
2 cloves garlic, peeled, crushed

Preheat oven to 325°. Mix all ingredients and shape into balls. Arrange on a greased baking pan.

SAUCE:
1 cup packed brown sugar
½ cup cider vinegar
1 teaspoon dry mustard
1 cup crushed pineapple with juice

Mix Sauce ingredients in a saucepan, bring to a boil, and cook, stirring constantly, for 2–3 minutes. Pour Sauce over meatballs and bake uncovered for 1 hour, basting frequently. Serves 8.

From Mother's Cupboard (Pennsylvania)

Baked Vermont Ham

1 (10-pound) ham, cooked and skinned	1 teaspoon dry mustard
1 cup sugar	¼ teaspoon allspice
2 tablespoons dark molasses	¼ teaspoon ginger
¼ teaspoon cinnamon	Whole cloves
	Bread crumbs

The only skin that needs to be removed from my favorite ham is a piece around the shank. Yours may need more removed. Score the fat in diagonal lines about ¾-inch apart, making diamonds. Mix sugar, molasses, and spices together and rub mixture into the surface of the ham. Press whole cloves into the intersections of scored lines. Sprinkle fine bread crumbs over the whole surface.

BASTING SAUCE:

½ cup ginger ale	½ teaspoon ginger
½ cup fizzy cider	

Mix ginger ale, cider, and extra ginger and pour mixture into a roasting pan. Place the ham on a rack in the roaster. Insert meat thermometer so that it touches neither fat nor bone. Set the pan into a preheated 200° oven. Baste ham twice during the first hour, then cover with aluminum foil and forget it until morning.

The next day the thermometer should register 165° and the ham should be a golden brown. If necessary, let it go on cooking until it reaches this stage. Set in a cool place but do not refrigerate it. Serve at room temperature.

Mrs. Appleyard's Family Kitchen (Vermont)

Vermont government is distinctive for its local tradition of Town Meeting Day, held the first Tuesday in March. In many towns and villages, municipal and school budgets are voted from the floor as they have been for nearly 200 years.

Sebago Pig & Poultry Rub

Nephew Jonny, Uncle Billy and some of their friends were up to camp on Sebago Lake visiting relatives when, as usually happens, Jonny was designated that evening's cook. He was in the kitchen, pondering possible dinner entrées, when a bunch of chickens burst through the screen door, chased by an assortment of children, angry adults, and one wet dog. The chickens headed for the pantry and ran straight into the spice shelf. An open jar of Oriental Five Spice Powder fell down, covering the chickens, pantry, dog, and one of the kids with a pretty liberal dose of the spice powder.

A good-sized mess was the result. Jonny lost his characteristic laissez-fare attitude, and since the kid belonged to a relative and everyone was partial to the dog, dinner that night was arrived at by deductive reasoning—it would be chicken.

To this day Jonny swears the story is true, and what's more, he said those chickens, all tossed with Oriental Five Spice Powder, were the best he'd ever eaten. Which is exactly why he puts it in his Sebago Pig & Poultry Rub.

3½ ounces granulated garlic	1½ ounces salt
3 ounces Hungarian paprika	1½ ounces black pepper
2½ ounces granulated sugar	½ ounce ground marjoram
2½ ounces Oriental Five Spice Powder	½ ounce ground anise
	¼ ounce ground sage
	⅛ ounce ground allspice
	⅛ ounce ground ginger

Combine all ingredients. There's enough here for a pound of rub. Store it on a shelf (minding the kids and dogs); it'll come in handy time and time again.

Uncle Billy's Downeast Barbeque Book (Maine)

Lamb Shanks

½ cup flour
4 whole lamb shanks,
  trimmed
¼ cup oil
1 tablespoon cornstarch
2 teaspoons salt
½ teaspoon dry mustard
¼ teaspoon pepper

¼ teaspoon ginger
¼ teaspoon cloves
¼ teaspoon onion salt
⅛ teaspoon garlic salt
½ teaspoon celery salt
1 teaspoon paprika
1 teaspoon minced parsley
3 cups chicken stock

Flour shanks; brown in oil. Place in large, greased, ovenproof casserole. Combine cornstarch and seasonings; add to pan drippings; blend. Gradually add stock. Cook over low heat until smooth and thickened. Pour over shanks. Bake, covered, at 350° for about 2½ hours, turning once. Serve with rice. Yields 4 servings.

The Albany Collection: Treasures & Treasured Recipes
(New York)

Roast Leg of Lamb
with Herb Crust

2 tablespoons olive oil
3 cloves garlic, minced
1 teaspoon crushed rosemary
1 teaspoon thyme
Salt and pepper to taste

1 boned and rolled leg of
  lamb, 3½–4 pounds
2 ounces bread crumbs
4 tablespoons finely chopped
  parsley

Mix together olive oil, garlic, rosemary, and thyme. Season generously with salt and pepper. Spread the mixture over the lamb and let it marinate 3 hours.

Preheat oven to 300° and roast the lamb for 1½ hours. Mix bread crumbs and parsley. Add sufficient meat juices to make a paste. You may need to add a little butter. Spread the paste over the lamb and bake another 30 minutes to finish cooking and to brown the crust. Yields 6–8 portions.

Hospitality (Massachusetts)

Seldom Seen Farm Lamb Chops in Foil

So easy, anyone will become the "Chef of the Day."

FOR EACH SERVING ALLOW:

2 lamb chops	1 small tomato, quartered
1 sliced zucchini, unpeeled	Dash of basil
1 small onion, sliced	Salt and pepper
1 small green pepper, cored and sliced	Garlic powder

Make a packet with the above in each, wrapped tightly. Grill on low about 25–30 minutes. Be sure to turn several times. Another great way to use this recipe is to bake at 350° for 1¼–1½ hours.

A recipe from Seldom Seen Farm, Harmony
The Island Cookbook (Rhode Island)

Veal in Wine

A great winter buffet dish served over noodles with crusty French bread and salad. I use Gallo Hearty Burgundy. It's a terrific cooking wine.

2 pounds veal steak, cut into serving portions	1 tablespoon oil
	1 tablespoon butter
Salt and pepper	1 cup red wine (to cover meat)
Flour	¼ teaspoon thyme
2 eggs, beaten	¼ teaspoon rosemary
1 cup bread crumbs	1 bay leaf

Coat veal pieces with seasoned flour; dip in eggs, then in bread crumbs. Brown veal pieces quickly in oil and butter. Arrange meat in casserole. Add wine (enough to cover meat) and herbs. Cook at 350° for at least 30 minutes. This dish can be kept in a warm oven for up to 1 hour. Add more wine if necessary. Serves 4–6.

The East Hampton L.V.I.S. Centennial Cookbook (New York)

Venison Steak Strips

This dish is very good served with wild rice or mashed potatoes and comes to us from the Seneca Indian Reservation.

1½ cups seasoned bread crumbs
½ cup freshly grated Parmesan cheese
½ teaspoon garlic powder
½ teaspoon freshly ground black pepper
2 large eggs
½ cup milk
¼ cup vegetable oil

1½ pounds venison steaks, sliced into ½-inch-thick strips
4 medium onions, sliced
1½ pounds fresh mushrooms, sliced
Flour
2 cups water
5 beef bouillon cubes
Cornstarch or flour for gravy

In medium bowl, mix bread crumbs, cheese, garlic powder, and pepper. In another bowl, beat eggs and milk. Place oil in large non-stick skillet and heat on medium-high. Dip steak strips into egg/milk mixture, then roll in bread crumb mixture. Brown steak strips quickly in hot skillet.

In a medium-sized roaster, layer the steak strips, onions, and mushrooms. Dust lightly with flour. Repeat layering until steaks, onions, and mushrooms are used up. Add water mixed with bouillon cubes. Bake 2 hours in preheated 275° oven.

Just before serving, gently drain liquid from roaster into a large saucepan. Make gravy with cornstarch or flour. Pour over steaks and serve.

Specialties of the House (New York)

The Scoville Memorial Library was established in 1803 in Salisbury, Connecticut, the first in the United States open to the public free of charge. The library collection began in 1771, when Richard Smith, owner of a local blast furnace, used community contributions to buy 200 books in London. Patrons could borrow and return books on the third Monday of every third month. Fees were collected for damages, the most common being "greasing" by wax dripped from the candles by which the patrons read.

Old-Country Roast Venison

1 venison roast
4 ounces wine
2 carrots
2 potatoes
2 onions

¼ stick butter, melted
½ clove garlic
Salt to taste
Black pepper to taste
1 can mushrooms

Preheat oven to 325°. Place venison roast in a large roasting pan. Pour wine over meat, allowing it to run over for basting. Slice carrots in quarters, lengthwise. Cut potatoes in quarters. Place both in pan along with whole onions, and brush roast heavily with butter. Finely mince garlic, and sprinkle evenly over meat. Add a pinch of salt and a dash of pepper.

Allow 30 minutes cooking time for each pound of meat to cook venison roast properly. Baste frequently with juices from bottom of pan. After roast is completely cooked, and while oven is still hot, toss mushrooms in the pan. Stir mushrooms in juices a few moments for flavor, then serve everything hot. Serves 4–6.

Wild Game Cookbook & Other Recipes (New York)

Poultry

Independence Hall in Philadelphia is the centerpiece of Independence National Historical Park, America's most historic square mile. Built 1732–1756 as the Pennsylvania State House, Independence Hall is the site where the Declaration of Independence was first adopted and the U.S. Constitution was written.

Buttermilk Fried Chicken

2 cups buttermilk
¼ cup Dijon mustard
1 tablespoon chopped onion
4 teaspoons salt, divided
1 tablespoon parsley flakes
4 teaspoons dry mustard, divided
4 teaspoons cayenne pepper, divided
2½ teaspoons ground black pepper, divided
1 (3-pound) fryer chicken, cut up
3 cups all-purpose flour
1 tablespoon baking powder
1 tablespoon garlic powder
1 tablespoon oregano
5 cups peanut oil

In a 1-gallon resealable plastic bag, mix buttermilk, Dijon mustard, onion, 1 teaspoon salt, parsley, 1 teaspoon dry mustard, 1 teaspoon cayenne pepper, and 1 teaspoon black pepper. Add chicken pieces. Seal bag and turn to coat chicken; refrigerate overnight.

Whisk flour, baking powder, garlic powder, 3 teaspoons salt, 3 teaspoons each dry mustard and cayenne, and 1½ teaspoons black pepper in 13x9x2-inch glass dish. With marinade still clinging to chicken pieces, add chicken to flour mixture; turn to coat. Let chicken stand in flour mixture for 1 hour, turning occasionally. Pour oil to depth of 1¼-inch into a deep frying pan. Heat oil to 350°. Fry chicken to a golden brown, turning frequently and keeping the oil bubbling constantly. Use wooden spoons or tongs to turn chicken, and remove when done to a rack to cool and drain.

Thou Preparest a Table Before Me (New York)

Happy New Year! Bringing in the New Year at New York City's Times Square began in 1904 when the owners of One Times Square began conducting rooftop celebrations to usher in the New Year. The ball-lowering celebration began in 1907.

Chicken Breasts in Champagne

1 carrot, finely chopped
1 small onion, finely
 chopped
3 large mushrooms, finely
 chopped
2 tablespoons butter

1 cup champagne or dry white
 wine
2 chicken breasts (halved,
 boned, and skinned)
Salt and pepper to taste

SAUCE:
½ cup heavy cream
¼ cup champagne or white
 wine

Salt and pepper to taste
Parsley, finely chopped

In a heatproof casserole, make a bed of carrot, onion, and mushrooms. Add butter cut into thin slices and add champagne or wine. Place chicken breasts on top of the mixture. Sprinkle the chicken with salt and pepper, cover the casserole, and bake chicken in a moderate oven (325°) basting it frequently with the liquid from the casserole for 50–60 minutes or until it is tender.

Remove chicken to a platter and keep warm. Cook sauce uncovered over moderate heat until it is reduced by half.

Stir in heavy cream and champagne or wine and pour sauce through a sieve. Season with salt and pepper and a little finely chopped parsley. Pour sauce over the chicken breasts and garnish the platter with braised celery and sautéed pimentos. Serves 2.

The Hammersmith Farm Cookbook (Rhode Island)

DIDIER B, WIKIPEDIA.ORG

Times Square

Chicken Stoltzfus and Pastry Squares

Named for our friends Elam and Hannah Stoltzfus, this has become one of the trademarks of Groff's Farm Restaurant. It is like the patty shells filled with chicken that were served to wedding guests at our family banquets, but are served like the Amish serve their "Wedding Chicken."

1 (5-pound) roasting chicken, cleaned, giblets removed
1½ quarts water
2 teaspoons salt
⅓ teaspoon pepper
Pinch of saffron
12 tablespoons butter
12 tablespoons flour

1 cup light cream, or ½ cup each: milk and evaporated milk
¼ cup finely chopped fresh parsley, or ⅛ cup dried parsley
Parsley for garnish

Put the chicken in a 6-quart kettle. Add the water, salt, pepper, and saffron and bring to a boil. Reduce the heat to medium and simmer, partially covered, for 1 hour. Remove the chicken and cool enough to debone. Strain the stock. Reduce the stock to 4 cups. Remove the skin and bones from the pieces. Melt the butter in the pot in which the chicken was cooked and mix in the flour. Cook over medium-low heat until golden and bubbling. Add the 4 cups chicken stock and the cream, stirring constantly. Cook over medium-high heat until the sauce comes to a boil. Simmer until thickened and smooth. Reduce heat and add chicken pieces and chopped parsley. Serve hot over Pastry Squares.

PASTRY SQUARES:
These may be made beforehand. Store in an airtight container.

½ cup lard or vegetable shortening
½ cup butter

2 cups all-purpose flour
1 teaspoon salt
About ½ cup ice water

Cut the lard and butter into the flour and salt with a pastry blender, or mix by hand, until it forms crumbs. Sprinkle ice water over the crumbs with one hand, while tossing them lightly with the other hand. Use only enough water to hold the dough together. Press the

(continued)

(Chicken Stoltzfus and Pastry Squares continued)

dough into a ball and put on a lightly floured surface. Divide into 2 or 3 parts. Roll each part ⅛ inch thick to fit an ungreased cookie sheet. On the cookie sheets, cut the dough into 1-inch squares with a pastry wheel or sharp knife. Bake in a preheated 350° oven for 12–15 minutes until lightly browned. Arrange pastry squares on a heated platter. Spoon the chicken on top. Garnish with fresh parsley.

Betty Groff's Up-Home Down-Home Cookbook (Pennsylvania)

Crab and Chicken Casserole

4 chicken breasts
¼ cup chopped onion
1–2 tablespoons butter
1 (3-ounce) can chopped, drained mushrooms
½ pound crabmeat
2 tablespoons snipped parsley
½ cup crumbled saltine crackers

Pepper to taste
4 tablespoons butter
¼ cup flour
¾ cup milk
¾ cup chicken broth
⅓ cup dry white wine
½ pound grated Swiss cheese
Paprika

Cut deboned chicken breasts in half and pound between Saran Wrap until flat. Place in buttered rectangular Pyrex dish. Sauté the onion in skillet in 1–2 tablespoons butter until soft. Add mushrooms, crabmeat, parsley, saltine crackers, and pepper to taste. Toss to blend and spoon mixture generously atop each piece of chicken. Melt 4 tablespoons of butter in a saucepan. Add flour and stir. Gradually stir in milk, chicken broth, and wine, whisking to keep a smooth sauce. Pour the sauce over the chicken-crab. Cover with aluminum foil and bake at 350° for 1 hour. Uncover, sprinkle with Swiss cheese and paprika, returning to oven to melt. Serves 6–8.

A Hancock Community Collection (New Hampshire)

Chicken Baked in Sour Cream

½ cup sour cream
1 tablespoon lemon juice
1 tablespoon Worcestershire
1 teaspoon celery salt
½ teaspoon paprika
2 cloves garlic, minced

½ teaspoon salt
Dash of pepper
1 cup bread crumbs
1 chicken (about 3½ pounds),
    cut up

Heat oven to 350°. Combine all the ingredients except the bread crumbs and chicken. Dip pieces of chicken into mixture, and then into bread crumbs. Place chicken on greased baking pan and bake for 50–60 minutes, until cooked through. Serves 4–6.

La Cocina de la Familia (New York)

Lemon-Garlic Chicken

This dish can be prepared the night before, covered and refrigerated. It can be cooked the following day.

4 ounces salted butter
8 garlic cloves, minced
1 cup bread crumbs, plain or
    flavored
1 cup freshly grated Parmesan
    cheese

¼ cup minced fresh parsley
8 skinless and boneless
    chicken breast halves
1–2 whole lemons, halved
Paprika (optional)

In a small saucepan over medium heat, melt butter with minced garlic. Set aside. Combine crumbs, cheese, and parsley on a plate; set aside. Pound each chicken breast between sheets of plastic wrap to flatten slightly. Dip in melted butter mixture, then coat well with crumbs. Roll each piece of chicken jellyroll-fashion. Place chicken rolls, seam-side-down in a glass 9x13-inch casserole dish that has been coated with vegetable spray. Pour any leftover butter and crumb mixture over chicken. Squeeze lemon generously over entire surface. Sprinkle with paprika. Bake 1 hour, uncovered, in pre-heated 350° oven. Yields 6–8 servings.

Specialties of the House (New York)

Pine Point Chicken Paprika

3 pounds boneless chicken breasts
1 lemon, cut in half
3 tablespoons sweet butter
3 yellow onions, chopped
1 tablespoon paprika (maybe more)

1½ teaspoons salt
¾ pint sour cream (more or less)
16 ounces wide egg noodles, cooked

Rub pieces of chicken with the cut sides of the lemon. Melt butter in a heavy large pan (one with a tight fitting lid). Sauté onions for 2–3 minutes until translucent. Remove from heat and blend in paprika. (Onions should be bright red.) Place chicken pieces in pan one-by-one making sure each piece is well-coated with onion mixture and salt. Turn heat on medium to medium-low and cover tightly with lid. Do not open lid for next 20 minutes. Adjust heat so there is a gentle sizzling. (The chicken should steam in its own juices.) Check chicken after 20 minutes and continue steaming until chicken is tender (usually within 5 minutes).

Remove chicken pieces to bowl. Add sour cream to pan containing the juices, turning up heat to almost a boil. Place chicken pieces back in pan making sure each piece is thoroughly coated with cream mixture. Replace lid and heat chicken on medium to low heat until heated through. Recheck for seasonings, adding more paprika and salt, if needed. Serve over egg noodles. Serves 6–8.

Simply...The Best (New York)

Chicken with Tri-Color Peppers

1 medium onion, finely
  chopped
Olive oil
2 boneless, skinless chicken
  breasts, cut in chunks
1 clove garlic, peeled and
  chopped

½ red, yellow and green
  peppers, seeded and cut into
  chunks
½ cup white wine

Sauté onion in olive oil until soft, then add chicken pieces and garlic. Cook until chicken is cooked through. Add peppers and wine and cook until peppers are cooked, but still firm, and liquid is slightly reduced. Serve with pasta of your choice.

Dishing It Out (New York)

Braised Chicken with White Wine and Mushrooms

1 pound fresh mushrooms,
  sliced
1 cup green onions, chopped
4 tablespoons butter or
  margarine, divided
¾ cup flour

4 teaspoons garlic salt
Ground pepper to taste
1 tablespoon rosemary
6 chicken breasts, halved,
  boned, and skinned
2½ cups dry white wine

Sauté mushrooms and onions in 2 tablespoons of the butter; set aside. Mix flour, garlic salt, pepper, and rosemary. Dust chicken lightly with flour mixture. Brown chicken on both sides in the remaining butter; set aside. Deglaze pan with white wine. Add chicken, mushrooms, and onions to wine, cover and cook on medium low for 15–20 minutes.

For flavor variations, use dry vermouth in place of wine, or add canned artichoke hearts at the last step.

In the Village (New York)

Blue Ribbon Chicken Spiedies

Broome County is home to the original "spiedie." These regional specialties are essentially chunks of meat marinated for days before being skewered and grilled. Fantastically tender bitefuls of pure flavor result. Spiedies are traditionally served in a slice of Italian bread.

3½ pounds boneless chicken breast, cut into chunks
2 cups olive oil
5 tablespoons balsamic vinegar
2 tablespoons light beer
2 tablespoons grated Romano cheese

2 tablespoons parsley
2 teaspoons salt
1 teaspoon garlic powder
1 teaspoon minced onion
1 teaspoon pepper
1 teaspoon oregano

Combine all marinade ingredients. Add chicken and marinate at least 24 hours (preferably 48), turning occasionally. Skewer and grill chicken, basting with marinade.

Family & Company (New York)

Spinach Stuffed Chicken Breasts

1 tablespoon butter
4 ounces mushrooms, finely chopped
1 (10-ounce) package frozen, chopped spinach, thawed and squeezed dry

2 (3-ounce) packages cream cheese, room temperature
½ cup chopped black olives
6 chicken breast halves
6 tablespoons Dijon mustard

Preheat oven to 450°. Melt butter in heavy skillet over medium heat. Add mushrooms and sauté until tender (5 minutes). Cool slightly. Blend spinach, cream cheese, and olives in medium bowl. Mix in mushrooms and season to taste with salt and pepper. Run finger under skin of each chicken breast, creating a pocket. Spread ⅙ of cream cheese mixture between chicken and skin of each breast. Arrange on baking sheet. Spread one tablespoon Dijon mustard over each. Bake until golden brown and cooked through (20 minutes). Serves 6.

Great Taste of Parkminster (New York)

Chicken Pillows

1 whole chicken breast,
  halved, skinned, boned
1 clove garlic, halved
2 slices ham (1 ounce)
2 slices mozzarella cheese
  (1 ounce)
2 tablespoons seasoned
  bread crumbs

2 tablespoons medium-dry
  sherry
2 tablespoons clarified
  butter
1 tablespoon chopped parsley

Pound chicken breasts to ¼ inch. Rub each with garlic. Place ham and cheese over chicken. Sprinkle with crumbs. Roll up and secure with wooden picks; place in lightly greased pan. Combine sherry and butter; heat briefly. Pour over chicken. Bake at 350° for 20–25 minutes. Sprinkle with parsley. Serves 2.

The Marlborough Meetinghouse Cookbook (Connecticut)

Woodie's Roux-the-Day Casserole

1½ pounds veal or chicken,
  boned, trimmed and cubed
¼ cup olive oil
1 tablespoon butter
1 tablespoon flour

½ cup chicken broth
½ cup white wine
1 teaspoon green peppercorns
  in vinegar, drained, reserve
  ½ teaspoon vinegar)

Preheat oven to 350°. In a heavy pan, brown veal or chicken in oil; drain and set aside. In a saucepan, melt butter, stir in flour until it is lightly browned. Gradually add broth and white wine to flour mixture, stirring constantly until well blended. Bring to a boil, reduce heat and simmer, stirring constantly, until sauce has thickened. Remove from heat and stir in green peppercorns and vinegar. Place veal or chicken in a casserole and pour sauce over it; bake for one hour.

Recipe by Heywood Hale Broun, commentator/journalist
Famous Woodstock Cooks (New York)

Broccoli and Chicken

2 (10-ounce) packages frozen broccoli, cooked, or 2 bunches fresh broccoli, cooked

2 cups sliced cooked chicken, or 2 chicken breasts, cooked and boned

2 (10¾-ounce) cans cream of chicken or celery soup

½ cup mayonnaise or salad dressing

1 teaspoon lemon juice

½ teaspoon curry powder

1 teaspoon butter or margarine

½ cup soft bread crumbs, or 1 cup instant rice

½ cup shredded sharp processed cheese

Pimento strips and nuts (optional)

Arrange broccoli and chicken in a greased 7x11-inch baking dish. Combine soup, mayonnaise, lemon juice, and curry powder. Pour over chicken and broccoli. Combine crumbs and butter. Sprinkle cheese over contents of baking dish, then crumbs over cheese. (You can start with 1 cup instant rice in bottom of dish and omit the bread crumbs.) Bake at 350° for 30 minutes or until heated through. Trim with pimento strips and nuts, if desired. Makes 6–8 servings.

Our Favorite Recipes (Pennsylvania)

In 1969, the Woodstock Festival actually took place fifty miles southwest of Woodstock on a dairy farm in Bethel, New York—not in Woodstock, as many people believe. The Woodstock town board voted against hosting the festival due to inadequate resources, but the name of Woodstock was already printed on the posters and publicity material.

Cheesy Chicken Florentine

Always requested for a repeat performance.

3 packages frozen chopped
spinach, thawed and
squeezed dry
3 whole chicken breasts,
cooked and cut into pieces
2 (8-ounce) packages cream
cheese
14 ounces extra sharp
Cheddar cheese, grated
2 cups milk

¼ teaspoon salt
¼ teaspoon pepper
½ teaspoon dill
½ teaspoon garlic
1 tablespoon parsley flakes
1 cup Parmesan cheese
1 cup bread crumbs
¼ cup (½ stick) butter,
melted

Preheat oven to 375°. Lightly butter a 13x9-inch casserole. Line with uncooked spinach. Add chicken. Set aside.

Make sauce by melting cream cheese, Cheddar cheese, milk, seasonings, and ⅔ cup Parmesan cheese. (Reserve ⅓ cup of Parmesan cheese for bread crumb mixture.) Blend over low heat until smooth. Pour cheese sauce over spinach and chicken. Combine bread crumbs with melted butter. Add ⅓ cup Parmesan cheese. Sprinkle mixture on top of mixture. Bake uncovered for 30 minutes. Serves 4–6.

Moveable Feasts Cookbook (Connecticut)

The song "Yankee Doodle" had its origins in Norwalk, Connecticut. In 1756, a brigade of volunteers assembled at the home of Colonel Thomas Fitch where the young recruits set out to assist the British during the French and Indian War. Fitch's young sister stuck a feather into the hatband of each soldier as he pulled out on his plow horse. The British, amused by the appearance of the troops, wrote and sang the jingle in mockery. The rest is history. "Yankee Doodle" became the rallying song for the colonial troops during the Revolution and in 1979 became the official song of Connecticut.

Marge's Parmesan Squash Ring Centered with Chicken

This is delicious served hot or cold with either chicken or turkey and is an excellent way to use leftover turkey.

SQUASH RING:

½ cup chopped green onion
2 tablespoons butter or margarine
4 eggs
¼ teaspoon salt
¼ teaspoon red pepper

2 (12-ounce) packages frozen squash, defrosted, or 4 cups fresh squash, cooked, mashed
1 cup Parmesan cheese

In skillet, cook onion in butter until tender. Set aside. Beat eggs in mixer until blended and add the salt, pepper, squash, Parmesan cheese, and onion mixture. Pour into oiled baking ring. Bake at 350° for 30–40 minutes or until set. Let stand 8 minutes. Loosen edges and turn onto serving dish.

CHICKEN MIXTURE:

2 cups cooked chicken
2 cups finely sliced celery
½ cup chopped toasted almonds
½ teaspoon salt

1 cup mayonnaise
2 tablespoons lemon juice
2 teaspoons grated onion
½ cup grated Parmesan cheese

While squash is baking, combine chicken, celery, almonds, salt, mayonnaise, and lemon juice. Grate the onion on top. If chicken is served cold, place in center of ring and top with cheese. If served hot, heat the mixture in a casserole about 10 minutes in a 450° oven. Add to ring and add the cheese.

Memories from Brownie's Kitchen (Maine)

Ski Day Chicken Casserole

Actually, good for any day.

8 tablespoons butter or margarine
¼ cup flour
1½ cups chicken broth
1 cup sour cream
⅛ teaspoon nutmeg
⅛ teaspoon pepper
Salt to taste
¼ cup dry sherry

½ pound flat egg noodles, cooked and drained
4½ cups cut-up cooked chicken
½ pound mushrooms, sliced and sautéed
1 cup soft bread crumbs
½ cup freshly grated Parmesan cheese

Melt 4 tablespoons butter; stir in flour, and add broth and sour cream, stirring until thick. Add nutmeg, pepper and salt. Remove from heat and stir in sherry. Arrange noodles in 9x13-inch baking dish. Cover with chicken, mushrooms, and sauce. Melt remaining 4 tablespoons butter and mix with crumbs. Top casserole with crumbs and cheese. Bake in preheated 350° oven for 30 minutes or until hot and bubbly. May be made day in advance, refrigerated, and baked when needed. Serves 8.

Merrymeeting Merry Eating (Maine)

Phyllo Chicken Pie

Tour luncheon guests will exclaim at the puffy, fluffy crust; they will exclaim again when they taste the pie—and they will come back for more.

1 cup chopped onions	¾ (10¾-ounce) can cream
½ pound mushrooms,	of mushroom soup
coarsely chopped	1½ cups sour cream
½ cup cubed celery	2 tablespoons sherry
¾ cup plus 2 tablespoons	1 tablespoon soy sauce
(1¾ sticks) margarine	1 tablespoon catsup
3 cups chopped cooked	1 teaspoon prepared mustard
chicken	8 leaves phyllo, thawed

Sauté onions, mushrooms, and celery in 2 tablespoons margarine. Mix in chicken, mushroom soup, sour cream, sherry, soy sauce, catsup, and mustard. Combine well. (Can be prepared 1 day in advance and refrigerated.)

The remaining preparation can be done several hours before cooking. Remove chicken mixture from refrigerator. Slowly melt ¾ cup (1½ sticks) margarine. Grease a 9x13-inch baking dish. Handle phyllo according to package directions. Place 4 foil phyllo leaves, 1 at a time, on bottom of dish. This is done in the following way: The leaves measure approximately 18x13-inches. Hold first leaf at right angles to dish and smooth half of it in bottom of dish. Brush all over with melted margarine—not too much. Fold other half of phyllo leaf into dish and brush with margarine. Repeat process with 3 more leaves, thus making 8 layers of phyllo. Spread phyllo with chicken mixture. Cover with 8 more layers (4 full leaves) of phyllo, each brushed with melted margarine. Spread top with any remaining margarine. Finally, with a sharp knife, cut the pie into 12 pieces. Store in refrigerator until ready to cook. Bake in a preheated 350° oven for 45 minutes and serve at once. Serves 12.

The Lymes' Heritage Cookbook (Connecticut)

Quick Stir-Fried Chicken

3 tablespoons peanut oil
4 tablespoons soy sauce
¾ teaspoon garlic salt
2 teaspoons cornstarch
3 tablespoons cold water
2 cups raw chicken, sliced
  julienne
1 (6-ounce) package frozen
  Chinese pea pods
1 (8-ounce) can water
  chestnuts, drained and
  sliced

¾ cup chopped fresh
  broccoli
2 oranges, sectioned
1 bunch green onions,
  trimmed and quartered
¼ cup sliced mushrooms
2 cups cooked rice or chow
  mein noodles

Heat oil in wok or skillet over medium heat. When hot, add soy sauce and garlic salt, and stir. Combine cornstarch and water, and set aside. Add chicken to pan and stir-fry, about 3 minutes. Add pea pods, water chestnuts, and broccoli, and stir-fry 2 minutes. Reduce heat then add orange sections, green onions, mushrooms, and cornstarch. Stir until thickened and serve over rice or noodles.

What's Cooking at Moody's Diner (Maine)

Buffalo Chicken Wings

20–25 chicken wings
Vegetable oil for deep-frying
¼ cup melted butter or
    margarine

½ small bottle hot sauce
Bleu Cheese Dressing
Celery sticks

Disjoint the chicken wings and discard the tips. Rinse and pat dry. The wings must be completely dry to fry properly since there is no batter or breading. Preheat the oil in a deep fryer or a large deep pan to 365°. Add the chicken wings a few at a time to the hot oil. Do not allow the oil to cool as the chicken is added. Deep-fry for 6–10 minutes or until crisp and golden brown. Drain well by shaking in the fryer basket or a strainer. Blend the butter with hot sauce for medium-hot wings. Add additional hot sauce for hotter wings, or additional butter for milder wings. Combine the wings and the hot sauce in a large container. Let stand, covered. Serve the chicken wings with Bleu Cheese Dressing and celery sticks. Makes 20–25 chicken wings.

BLEU CHEESE DRESSING:

2 cups mayonnaise
3 tablespoons cider vinegar
½ teaspoon dry mustard
½ teaspoon white pepper

¼ teaspoon salt
8 ounces bleu cheese,
    crumbled
¼ to ½ cup cold water

Combine the mayonnaise, vinegar, dry mustard, pepper and salt in a large bowl and beat until well blended. Mix in the bleu cheese. Add enough cold water gradually to make the dressing of the desired consistency, whisking constantly. Store in an airtight container in the refrigerator. Makes 3½ cups.

Great Lake Effects (New York)

Buffalo wings are named after the culinary dish from, Buffalo, New York. The local residents of Buffalo generally refer to them as "wings" or "chicken wings" rather than "Buffalo wings." Classic Buffalo-style chicken wing sauce is composed of a vinegar-based cayenne pepper hot sauce and butter. Buffalo wings are traditionally served with celery sticks and blue cheese dressing.

Pilgrim Roasted Turkey

1 (4- to 6-pound) turkey
¼ stick butter
3 tablespoons wine
Salt
Black pepper
1 clove garlic, chopped

2 yams, peeled
2 carrots, peeled
2 bay leaves
1 can mushrooms
Handful bread crumbs

Preheat oven to 450°. Place bird on grill rack in roasting pan. This allows juices to run, causing steam, which cooks the turkey better. Baste with butter. Pour wine onto meat. Mix and sprinkle salt, pepper, and chopped garlic on top. Cut yams lengthwise in half, and quarter the carrots lengthwise. Line around turkey. Put bay leaves in pan for flavor only.

Roast approximately 3 hours, basting a few times with its juices. Ascertain that bird is cooked properly. Use a meat thermometer for best cooking results after the 3-hour period (or test earlier, if preferred). Stick the thermometer into a thick section of thigh; avoid touching bone (which gives a false, higher reading). Turkey should be completely cooked when temperature reaches 180°.

Toss in mushrooms and bread crumbs during the last 5 minutes and swish around once or twice. Serves 2–4.

Wild Game Cookbook & Other Recipes (New York)

Why Be Normal Burger

This original recipe was entered in the Stowe, Vermont, Annual Best Burger Contest—it took First Place!

1 pound ground turkey
2 cups cooked wild rice
¾ cup whole cranberry
  sauce

¼ cup cooking wine
1½ cups bread crumbs
Chopped onions (½–1 cup)

Combine all ingredients. Shape into patties and grill. Serves 6–7.

Note: Cooking time for these burgers is longer than for regular hamburgers—about 7 minutes a side.

The Marlborough Meetinghouse Cookbook (Vermont)

Seafood

GREATER BOSTON CONVENTION & VISITORS BUREAU

The Head of the Charles Regatta is the world's largest two-day regatta attracting more than 8,500 rowers and 300,000 spectators to the banks of the Charles River in Boston, Massachusetts. This two-day event encompasses 55 different events, all taking place amidst the unmistakable beauty of foliage season in Boston.

Baked Bluefish Stuffed with Wellfleet Oysters

1 (5-pound) bluefish

Take a whole 5-pound bluefish and stuff it with a Wellfleet oyster dressing made as follows:

OYSTER DRESSING:

3 dozen oysters with liquor
1 cup white wine
Fresh ground pepper to taste

3–4 slices French bread
Melted butter for brushing

Place oysters and their liquor and a cup of white wine in a pan, and add a little fresh ground black pepper (the liquor furnishes the salt); poach the oysters gently until their edges curl. Drain off the broth and use it to wet down and knead 3 or 4 slices of French bread into a paste. Mix this paste with the oysters and stuff the bluefish with it.

Sew the fish up, lay it on greased aluminum foil in a baking pan, and bake in a preheated oven at 350° for 30 minutes or until it is browned and cooked through. Brush it a couple of times with melted butter during the baking to keep it from drying out. Lay the whole fish out on a platter on a bed of lettuce leaves. Serve a tomato sauce on the side and a bottle of white wine moderately chilled.

Provincetown Seafood Cookbook (Massachusetts)

 One of the laws regulating oysters prohibited their taking during the months without an "R." Although this was done as a conservation measure during spawning, people erroneously came to believe that oysters were inedible in May, June, July, and August.

Bluefish Grilled in Foil

This recipe comes from Fishers Island and is a DuPont family favorite. The packet can be prepared ahead and stored for up to 12 hours before grilling.

2 large bluefish fillets
  (about 1 pound each)
1 medium onion, thinly
  sliced
1 green pepper, seeded and
  thinly sliced
1 large firm tomato, thinly
  sliced

1 cup bottled Italian salad
  dressing
Lemon wedges for garnish
Large pieces of aluminum
  foil

Prepare a barbecue fire. Coals should burn down until they are covered with a white ash.

Rinse and dry the bluefish. Tear off 2 pieces of aluminum foil large enough to wrap around the fish and seal it tightly. On 1 sheet of foil, place 1 of the bluefish fillets, skin-side-down. Layer sliced onion, green pepper, and tomato on top. Top with the second fillet, skin-side-up.

Raise the sides of the foil and pour the salad dressing over the fish. Seal foil by crimping the edges together and wrap again with the second sheet of foil. Place the packet on the grill and cook for 20 minutes, turning once. Poke holes in foil with fork to let liquid escape and grill for another 5 minutes or so per side or until fish tests done. Remove from grill, open foil, and serve with lemon wedges. Yields 4–6 servings.

Off the Hook (Connecticut)

Baked Salmon with Dill

1 medium onion, cut into
⅛-inch slices
1 fresh red pepper, cleaned
and cut in ⅛-inch slices
2 tablespoons butter
1 pound salmon fillet, with
skin removed

1 cup minced fresh dill (no
stems)
2 slices of lemon, ¼-inch
thick
1 teaspoon chopped garlic
4–6 ounces Italian dressing

Sauté onion and red pepper slices in butter over medium heat until they soften. Cover the bottom of a small baking dish evenly with the sautéed vegetables. Place salmon, skinned-side-down, on top of the vegetables. Completely blanket with fresh dill. Place lemon slices side by side on top of dill and salmon. Sprinkle with garlic. Pour Italian dressing over dish until lightly saturated (like mist on grass). Bake at 350° for 30 minutes. Serve hot. Any left-over salmon can be served cold sprinkled over a fresh garden salad the next day. Serves 2–3.

The East Hampton L.V.I.S. Centennial Cookbook (New York)

Baked Salmon with Carrots and Zucchini

1 tablespoon olive oil
1 onion, chopped fine
2 zucchini, cut in matchstick-
size pieces or shredded
coarsely
2 carrots, shredded coarsely
¼ cup chopped fresh parsley

2 tablespoons chopped fresh
basil
4 salmon fillets
1 tablespoon lemon juice
½ teaspoon salt
½ teaspoon pepper

Heat oven to 350°. In a nonstick skillet, heat oil. Add onion, sauté until tender. Add zucchini, carrots, parsley, and basil, mixing light-ly. Place vegetable mixture into a lightly greased 10x10-inch baking dish. Arrange salmon steaks over vegetables and drizzle with lemon juice, salt and pepper. Cover; bake 30 minutes. Uncover and bake 10 more minutes. Serves 4.

Thou Preparest a Table Before Me (New York)

Smoked-Salmon and Cream-Cheese Quesadillas

This is one of our most popular summer breakfast dishes. Some of our return-ing guests now request this breakfast when they make their reservations. We usually make extra so that we can enjoy it for a cool summer lunch.

6 ounces low-fat cream cheese, softened
2 tablespoons chopped fresh dill, plus 2 teaspoons for garnish
Salt and pepper
1 tablespoon fresh lemon juice

6 (8-inch) flour tortillas (white or whole-wheat)
12 ounces smoked salmon
3 scallions chopped, green parts only
1 lemon, thinly sliced into rounds

In the bowl of an electric mixer, combine cream cheese, 2 table-spoons dill, salt and pepper to taste, and lemon juice. Beat until smooth and well-blended. Set aside.

In a 10-inch non-stick skillet, warm each tortilla over low heat until lightly browned on each side. Set aside on a cookie sheet.

For each quesadilla: Spread 2 tablespoons cream cheese mixture evenly on a tortilla, covering to the edges. Arrange 2 ounces of sliced smoked salmon over the cheese, covering to the edges. Repeat with remaining tortillas. Sprinkle with reserved 2 teaspoons chopped dill. Cut each tortilla into 6 wedges per serving. Garnish with lemon slices and sprinkle with scallions. Yields 12 servings.

Tasting the Hamptons (New York)

The Southern New England Telephone Company in Connecticut (com-monly referred to as SNET by its customers) started operations on January 27, 1878 as the District Telephone Company of New Haven. It was the founder of the first telephone exchange, as well as the world's first telephone book, which contained only fifty names.

Grilled Lime Salmon Steaks

4 salmon steaks
¼ cup lime juice
½ cup oil

1 teaspoon dried tarragon
Salt and pepper

Whisk lime juice together with oil. Add tarragon, salt, and pepper. Place salmon steaks in a shallow dish. Pour marinade over salmon. Refrigerate 4 hours or overnight.

Grill over hot coals until cooked to desired degree of doneness, approximately 5 minutes per side.

Dining on Deck (Vermont)

Dilled Haddock Parmesan

1 cup sour cream
¼ cup freshly grated
  Parmesan
¼ cup grated Swiss cheese
1 teaspoon fresh minced dill
  (or ½ teaspoon dried)
¼ cup very soft butter

Salt and pepper to taste
3 pounds haddock fillets
Sprinkle of sweet Hungarian
  paprika
6 sprigs of dill for garnish
6 lemon wedges

In a small bowl, mix the sour cream, cheeses, minced dill, and butter. Add salt and pepper to taste. Set aside.

Preheat oven to 375°. Cut fillets into 6 individual servings and place them on a buttered baking sheet. Top each piece with cheese mixture and bake for 15–20 minutes. Sprinkle lightly with paprika, garnish with dill sprig, and serve with a lemon wedge. Serves 6.

Recipes from a New England Inn (New Hampshire)

Baked Boston Scrod

Scrod, a young cod, is strictly a New England dish, and abundantly available. It is firm, tender, and moist—a delightful fish.

4 pieces scrod fillet (6–8 ounces each)
Salt and pepper to taste
2 tablespoons lemon juice
1½ cups white wine
½ cup butter, melted
1 cup dried bread crumbs

Preheat the oven to 350°. Butter a baking pan large enough to hold the scrod in a single layer. Place the scrod in the prepared baking pan, and add the salt, pepper, lemon juice, and wine. Drizzle ¼ cup of the melted butter over the fish. Bake at 350° for approximately 20 minutes, or until the fish flakes but is still moist. Remove the pan from the oven and preheat the broiler. Scatter the bread crumbs over the fish, and drizzle with the remaining ¼ cup butter. Brown under the broiler for 2–5 minutes only, until lightly browned, and serve. Serves 4.

The Red Lion Inn Cookbook (Massachusetts)

Marinated Cod

This is a good all-purpose seafood marinade and excellent for other fish such as red snapper, swordfish, or any fairly thick, firm fleshed fish.

1 pound cod
¼ cup corn oil
1 tablespoon Dijon mustard
1 tablespoon Na Soy Sauce
⅛ cup lemon juice
1 tablespoon chopped onion
1 garlic clove, minced
1½ teaspoons Worcestershire
½ teaspoon pepper

Blend in blender or food processor all of the above ingredients except the cod. Pour over cod and marinate for several hours. Place on greased broiling pan, pouring extra marinade on top of fish. Broil until fish flakes easily, about 7–10 minutes. Serves 2–3.

Hasbro Children's Hospital Cookbook (Rhode Island)

Poached Cod with Lemon Butter Sauce

1¾ pounds cod fillets	4 sprigs fresh parsley
1 cup milk	4 whole peppercorns
1½ cups water	2 whole cloves
1 bay leaf	Salt to taste (optional)

Cut cod fillets crosswise into 4 equal pieces. In a large skillet, arrange fillets in a single layer. Pour milk into skillet; add enough water to just cover fillets. Add bay leaf, parsley sprigs, peppercorns, and cloves to skillet. Season with salt, if desired. Bring to a simmer; cover and cook gently, approximately 3–4 minutes, until fish flakes easily with a fork. Remove skillet from heat; set aside.

LEMON BUTTER SAUCE:

4 tablespoons chilled butter, divided	Juice of ½–1 lemon to taste
½ teaspoon finely minced garlic	2 tablespoons finely minced fresh parsley
3 tablespoons finely chopped shallots	Salt and freshly ground black pepper to taste

In a small saucepan, heat 1 tablespoon butter. Add garlic and shallots; sauté just until softened. Remove ¼ cup of cooking liquid from skillet; add to saucepan and stir. Bring sauce to a boil; cook until reduced by ½. Add lemon juice. Remove sauce from heat. Whisk in remaining butter until melted. Season with minced parsley, salt and pepper. Drain cod. Serve with sauce. Serves 4.

The Heart of Pittsburgh II (Pennsylvania)

Baked Swordfish Steak

Swordfish is the king of the fish that cut well into steaks. It is a toss-up whether my off-Cape friends prefer swordfish or lobster when they visit here. Swordfish can be baked (as in this recipe), charcoal-broiled, or broiled in the range broiler. It is one fish that I would not pan-fry if facilities for the other cooking methods were available. All swordfish recipes can also be prepared with Mako shark or salmon.

2 pounds swordfish steak, 1-inch thick
Cooking oil
Flour seasoned with salt, pepper, and paprika
½ cup finely chopped onion
2 tablespoons chopped fresh dill (or more to taste)
4 tablespoons melted butter
½ cup dry white wine

Dip steaks in cooking oil and then in seasoned flour. Place steaks in 1 layer in an oiled flat baking pan. Sprinkle with onion, dill, and melted butter. Pour wine around fish.

Bake at 400° for 20–25 minutes or until fish flakes easily, basting twice with wine. Serve fish with pan sauce. Makes 4 servings.

Note: With Baked Swordfish Steak, put 4 potatoes in the oven to bake about 35 minutes before the fish. Steamed broccoli, watercress salad, and fresh or frozen sliced peaches can complete the dinner.

A Cape Cod Seafood Cookbook (Massachusetts)

 Provincetown, Massachusetts, the birthplace of the commercial fishing industry of the United States, was the wealthiest town per capita in New England in the 1840s and 1850s. It is still considered the gourmet seafood capital of the Atlantic seaboard, supplying fresh fish for the tables of gourmets everywhere.

Baked Wild Trout

1 filleted trout	1 clove garlic
2 ounces oil	1 teaspoon oregano
3 ounces wine	Handful bread crumbs
Salt	2 slices bacon
Black pepper	2 onions
1 tablespoon parsley, minced	Several small potatoes

Preheat oven to 350°. Slice trout fillets in half lengthwise. Arrange fillets in well-oiled pan, open halves facing up. Mix oil and wine; pour onto fillets. Then sprinkle salt, pepper, minced parsley, minced garlic, oregano, and bread crumbs over fish. Lay bacon slices across tops of fillets. Arrange whole onions and quartered potatoes in pan alongside fish. Bake 30 minutes. Baste, using juices from bottom of pan. When bread crumbs are browned sufficiently, fish should be ready. Serve hot with warm bread. Brook trout serves 2–4; rainbow, brown and lake trout serves 6–12.

Wild Game Cookbook & Other Recipes (New York)

Stuffed Sole

A light and delicious dish!

1 small onion	1 (7-ounce) can crabmeat
2 stalks celery	Fillet of sole for four
½ green pepper	Parsley
4 tablespoons butter, melted	Lemon slices
¼ cup bread crumbs	

Dice onion, celery, and green pepper. Mix butter and bread crumbs. Break up crabmeat and add it along with onion, celery, and pepper to bread crumb mixture. Place mixture on sole and roll up. Bake at 350° for 20 minutes. Serve with parsley and lemon slices. Serves 4.

Thru the Grapevine (New York)

Halibut Provençal

2 (7-ounce) halibut steaks,
  1 inch thick
½ cup diced tomatoes
1 tablespoon olive oil
½ cup fresh bread crumbs
2 cloves garlic, chopped
2 whole basil leaves, chopped
  (or ¼ teaspoon dry)

½ teaspoon salt
¼ teaspoon fresh ground
  black pepper
¼ cup fresh grated Parmesan
  cheese

Preheat oven to 425°. Spray bottom of a medium glass baking dish with non-stick cooking spray. Rinse fish and drain on paper towels. Place fish in baking dish. Top with diced tomatoes. In a small skillet, heat oil over medium-high heat. Add bread crumbs, garlic, and basil; sauté about 2 minutes or until aromatic, stirring so it will not burn. Add salt and pepper. Sprinkle bread crumb mixture over tomatoes. Top with Parmesan cheese. Bake 10–12 minutes or until fish flakes when pierced with a fork. Serves 2.

Note: A general rule when baking fish is to allow 10 minutes per inch of thickness, measured at the thickest part. That applies when using a temperature of 425°, a bit longer at a lower temperature.

Recipes from the Children's Museum at Saratoga (New York)

"Rip Van Winkle" is a short story by Washington Irving who was born in Manhattan in 1783. Published in June 1819, the story, which has become a legend, is set in the Catskill Mountains of New York before and after the American Revolution. The title character is a young married Dutch American of a kind and generous disposition. Averse to profitable labor, he prefers rambles in the mountains, playing with the village children, and sitting in the shade gossiping with his cronies. One day he wanders into the mountains and happens upon the ghosts of Henry Hudson and his crew playing nine pins in a mysterious hollow. He drinks their brew and falls asleep. Twenty years later, he wakes as an aged man and wanders back to his village, where he is astonished by the changes that have taken place. After some ado, he is reunited with his now-grown daughter and her children.

Sesame Balsamic Tuna

2 (½-inch) tuna steaks
½ cup balsamic vinegar
¼ cup dark sesame oil
2 tablespoons freshly grated
  gingerroot
2 tablespoons chopped fresh
  cilantro

2 green onions, chopped
4 teaspoons sugar
8 ounces mushrooms, sliced
2 tablespoons sesame oil

Rinse the tuna steaks and pat dry. Arrange in a shallow dish. Combine the balsamic vinegar, ¼ cup sesame oil, gingerroot, cilantro, green onions, and sugar in a bowl and mix well. Pour over the tuna, turning to coat. Marinate, covered, in the refrigerator for 1 hour, turning occasionally. Drain, reserving the marinade.

Preheat the grill on high for 10 minutes. Place the tuna steaks on the grill rack. Grill for 3–4 minutes per side or until the tuna flakes easily. Sauté the mushrooms in 2 tablespoons sesame oil in a skillet until brown on both sides. Stir in the reserved marinade. Cook until heated through. Arrange the tuna steaks on a serving platter. Pour the mushroom sauce over the steaks. Serves 2.

Great Lake Effects (New York)

Taxis are a significant component of the New York City transportation network, with over 40,000 licensed taxi drivers and 12,000 licensed taxi-cabs in service. Yellow became the uniform color for all licensed cabs in 1969. Manhattan residents hail cabs an average of 100 times a year. Sixty-nine percent of all trips carry one passenger.

Ceviche

The acid in the lime "cooks" the fish so that it no longer has the texture nor the taste of raw fish.

1 pound firm white ocean fish (like scrod), or scallops, cut into small cubes
Juice of 8–10 limes
1 tomato, peeled and diced
½ white onion, thinly sliced into rings
2 jalapeño peppers, seeded and chopped, or to taste

2 tablespoons olive oil
2 tablespoons red wine vinegar
2 tablespoons chopped cilantro leaves
10 Spanish olives (with pimiento) whole, or to taste
1 ripe avocado (preferably Haas), peeled and sliced*
Saltine crackers

Place the fish in a glass or porcelain bowl. (Do not use metal.) Pour lime juice over fish. Marinate in refrigerator overnight or for at least 4 hours, stirring occasionally until fish is opaque. Add tomato, onion, jalapeño, oil, vinegar, cilantro, and olives, and mix gently. Refrigerate another 2 hours. Garnish with avocado slices and serve with saltine crackers. Serves 4.

*Do not peel and slice avocado until you are ready to serve the dish. Otherwise, the flesh will turn brown when exposed to air.

La Cocina de la Familia (New York)

Baked Stuffed Flounder

1 pound frozen flounder
  fillets, thawed
1 (4-ounce) can mushroom
  stems and pieces
2 teaspoons minced onion
¼ cup soft bread crumbs

1 teaspoon Worcestershire
1 tablespoon butter
2 teaspoons milk
¼ cup mayonnaise
1½ teaspoons lemon juice
Paprika for garnish

Pat moisture off flounder and arrange half in bottom of a greased, shallow baking dish. Drain mushrooms and save juice. Mix mushrooms with onion, bread crumbs, Worcestershire, and 3 tablespoons mushroom juice. Spread mixture on fillets and dot with butter. Place remaining fillets on top. Mix milk, mayonnaise, and lemon juice well and spread on top of fish. Garnish with paprika. Bake in 375° oven for 40 minutes. Serves 3–4.

Dinner Bell (Pennsylvania)

Lobster Thermidor

2 lobsters, boiled
¼ pound fresh mushrooms
2 tablespoons butter
Salt and pepper, to taste
2 ounces sherry or cooking
  wine (optional)

2 tablespoons flour
1 cup milk or cream
¼ cup diced Cheddar cheese
Paprika
2 egg yolks

Boil lobsters and remove meat. Reserve shells. Sauté lobster meat and sliced mushrooms in butter for 5 minutes. Add salt and pepper to taste. Add sherry and braise for 2 minutes. Blend flour into mixture, then slowly stir in milk. Add cheese and stir until it melts. Sprinkle with paprika. Remove from heat and blend in egg yolks. Fill lobster shells. Sprinkle with Parmesan cheese and a dash of paprika. Place under broiler to brown.

A recipe from Ron Machtley, Congressman from Rhode Island
Celebrities Serve (Rhode Island)

Merrymount Lobster

Can be prepared ahead of time. Excellent for large buffets.

3 cups cut-up lobster, crab, shrimp, or sea legs
1 tablespoon lemon juice
2 eggs, slightly beaten
2 cups light cream
2 tablespoons butter
1 cup soft bread crumbs
1 cup buttered cracker crumbs (or saltines)

1 heaping teaspoon prepared mustard
Dash of cayenne pepper
Black pepper, freshly ground (about ¼ teaspoon)
Salt to taste

Lobster may be frozen, canned, or fresh. Sprinkle lemon juice and beaten eggs over lobster. Bring cream, butter, and bread crumbs just to a boil; stir well together and pour over lobster. Stir mustard, cayenne pepper, black pepper, and salt carefully into lobster mixture. Pour into a buttered casserole dish and top with 1 cup buttered cracker crumbs. Bake, uncovered, in a preheated oven at 350° until crumbs are brown and lobster is bubbly—no more. Serves 8.

Sandy Hook Volunteer Fire Co. Ladies Aux. Cookbook
(Connecticut)

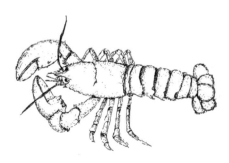

Lobster à la Newburg

½ pint of cream
1 tablespoon butter
1 tablespoon flour
Yolks of 2 eggs
Salt and cayenne pepper (few
   grains)

1 large lobster, cooked, cut
   in pieces
Juice of half a lemon
Wine glass of sherry

Make a cream of the cream, butter, flour, and egg yolks; season with salt and very little cayenne. Put the lobster meat in a double boiler and when hot, add the creamed mixture, allowing it to come just to a boil, then add the juice of half a lemon and a wine glass of sherry.

All-Maine Cooking (Maine)

Baked Shrimp Scampi

Everybody's favorite! This makes a great appetizer. It is so fast and easy.

1 pound shrimp, peeled and
   deveined
½ cup butter
3 cloves garlic, minced
2 tablespoons finely chopped
   fresh parsley
1 tablespoon lemon juice

½ teaspoon crushed red
   pepper flakes
1 teaspoon Worcestershire
½ teaspoon oregano
¼ teaspoon seasoned salt
½ cup bread or cracker
   crumbs

Arrange shrimp in a single layer in a shallow baking dish. In a small saucepan, combine all remaining ingredients except bread or cracker crumbs. Heat until butter has melted, stirring to mix seasonings. Pour evenly over shrimp, reserving 2 tablespoons.

Add reserved seasoned butter to bread or cracker crumbs; mix well. Sprinkle crumbs over shrimp. Bake at 450° for 8–10 minutes, or until browned. Serves 2–4.

Family & Company (New York)

Roasted Red Pepper and Shrimp Grits

In the White Dog kitchen, we have very few fixed rules about food, however one of them is to never combine fish and cheese. Of course, there are exceptions to every rule, and these rich creamy grits are a glorious one.

2 tablespoons unsalted butter
1 large yellow onion, minced
  (about 2 cups)
1 tablespoon minced garlic
1 cup quick-cooking grits
4 cups whole milk, divided
1 cup water
2 teaspoons salt
½ teaspoon freshly ground
  black pepper

¼ teaspoon Tabasco
2 red bell peppers, roasted,
  peeled, seeded, puréed
8 ounces shrimp, peeled,
  deveined
8 ounces (2 cups) grated
  Cheddar or Monterey Jack
  cheese

Melt butter in a saucepan set over medium heat. Add onion and sauté until soft, about 5 minutes. Add garlic and cook 2 minutes. Stir in grits. Stir in 2 cups of milk and simmer until liquid is absorbed, about 5 minutes. Add remaining 2 cups milk and simmer, stirring occasionally, until it is absorbed, about 5 minutes. Add water and simmer until grits are soft and thick, 35–40 minutes.

Preheat oven to 400°. Add salt, pepper, Tabasco, and puréed bell peppers to grits; mix well. Pour mixture into a 6x10x1¾-inch casserole. (The grits may be prepared to this point 1 day in advance. Let cool to room temperature, cover, and refrigerate overnight. Bring to room temperature before proceeding.)

Spread shrimp evenly over grits and top with grated cheese. Bake on top rack of oven until shrimp are cooked through and cheese is melted, about 15 minutes. Serves 6.

White Dog Cafe Cookbook (Pennsylvania)

Garlic Broiled Shrimp

2 pounds large fresh shrimp,
  peeled and deveined
½ cup (8 tablespoons)
  butter, melted
½ cup olive oil
¼ chopped cup fresh parsley

1 tablespoon chopped green
  onion
3 cloves garlic, minced
1½ tablespoons fresh
  lemon juice
Freshly ground black pepper

Combine butter, olive oil, parsley, green onion, garlic, and lemon juice in a large shallow dish. Add shrimp, tossing to coat. Cover and marinate at least 30 minutes, stirring occasionally. Set oven to broil. Place shrimp on broiler pan and broil 4 inches from the heat source for 3–4 minutes. Turn and broil for another 3 minutes or until done. Top with a few turns of the peppermill and serve with the pan drippings with pasta or rice. Yields 4–6 servings.

Note: I prefer to use shrimp that have been peeled but with the tails left on and split (or "butterflied") up the back. You can ask your fish market to do this for you.

Off the Hook (Connecticut)

New England Shrimp Casserole

1 small onion, minced
1 green pepper, chopped
½ cup chopped celery
¼ cup butter, melted
½ cup chopped pimento
1 (27-ounce) can stewed
  tomatoes

1 tablespoon cornstarch
2 tablespoons water
Salt and pepper to taste
1 tablespoon parsley
1 pound cooked shrimp

Add onion, green pepper, and celery to melted butter. Cook until tender. Add pimento and tomatoes. Bring to boil and simmer until well blended. Mix cornstarch with water and add to mixture. Season to taste. Add parsley and cooked shrimp. Serve over hot rice.

A Taste of New England (Massachusetts)

Shrimp Stir-Fry with Lemon

½ pound peeled raw shrimp
¾ cup thin sliced celery
½ medium green pepper, cut in strips
2 scallions, sliced, including tops
½ cup bamboo shoots
1 (4-ounce) can sliced mushrooms (drained, reserve liquor)
2 or 3 pimentos, cut in strips
1 tablespoon oil
1½ tablespoons cornstarch
1½ teaspoons soy sauce
1 tablespoon lemon juice
1 chicken bouillon cube
Salt and pepper to taste
½ teaspoon grated lemon peel

Stir-fry the shrimp, celery, green pepper, scallions, bamboo shoots, mushrooms, and pimentos in oil for 3 minutes in a 10-inch skillet. Add enough water to mushroom liquid to make 1 cup. Combine liquid with cornstarch, soy sauce, lemon juice, bouillon cube, and seasonings. Cook until sauce is clear and thickened, 1–3 minutes. Stir sauce into shrimp mixture. Serve over hot rice.

Heritage Fan-Fare (Massachusetts)

U.S. NAVY PHOTO BY TODD STEVENS

The *U.S.S. Constitution*, more commonly known as "Old Ironsides," is the world's oldest commissioned war ship. The wooden-hulled, three-masted heavy frigate of the United States Navy was commissioned in 1797, and retired from active service in 1881. *Constitution* was designated a museum ship in 1907, and in 1997 she finally sailed again under her own power for her 200th birthday. As a fully commissioned US Navy ship, her crew of 60 officers and sailors participate in ceremonies, educational programs, and special events while keeping the ship open to visitors year-round and providing free tours. She is berthed at Pier 1 of the Boston Navy Yard, Massachusetts.

Sweet-Sour Shrimp

8 uncooked large shrimp,
  shelled, deveined, and tails
  removed
¼ cup peanut oil or
  vegetable oil
1 medium onion, chopped
1 stalk celery, sliced thin
1 green pepper, seeded and
  cut into bite-size chunks
1 sweet red pepper, seeded,
  cut into bite-size chunks

1 tablespoon cornstarch
1 tablespoon lemon juice
1 (13-ounce) can pineapple
  tidbits, not drained
1 tablespoon brown sugar
1 tablespoon soy sauce
1 cup chicken stock
2 cups cooked rice
Watercress for garnish

Melt oil in a large skillet or wok. Add onion and celery and sauté slowly 3 minutes. Add shrimp, green, and red pepper and sauté 3 minutes. Mix cornstarch with lemon juice. To shrimp mixture add pineapple, brown sugar, and soy sauce. Stir in cornstarch mixture, then chicken stock. Simmer until thickened. Add rice, and heat until hot. Spoon shrimp mixture onto heated plates.

Seafood Expressions (Rhode Island)

Alice's Special Shrimp

This dish was created for visual as well as culinary effect, with different shapes and colors, all retaining their own individuality. It turned out to be an all-time favorite at Alice's Restaurant, the famous Berkshire eatery immortalized by the 60's movie of that name, starring Arlo Guthrie and a contingent of Berkshire locals.

1 or more tablespoons butter
5 raw jumbo shrimp, shelled
  and deveined
4 black olives, pitted
4 green olives, pitted
4 ripe cherry tomatoes
3–4 artichoke hearts (packed
  in oil, lightly drained)

1 handful freshly chopped
  scallions and parsley
1 tablespoon sherry
Generous pinch of crumbled
  dried tarragon
One portion of cooked orzo

Melt the butter in a sauté pan over fairly high heat. Toss in the remaining ingredients, except the orzo, all at once. Let it all sizzle up, turning the shrimp once, and immediately serve over the orzo the moment the shrimp are cooked. It takes just minutes.

In the restaurant, each portion was cooked to order in its own little pan. Four or so portions can be prepared at a time in a 12-inch or larger pan. The ingredients should not be crowded. Serves 1.

Best Recipes of Berkshire Chefs (Massachusetts)

Shrimp and Crabmeat Casserole

We can't explain why, exactly, but this is the most popular dish we've ever served. Nobody has ever failed to ask for the recipe. It's also easy to make and can be put together in advance, then baked at the last minute.

½ pound macaroni
1 tablespoon salt
1 tablespoon vegetable oil
4 tablespoons butter or
  margarine
½ pound fresh mushrooms,
  sliced
2 tablespoons butter or
  margarine
1 cup light cream

1 (10-ounce) can cream of
  mushroom soup
¾ cup grated sharp Cheddar
  cheese
1 pound cooked shrimp,
  shelled and deveined
1 cup cooked crabmeat
1 cup soft bread crumbs
1 tablespoon butter or
  margarine

Add the salt and vegetable oil to 3 quarts boiling water. Add the macaroni and boil rapidly for 10 minutes. Drain and toss with 4 tablespoons butter or margarine.

Sauté the mushrooms in 2 tablespoons butter or margarine for about 5 minutes, shaking the pan frequently. Mix the cream, mushroom soup, and Cheddar cheese together and add to the macaroni. Add the mushrooms, shrimp, and crabmeat, which have been cut into bite-size pieces.

Place in a buttered 9x13-inch casserole; top with soft bread crumbs which have been tossed with the 1 tablespoon melted butter or margarine. Bake in a 350° oven for 25 minutes. Season to taste. Serves 6.

The Country Innkeepers' Cookbook (Vermont)

 Ben & Jerry's Ice Cream company was founded in 1978 in Burlington, Vermont, in a renovated gas station by Ben Cohen and Jerry Greenfield. Supposedly, waste from Ben and Jerry's Ice Cream company is given to local farmers in Vermont to feed to their hogs. It is said the hogs like almost all the flavors, but don't particularly care for the Mint Oreo.

Crab Casserole

1 pound crabmeat (claw), or
  1 pound small scallops
1 small onion, diced
1 tablespoon parsley
½ teaspoon oregano
1 cup mayonnaise
1 cup half-and-half

2 or 3 hard-boiled eggs,
  chopped
½ package Pepperidge Farm
  Stuffing Mix, crushed fine
1 (4-ounce) can diced
  mushrooms, drained

Mix all ingredients together well. Pour into casserole and bake 30 minutes at 350°. Serves 4.

Dinner Bell Encore (Pennsylvania)

Phyllis Lake's Hudson River Crab Cakes

Phyllis Lake, wife of Hudson River fisherman Tom Lake, is known for her crab cakes. For the cakes she uses Old Bay, from the Baltimore Spice Company, a seafood seasoning favored by the crabbers on the Hudson.

1 pound Hudson River
  blue crab meat
1 teaspoon Old Bay Seasoning
¼ teaspoon salt
1 tablespoon mayonnaise
1 tablespoon Worcestershire
1 tablespoon chopped parsley

1 tablespoon baking powder
1 egg, lightly beaten
2 slices crustless white or
  whole-wheat bread, torn into
  small pieces and moistened
  with a little milk
Vegetable oil, for frying

Mix all ingredients but oil and shape into 2-inch flat cakes. In a frying pan, heat about ¼ inch of oil and fry the cakes on both sides until golden (about 6 minutes). Makes 1 dozen cakes.

Foods of the Hudson (New York)

Scallops en Casserole

If you have scallop-shaped individual shells or casseroles, use them for this recipe. Fresh or frozen peas cooked with sliced water chestnuts, steamed acorn squash, peach and cottage cheese salad on lettuce, and applesauce with cookies could complete the menu.

4 tablespoons butter or margarine
½ pound fresh mushrooms, sliced
1 green onion, chopped
2 tablespoons flour
1 cup dry white wine
1 tablespoon lemon juice
½ teaspoon salt
Freshly ground pepper to taste
1½ pounds bay or ocean scallops
2 tablespoons chopped fresh parsley
1 cup buttered crumbs

Heat butter in skillet and sauté mushrooms and onion until tender. Stir in flour and cook 2 minutes. Add wine and cook and stir until mixture boils and is thickened. Add lemon juice, salt, and pepper. Stir in scallops (if ocean scallops are used, cut in half) and parsley. Spoon into a buttered shallow casserole or individual casseroles and sprinkle with crumbs. Bake at 400° for 25 minutes. Makes 6 servings.

A Cape Cod Seafood Cookbook (Massachusetts)

Dill Sauce with Scallops Over Angel Hair Pasta

1¼ tablespoons chopped
  shallots
1½ tablespoons butter
2 tablespoons flour
1 cup heavy cream
1¼ cups half-and-half
6 drops of Tabasco sauce
2½ tablespoons chopped
  fresh dill

⅓ teaspoon salt
¼ teaspoon freshly ground
  white pepper
1¼ pounds bay scallops
1 tablespoon butter
½ cup dry white wine
1½ pounds angel hair
  pasta, cooked

Sauté shallots in 1½ tablespoons butter in 1½-quart saucepan until translucent. Stir in flour. Cook for 5 minutes to make roux, stirring frequently. Bring cream and half-and-half to the simmering point in saucepan. Whisk into roux. Cook for 5–10 minutes or until thickened to desired consistency, stirring frequently. Stir in Tabasco sauce, dill, salt and white pepper; keep warm. Sauté scallops in 1 tablespoon butter in skillet for 2–3 minutes. Stir in wine. Add to cream sauce. Serve over pasta. Yields 6 servings.

Rhode Island Cooks (Rhode Island)

Roger Williams, the first American proponent of religious freedom and the separation of church and state, founded Rhode Island. He established the first practical working model of democracy after he was banished from Plymouth, Massachusetts, because of his "extreme views." Thomas Jefferson and John Adams publicly acknowledged Roger Williams as the originator of the concepts and principles reflected in The First Amendment, among which were freedom of religion, freedom of speech, and freedom of public assembly.

WIKIPEDIA.ORG

Clam Fritters

(Fritura de Marisco)

1 cup flour
½ teaspoon pepper
½ teaspoon chopped parsley
½ teaspoon baking powder
2 cups ground sea clams

1 onion, ground with the clams
2 eggs, beaten
Olive oil or other shortening
  for frying

Mix flour, pepper, chopped parsley, and baking powder together. Add ground clams and onion and mix well. Add beaten eggs and mix well again.

Drop teaspoonsful of the mixture into hot fat. Fry until fritters are lightly browned on one side. Turn them and brown the other side. Drain and serve. Always taste the first fritter to see if they need more seasoning.

Note: These clam fritters make a good meal accompanied with home-made baked beans and a green salad. They may also be served as an appetizer at parties, either hot or cold.

Traditional Portuguese Recipes from Provincetown
(Massachusetts)

Cakes

Flowing 315 miles through eastern New York, the Hudson River is one of America's most important commercial and recreational waterways. Deeply connected to our nation's heritage, it was the first great river settlers encountered in the New World, and the precedent for the National Environmental Policy Act established there.

Sour Cream Chocolate Cake

Enjoy the wonderful smell of baking chocolate cake! You can frost this, of course, but it is rich and moist alone or with a plop of whipped cream on top!

1 stick butter
1 cup boiling water
2 cups sugar
5 heaping tablespoons cocoa
1 teaspoon vanilla

2 beaten eggs
½ pint sour cream
1½ teaspoons baking soda
2 cups flour

Put butter in bowl and pour boiling water over it; let the butter melt or at least become more liquid. Add sugar and cocoa and mix. Add vanilla, eggs, and sour cream and mix. Add baking soda and flour and mix by hand or 2 minutes on medium with mixer. Pour into greased 9x13-inch baking pan and bake for 20–25 minutes at 350°.

Dishing It Out (New York)

Chocolate Upside-Down Cake

10 tablespoons butter, divided
¼ cup packed brown sugar
⅔ cup Karo syrup
¼ cup heavy cream
1 cup broken walnuts
1¾ cups sifted flour
2 teaspoons baking powder

¼ teaspoon salt
1½ cups sugar
2 eggs, separated
3 squares unsweetened
  chocolate, melted
1 teaspoon vanilla
1 cup milk

Melt 4 tablespoons butter in small saucepan. Stir in brown sugar and heat until bubbly. Stir in Karo and cream; heat, stirring constantly, just until boiling. Add nuts and pour into buttered 10-inch tube pan.

Sift flour, baking powder, and salt and set aside. Beat remaining butter until soft. Gradually beat in sugar, egg yolks, chocolate, and vanilla. Add dry ingredients and mix, alternately, with milk. Beat egg whites until stiff and fold into cake batter. Spoon batter evenly over nut mixture in pan. Bake at 350° for 45 minutes. Invert and serve with cream.

Friend's Favorites (New York)

Easy Chocolate Chip Cake

A simple cake with a brownie-like texture.

1 (3½-ounce) package
   chocolate pudding
2 tablespoons milk
1 (18.25-ounce) box chocolate
   cake mix with pudding

1 (12-ounce) package
   chocolate chips
1 (2- to 3-ounce) package
   chopped walnuts or pecans

Cook the pudding mixture according to instructions on the package. Add the additional 2 tablespoons milk to the hot pudding mixture and stir thoroughly. Preheat oven to 350°.

Butter and flour a 9-inch square or round baking dish.

In a large bowl, pour in the chocolate cake mix. Add the prepared pudding mix and blend well. Pour into the baking dish. Sprinkle chocolate chips and chopped nuts on top. Bake for 30 minutes. Remove from oven and cool. When cooled, cut into squares or wedges. Serves 6–8.

The Original Philadelphia Neighborhood Cookbook
(Pennsylvania)

Tasty Cakes

4 eggs
⅛ teaspoon salt
2 cups sugar
1 cup milk
1 teaspoon vanilla

2 teaspoons baking powder
2 cups all-purpose flour
2 teaspoons margarine or
   butter, melted

TOPPING:

Peanut butter

2 large chocolate bars

Combine all cake ingredients and mix well. Pour onto a greased and floured cookie sheet. Bake at 350° for 20 minutes. While cake is still warm, spread peanut butter over top until entire cake is covered. Set aside in refrigerator. Melt 2 large chocolate bars. Spread over the layer of peanut butter. Refrigerate until chocolate is set. Cut into squares.

Ladies of the Church (Pennsylvania)

Chocolate Mousse Cake

7 ounces semisweet chocolate
8 tablespoons (1 stick)
  unsalted butter
7 eggs, separated, at room
  temperature

1 cup sugar, divided
1 teaspoon vanilla extract
⅛ teaspoon lemon juice

Heat the oven to 325°. Melt the chocolate and butter in a double boiler over simmering water. Stir until smooth. Whisk the yolks and ¾ cup sugar until pale yellow and fluffy. Gradually stir in the chocolate and vanilla extract. Beat the whites with lemon juice until soft peaks form. Add the remaining sugar, 1 tablespoon at a time, and continue beating until stiff but not dry. Gently fold into the chocolate mixture. Pour three-fourths of the batter into a buttered 9-inch springform pan; cover and refrigerate the remaining batter. Bake the cake for 35 minutes. Let cool completely. (The cake will fall as it cools, but don't let it bother you.) Trim the edges with a sharp knife and spread the remaining batter over the top. Refrigerate for at least 8 hours. Makes 1 (9-inch) cake.

The Black Hat Chef Cookbook (Pennsylvania)

Rocky Roadhouse Cake

8 eggs
¼ cup oil
1¾ cups sour cream
1 (6-ounce) box butterscotch
  instant pudding mix
1 package devil's food
  chocolate cake mix

1 cup chopped walnuts
½ bag mini marshmallows
8 ounces mini chocolate
  chips
8 ounces mini butterscotch
  chips

Break eggs into a large bowl and mix in the oil, sour cream, and butterscotch pudding mix. Add cake mix. Stir, but do not overmix. Stir just long enough for the mix to be absorbed but not completely smooth. This will be a heavy mix. Add the rest of the ingredients. Spoon into a greased and floured cake pan. Bake at 350° for about ¾ hour.

A recipe from The Roadhouse Café, Hyannis
Cape Cod's Night at the Chef's Table (Massachusetts)

Apple Dapple

2 eggs
2 cups white sugar
1 cup cooking oil
3 cups all-purpose flour
  (scant)

½ teaspoon salt
1 teaspoon baking soda
3 cups chopped apples
2 teaspoons vanilla
Chopped nuts (optional)

Mix together eggs, sugar, oil, and flour, salt, and soda that have been sifted together. Add chopped apples, vanilla, and nuts. Mix batter well and pour into a greased 9x13-inch cake pan. Bake at 350° for 45 minutes or until done.

ICING:

1 cup brown sugar
¼ cup milk

¼ cup butter or margarine

Combine sugar, milk, and butter, and cook mixture 2½ minutes. Stir a little after removing from stove, but do not beat. Dribble over cake while cake is still hot. A few chopped nuts may be sprinkled over icing.

Amish Cooking (Pennsylvania)

Dutch Apple Cake

3 cups flour
2 cups granulated sugar
3 teaspoons baking powder
1 cup salad oil
½ cup orange juice

4 eggs
2 tablespoons vanilla
6 tablespoons sugar
3 tablespoons cinnamon
4–6 apples

Mix together all but 6 tablespoons sugar, 3 tablespoons cinnamon and apples. Peel and slice apples. Mix reserved sugar and cinnamon together. Layer in greased tube pan starting with one-third batter, cinnamon mixture, half apples, cinnamon mixture, one-third batter; repeat, ending with last one-third batter.

Bake at 350° for 1 hour and 10 minutes. Leave in pan to cool.

Our Favorite Recipes (Pennsylvania)

Apple Pie Cake

Mrs. Hunter cooked for my grandfather for years, and everything she cooked was good and made from scratch. Surely nothing this tasty comes from a mix. It's easy, bright with cinnamon, and delicious hot or cold.

½ cup (1 stick) margarine
¾ cup sugar
1 egg, slightly beaten
1 cup flour
1 teaspoon baking powder
1 teaspoon ground cinnamon
½ teaspoon salt

½ teaspoon ground nutmeg
¼ teaspoon ground cloves
⅛ teaspoon vanilla
2 cups chopped and peeled
  apples
½ cup chopped pecans

Thoroughly grease a 9-inch pie pan. Melt margarine, remove from heat, and blend with sugar and egg. Mix in flour, baking powder, cinnamon, salt, nutmeg, cloves, vanilla, apples, and pecans. Spread into pan. Bake in a preheated 350° oven for 40–45 minutes. Serve warm with ice cream. Serves 6–8.

The Lymes' Heritage Cookbook (Connecticut)

Blueberry Tea Cake

¼ cup margarine
1¼ cups sugar
1 egg
½ cup milk

1 teaspoon salt
2 cups flour
2 teaspoons baking powder
2 cups blueberries

Mix margarine, sugar, egg, milk, salt, flour, and baking powder. Fold in blueberries and mix thoroughly. Pour into greased 9x13-inch pan and sprinkle on Topping.

TOPPING:
½ cup sugar
1 teaspoon cinnamon

¼ cup flour
¼ cup margarine

Mix ingredients with a pastry blender till well blended. Sprinkle on top of cake. Bake at 375° for 45 minutes or until done.

The Proulx/Chartrand 1997 Reunion Cookbook (New York)

Melt-In-Your-Mouth Blueberry Cake

A wonderful light summer dessert and especially good for picnics. A family favorite!

2 eggs, separated
1 cup sugar, divided
½ cup margarine, softened
¼ teaspoon salt
1 teaspoon vanilla
1½ cups flour, sifted, and
  1 tablespoon for coating
  blueberries

1 teaspoon baking powder
⅓ cup milk
1½ cups fresh blueberries
Cinnamon sugar for topping

Preheat oven to 350°. Beat egg whites until stiff. Beat in ¼ cup of sugar. Cream margarine; add salt, vanilla, and remaining sugar gradually. Add egg yolks and beat until creamy. Sift flour with baking powder. Add alternately to creamed mixture with milk. Fold in beaten egg whites. Add 1 tablespoon of flour to coat blueberries. Fold in berries. Turn into 8x8-inch pan. Sprinkle cinnamon sugar on top. Bake in 350° oven 50 minutes. Cool on rack. Wrap any leftovers and store in refrigerator. May be frozen. Serves 8.

The Maine Collection (Maine)

Eastport, Maine, is the most easterly city in the United States. The residents of Washington County are usually the very first Americans to greet the sun each morning when it rises. On approximately 200,000 acres of open land in this county, 80% of the nation's wild blueberry crop is raised.

Pineapple Cake with Cream Cheese Ginger Frosting

2 eggs
1 (20-ounce) can crushed
  pineapple, undrained
2 cups flour

1 cup sugar
1 cup brown sugar
2 teaspoons baking soda
1 cup chopped walnuts

Combine all and pour into an ungreased, 13x9-inch Pyrex pan. Bake at 350° for 45–50 minutes.

CREAM CHEESE GINGER FROSTING:

1 (3-ounce) package cream
  cheese, softened
¼ cup butter, softened

1 teaspoon vanilla
2 cups powdered sugar
½ teaspoon ginger

Combine and spread on cooled pineapple cake.

Berkshire Seasonings (Massachusetts)

Lemonade Cake

1 package lemon Jell-O
¾ cup boiling water
1 package yellow cake mix
4 eggs

½ (6-ounce) can lemonade
¾ cup oil
Powdered sugar

Dissolve Jell-O in boiling water. Cool, but do not set. Mix remaining ingredients and add Jell-O. Pour into greased angel food pan. Bake at 350° for one hour. Cool and dust with powdered sugar.

Friend's Favorites (New York)

Eggnog Cake

CAKE:

1 package yellow cake mix
1 cup whipping cream
3 eggs
¼ cup oil

½ cup rum or ½ cup water
  and 1 teaspoon rum extract
½ teaspoon nutmeg

Heat oven to 350°. Grease and flour 12-cup fluted tube pan. In large bowl, blend cake ingredients until moistened. Beat 2 minutes at highest speed. Pour into prepared pan. Bake at 350° for 35–45 minutes or until toothpick inserted into center comes out clean.

GLAZE:

¼ cup margarine
¼ cup sugar
⅛ teaspoon nutmeg
1 tablespoon water

1 teaspoon rum or 1–2 drops
  rum extract
Powdered sugar (optional)

In small saucepan, heat margarine, sugar, nutmeg, and water until mixture boils and sugar is dissolved. Remove from heat; add rum. Pour half of the glaze around edges of hot cake. Cool upright in pan 5 minutes; invert onto serving plate. Slowly spoon remaining glaze over top of cake. Cool. Sprinkle with powdered sugar, if desired.

Great Taste of Parkminster (New York)

Black Walnut Cake

2¼ cups all-purpose flour
1½ cups sugar
3½ teaspoons baking powder
1 teaspoon salt
1 cup milk
½ cup butter, softened
1 teaspoon vanilla
4 egg whites
1 cup chopped black walnuts

Blend together in large bowl the flour, sugar, baking powder, and salt. Add milk, butter, and vanilla and beat with electric mixer 2 minutes. Add egg whites and beat 2 minutes. Fold in black walnuts. Pour into 2 greased and floured 9-inch round cake pans. Bake in preheated oven at 350° for 35–40 minutes. Serves 12.

Simply in Season (Pennsylvania)

Coconut Caramel Cake/Pie

CRUST:
1 cup graham cracker crumbs
⅛ cup sugar
3 tablespoons butter or margarine

Mix ingredients and pat in bottom of 9-inch springform pan.

FILLING:
1 (8-ounce) package cream cheese, softened
1 can condensed milk
1 (16-ounce) carton Cool Whip

Blend cream cheese and condensed milk together and then fold in Cool Whip. Put ½ of this mixture over crumb crust.

TOPPING:
¼ cup butter or margarine
½ cup chopped pecans
7 ounces flaked coconut
1 jar caramel ice cream sauce

Mix together butter, pecans, and coconut. Spread ½ of topping mixture over the filling. Repeat layers, ½ filling and ½ topping. Drizzle caramel ice cream sauce over top and freeze overnight. At serving time, remove from springform pan to plate and let warm up about 10 minutes before cutting. Can use 2 pie plates instead of springform pan, if desired.

The Cookbook AAUW (New York)

Carrot Cake

This is the best carrot cake I have ever tasted.

1½ cups vegetable oil
2 cups granulated sugar
3 whole eggs and 1 egg white, well beaten
2 cups flour
1 teaspoon salt

2 teaspoons ground cinnamon
2 teaspoons baking powder
1 cup chopped pecans
½ cup golden raisins
3 cups grated carrots

Preheat oven to 325°. Coat 2 (9-inch) square Teflon cake pans with vegetable spray. In a large bowl, mix vegetable oil and sugar and beat well. Add the eggs and blend. Sift together the dry ingredients and add to egg mixture. Add the nuts, raisins, and grated carrots, a small amount at a time, and blend thoroughly.

Pour the batter into prepared cake pans and bake 1 hour, or until toothpick inserted into center comes out clean. Turn onto wire rack to cool. When cool, spread Cream-Cheese Frosting between layers and on the top (but not on the sides) of the cake. Finish off with some fancy swirls. Yields 16 or more servings.

CREAM-CHEESE FROSTING:

4 ounces (1 stick) butter or margarine
1 (8-ounce) package cream cheese

2 cups powdered sugar
2 teaspoons vanilla extract (or substitute brandy if desired)

Allow the butter and cream cheese to reach room temperature. Then cream butter and cream cheese and gradually beat in powdered sugar and vanilla (or brandy). Spread between layers and on top of Carrot Cake. Yields enough frosting for top and filling for 2-layer cake.

Favorite New England Recipes (Maine)

Fudge Truffle Cheesecake

CHOCOLATE CRUMB CRUST:

1½ cups vanilla wafer crumbs   ⅓ cup cocoa
½ cup powdered sugar   ⅓ cup melted butter

Heat oven to 300°. Mix crumbs, sugar, cocoa, and butter firmly on bottom of 9-inch springform pan. Set aside.

FILLING:

1 (12-ounce) package (2 cups)   1 (14-ounce) can sweetened
   semisweet chocolate chips   condensed milk
3 (8-ounce) packages cream   4 eggs
   cheese, softened   2 teaspoons vanilla

In heavy saucepan over very low heat, melt chips, stirring constantly. In large mixer bowl, beat cheese until fluffy. Gradually beat in sweetened condensed milk until smooth. Add melted chips, eggs, and vanilla; mix well. Pour into prepared pan. Bake 1 hour and 5 minutes or until cheese center is set. Cool; chill. Refrigerate leftovers.

Recipes from the Children's Museum at Saratoga (New York)

In 1872, cream cheese was invented by American dairyman, William Lawrence of Chester, New York, who accidentally developed a method of producing cream cheese while trying to reproduce a French cheese called Neufchatel. Lawrence distributed his cream cheese in foil wrappers. He called his cheese Philadelphia Brand Cream Cheese, now a famous trademark. Kraft Cheese Company bought the brand in 1928. James L. Kraft invented pasteurized cheese in 1912, and that lead to the development of pasteurized Philadelphia Brand cream cheese. Kraft Foods still produces Philadelphia Cream Cheese, the most popular cheese used for making cheesecake today.

New York Cheesecake

⅓ stick butter
1 cup graham cracker crumbs
2 pounds cream cheese
1¾ cups sugar

4 eggs
1 teaspoon vanilla
3 tablespoons Grand Marnier
　or orange juice, divided

Melt butter and mix well through graham cracker crumbs. Press into bottom of greased aluminum pan* and set aside. Into one large mixing bowl, put all other ingredients with the exception of 1 tablespoon Grand Marnier or orange juice. Mix well with any type of electric mixer or place ingredients in a blender. Be sure all ingredients are thoroughly blended and creamy.

Pour mixture into pan. Shake gently to distribute contents evenly. Over top of cake, slowly pour remaining tablespoon Grand Marnier or orange juice (this will give a nice glaze). Now place pan into center of large roasting pan or any other container that will allow at least ½-inch air around cheesecake pan (sides of cheesecake pan must not touch lower pan). Now pour boiling water into lower pan until it reaches half-way up cheesecake pan.

Place into preheated 325° oven and bake 1½–2 hours. Cake should look firm and lightly browned. Turn oven off and let cake remain for additional 20 minutes. Remove and let cool down to room temperature. Turn upside down onto serving platter and refrigerate. This cake also freezes beautifully for future use.

*Recipe requires a solid-bottom cheesecake pan.

In the Village (New York)

Bavarian Apple Cheesecake

1⅓ cups sugar, divided
⅓ cup butter or margarine
1 tablespoon shortening
¾ teaspoon vanilla, divided
1 cup flour
⅛ teaspoon salt
4 cups sliced, peeled, and
  cored cooking apples
  (Golden Delicious or
  Granny Smith)

2 (8-ounce) packages cream
  cheese, softened
2 eggs
1 teaspoon ground cinnamon
¼ cup sliced almonds

In a medium mixer bowl, beat ½ cup sugar, butter or margarine, shortening, and ¼ teaspoon vanilla on medium speed with an electric mixer until combined. Blend in flour and salt until crumbly. Pat on the bottom of a 9-inch springform pan. Set aside.

Place apple slices in a single layer in a shallow baking pan. Cover with foil. Bake in a 400° oven for 15 minutes. Meanwhile, for filling, in a large mixer bowl, beat cream cheese, ½ cup sugar, and ½ teaspoon vanilla with an electric mixer until fluffy. Add eggs all at once, beating on low speed just until combined. Pour into dough-lined pan. Arrange warm apple slices atop filling. Combine remaining ⅓ cup sugar and cinnamon.

Sprinkle filling with sugar mixture and the almonds. Bake in a 400° oven for 40 minutes or until golden. Cool. Chill 4–24 hours before serving. Serves 12.

Hudson Valley German-American Society Cookbook (New York)

Every year since 1776, on July 4th, the Declaration of Independence is read from the same balcony it was first read from, the Old State House. Built in 1713, it is the oldest public building in Boston. The oldest wooden building in Boston is Paul Revere's house. It was nearly 100 years old when the patriot took his famous midnight ride to warn "every Middlesex village and farm" that the British were coming.

Amaretto Cheesecake

CRUST:

¼ pound lightly salted
  butter
¼ cup sugar

2 cups finely ground chocolate
  wafer cookie crumbs (1 box)

Preheat oven to 350°. Melt butter over very low heat. In a bowl, combine butter with sugar and crumbs with a fork. Press mixture over bottom and up sides of ungreased 10-inch springform pan.

FILLING:

2 pounds cream cheese
1½ cups sugar
1 tablespoon amaretto
  liqueur

1 teaspoon vanilla extract
1 teaspoon almond extract
Pinch of salt
4 eggs

In mixer, combine cream cheese and sugar and beat for 2 minutes or until soft. Add liqueur, extracts, and salt; blend thoroughly. Add eggs one at a time, keeping the mixture at low speed (to prevent too much air from destroying the proper consistency of the batter). Mix just until each egg has been mixed into batter. Pour filling into crust and bake for 40 minutes. If ingredients are not at room temperature, add 5 minutes to baking time. Remove from oven and let stand on a counter for 10 minutes while you prepare topping (this is very important).

TOPPING:

2 cups sour cream
¼ cup sugar
1 teaspoon almond extract

1 teaspoon amaretto liqueur
½ cup blanched, sliced
  almonds, toasted

Combine sour cream, sugar, extract, and liqueur with a spatula in a plastic bowl. Spread evenly over top of baked filling. Sprinkle with almonds and return to 350° oven for 10 minutes. Remove from oven and place in refrigerator immediately to cool. This prevents cracks from forming in the cheesecake.

Rhinebeck Community Cookbook Desserts of Good Taste
(New York)

Almond Cheesecake with Raspberries

1¼ cups graham cracker
  crumbs
⅓ cup butter, melted
¼ cup sugar
2 (8-ounce) packages cream
  cheese, softened
1 (16-ounce) can ready-to-
  spread vanilla frosting

1 tablespoon lemon juice
1 tablespoon grated lemon
  peel
3 cups Cool Whip
Raspberries
Sliced almonds

Stir together crumbs, butter, and sugar in a small bowl; press onto bottom and ½ inch up sides of a 9-inch springform pan or pie plate. Chill. Beat cream cheese, frosting, juice, and peel in a large mixing bowl at medium speed with electric mixer until well blended. Fold in whipped topping; pour over crust. Chill until firm. Arrange raspberries and almonds on top.

**Sandy Hook Volunteer Fire Co. Ladies Aux. Cookbook
(Connecticut)**

Cookies and Candies

WWOODS@WIKIPEDIA.ORG

Mount Washington is the highest peak in the Northeastern United States at 6,288 feet. Located in the Presidential Range of the White Mountains in Coos County, New Hampshire, it is known for its dangerously erratic weather with wind gusts up to 231 mph.

Hazelnut Chocolate Chip Cookies

2 sticks unsalted butter,
  softened
¾ cup sugar
¾ cup brown sugar
1 tablespoon hazelnut liqueur
1 tablespoon coffee liqueur
2 eggs

2½ cups flour
1 teaspoon baking soda
½ teaspoon salt
4 cups milk chocolate chips
1 cup chopped walnuts
1 cup chopped pecans

In a large bowl, beat butter, sugars, and liqueurs until light and fluffy. Add eggs. Beat well. Mix flour, baking soda, and salt in a small bowl. Stir flour mixture into butter mixture. Mix in chocolate chips and nuts. Drop batter by rounded teaspoonfuls onto greased baking sheet, one inch apart. Bake at 325° for 16 minutes or until golden brown.

Beyond Chicken Soup (New York)

Whoopie Pies

1 cup shortening
2 cups sugar
2 eggs
1 cup sour milk
2 teaspoons vanilla

4 cups flour
1 teaspoon salt
1 cup cocoa
2 teaspoons baking soda
1 cup (scant) hot water

Cream shortening and sugar; add eggs and beat well. Add sour milk and vanilla. Sift flour, salt, and cocoa; mix well into egg mixture. Combine soda with hot water and add last. Drop onto greased cookie sheet and bake at 400° for 8 minutes.

WHOOPIE PIE FILLING:

1½ cups Crisco
4 cups powdered sugar
4 tablespoons flour

4 tablespoons milk
1½ tablespoons vanilla
2 egg whites, beaten

Combine and beat all ingredients together, adding the beaten egg whites last. Put filling between 2 cookies.

Family Favorites (Pennsylvania)

Chocolate-Glazed Shortbread Cookies

1 cup (2 sticks) butter,
  softened
1 cup powdered sugar
2 cups flour

2 cups almonds or pecans,
  finely chopped
6 ounces semisweet chocolate

Cream butter and sugar; gradually add flour; stir in half the nuts. Chill dough 1 hour. Preheat oven to 325°.

Form 1 tablespoon dough into a 2-inch-long finger. Cut in half lengthwise and place cut-side-down on ungreased cookie sheet. Bake 15 minutes or until pale golden brown. Cool. Melt chocolate. Dip 1 end of cookie into chocolate then into chopped nuts. Cool on waxed paper until set. Yields about 5–6 dozen.

Christmas Memories Cookbook (Connecticut)

Cornflake Macaroons

These are chewy cookies. Delicious!

2 egg whites
½ teaspoon salt
½ cup sugar
½ cup white corn syrup

1 teaspoon vanilla
2 cups cornflakes
1 cup grated coconut

Beat egg whites until frothy. Add salt and continue to beat until very stiff but not dry. Add 2 tablespoons sugar at a time and continue to beat. Add syrup and vanilla and blend into mixture. Lightly fold cornflakes and grated coconut into mixture. Drop by teaspoonfuls onto greased baking sheet, spaced 2–3 inches apart. Bake at 350° for 15 minutes or until lightly browned. Makes about 3½ dozen cookies.

Mennonite Community Cookbook (Pennsylvania)

Chippy Peanut Butter Cookies

¾ pound butter, softened
  to room temperature
1½ cups peanut butter
1½ cups granulated sugar
1½ cups brown sugar
3 eggs, beaten
1 teaspoon vanilla extract

3¾ cups flour
2¼ teaspoons baking soda
1½ teaspoons baking powder
¾ teaspoon salt
18 ounces peanut butter chips
18 ounces butterscotch chips

Cream together butter, peanut butter, and both sugars until smooth. Beat in the eggs and vanilla. Sift together flour, baking soda, baking powder, and salt. Stir into creamed mixture and blend well. Stir in peanut butter and butterscotch chips. Chill in refrigerator for 30 minutes. Preheat oven to 350°. Shape dough into 1-inch balls and arrange on ungreased cookie sheet, or Pampered Chef stone, 2 inches apart. Press down on each cookie with the tines of a fork. Bake for 10–12 minutes (10 for chewy, 12 for crisp). Cooling them before taking them off the cookie sheet will let them firm up.

Our Daily Bread, and then some... (New York)

Soft Molasses Cookies

1½ cups sugar
2 eggs
1 cup shortening
1 cup molasses
1 cup hot water with
  2 teaspoons (slightly
  rounded) baking powder
1 cup raisins

5 cups flour
Pinch salt
2 teaspoons cinnamon
1 teaspoon ginger
½ teaspoon cloves (optional)
1 tablespoon sharp vinegar

Beat sugar, eggs, and shortening together. Stir in molasses followed by water mixture and raisins.

Add dry ingredients and mix well. Stir in vinegar. Drop on lightly greased cookie sheets. Bake at 350° for 12–15 minutes depending on size.

200 Years of Favorite Recipes from Delaware County (New York)

Country Raisin Gingersnaps

1½ cups seedless raisins
¾ cup shortening
1 cup sugar
1 egg
¼ cup molasses
2¼ cups sifted flour

2 teaspoons baking soda
½ teaspoon salt
1 teaspoon ginger
½ teaspoon cinnamon
½ teaspoon cloves

Chop raisins, as this makes the cookie chewy as well as crunchy. Beat together shortening, sugar, and egg. Blend in molasses. Blend in flour sifted with soda, salt, and spices. Mix in raisins. Chill dough. Shape dough into small balls and roll in additional sugar, if desired. Place on lightly greased baking sheet. Bake in moderately hot oven 375°, 8–10 minutes. Remove to cooling rack. Makes about 3 dozen cookies.

Maine's Jubilee Cookbook (Maine)

Kolacky

(Slovak: Sweet Dough with Filling)

2 cups flour
½ cup powdered sugar
½ pound butter, softened

1½ (3-ounce) packages
Philadelphia cream cheese
softened

Mix ingredients. Roll out thin and cut into squares. Fill with favorite filling. Bring the corners of the square folded to the center. Place on greased cookie sheet and bake 15–20 minutes in 350° oven.

FILLING SUGGESTIONS:

Nut: Combine 1 cup ground nuts, ½ cup sugar, and 2 beaten egg whites.

Prune: Sweeten to taste 1 cup pitted, mashed, and cooked prunes; add a pinch of nutmeg or 1 teaspoon lemon juice.

Poppy Seed: Combine 1 cup ground poppy seeds and ¼ cup milk with enough sugar or corn syrup to sweeten. Cook 5 minutes. Cool.

Pineapple: Combine 1 cup pineapple jelly with 1 teaspoon lemon juice.

The Whole Valley Cookbook (Pennsylvania)

Skip's Cookies

FILLING:

1 pound finely chopped
   walnuts
1 cup sugar

¼ stick butter
Evaporated milk to moisten

To make filling, put all ingredients into a saucepan and cook until sugar is dissolved and butter is melted.

DOUGH:

3 cups flour
1 package yeast
Dash salt
1 egg

½ (12-ounce) can evaporated
   milk
1 cup Crisco

To make dough, blend all ingredients. Knead until flour disappears. Roll dough and cut into squares with serrated-edge knife.

   Put small amount of filling into center of square. Fold on diagonal, overlapping slightly. Place on cookie sheet. Bake at 350° for 10 minutes or until golden brown.

Friend's Favorites (New York)

Spritz Butter Cookies

1 cup butter, softened
1 cup sugar
2 teaspoons vanilla extract,
   or more

2 eggs, unbeaten
3 cups sifted flour
¼ teaspoon salt

Cream together the butter, sugar, and vanilla. Add the eggs and beat well. Add the flour and salt and mix until well blended. Using a cookie press, press the dough into long strips onto an ungreased baking sheet. Cut the strips into pieces about 1½ inches long. Bake at 375° until golden brown, 10–12 minutes. About one-half minute after removing the baking sheet from the oven, loosen the cookies with a spatula to keep them from sticking to the pan. Cool on wire racks. Makes 4–6 dozen.

As You Like It (Massachusetts)

Sweet Butter Cookies
(Yiayia's Kourambiethes I)

. . . sometimes called "Greek Cloud Cookies."

1 pound unsalted butter
½ cup powdered sugar
2 egg yolks
⅔ cup finely chopped,
  blanched almonds

1½ ounces brandy
⅓ cup orange juice
1 teaspoon baking powder
4½–5 cups flour

TOPPING:
1 pound powdered sugar

Cream butter until very light in color; about 20 minutes. Beat in sugar, egg yolks, almonds, brandy, and orange juice.

Sift baking powder with flour and carefully blend into butter mixture. Mix with hands. Dough should be pliable. Shape into small crescents and place on ungreased baking sheets. Bake at 350° about 15–20 minutes until lightly golden.

Sift powdered sugar on a large sheet of wax paper. With spatula, place cookies on paper and sift additional powdered sugar over tops and sides. Cool thoroughly before storing. Yields 7 dozen small crescents.

Note: Sift sugar over hot cakes.

Treasured Greek Recipes (New York)

Vermont sugar maple trees yield their harvest in late winter when the days are warmer, but the nights are still cold. Four maple trees will yield 30–40 gallons of sweet, waterlike sap that boils down to make one gallon of maple syrup.

Lemon Whipper Snappers

1 (18¼-ounce) box lemon
  cake mix
2 cups Cool Whip

1 egg
½ cup powdered sugar, sifted

Combine lemon cake mix, Cool Whip, and egg in a large bowl; mix well. Drop by teaspoon in powdered sugar; roll to coat. Place 1½ inches apart on a greased cookie sheet. Bake at 350° for 10–15 minutes. Makes 4 dozen.

The Bloomin' Cookbook (Pennsylvania)

Cousin Serena's Easy Lemon Squares

2 cups plus 6 tablespoons
  flour, divided
Pinch of salt
½ cup powdered sugar
1 cup butter

2 cups sugar
4 eggs
Juice of 2 lemons
Grated rind of 1 lemon

Combine 2 cups flour, salt, and powdered sugar. Cut in butter with a pastry blender or in a food processor fitted with a metal blade. Pat with your hands into a 9x13-inch pan, evenly. Bake in a 350° oven for 20 minutes. While it bakes, mix together 6 tablespoons flour, sugar, eggs, lemon juice, and grated rind. Mix with a spoon or combine in food processor. Pour over the partly-baked crust. Bake 35 minutes more. Cool. Cut into squares and dust with powdered sugar. Trim off the edges for a clean look.

Temple Temptations (New York)

Brickle Bars

½ cup margarine or butter
2 squares (2 ounces)
  unsweetened chocolate
1 cup sugar
2 eggs

1 teaspoon vanilla
¾ cup all-purpose flour
¾ cup almond brickle pieces
½ cup miniature semisweet
  chocolate pieces

In a 2-quart saucepan, cook and stir margarine or butter and unsweetened chocolate over low heat until melted. Remove from heat; stir in sugar. Add eggs and vanilla; beat lightly with a wooden spoon just until combined (don't overbeat or brownies will rise too high, then fall). Stir in flour.

Spread batter in a greased 8x8x2-inch baking pan. Sprinkle almond brickle pieces and chocolate pieces evenly over batter. Bake in a 350° oven for 30 minutes. Remove pan from oven and cool brownies in pan on a wire rack. Cut into bars. Makes 16 bars.

Home Cookin' is a Family Affair (Connecticut)

You can still throw a bale of tea overboard just for the fun of it from the *Beaver II*, an authentic replica of one of the three British brigs moored that historic night, when 342 chests (equaling 90,000 pounds of tea) were dumped into Boston Harbor.

Amaretto Cheesecake Cookies

1 cup all-purpose flour
⅓ cup brown sugar, packed
6 tablespoons butter,
  softened
1 (8-ounce) package cream
  cheese, softened

¼ cup granulated sugar
1 egg
4 tablespoons amaretto
½ teaspoon vanilla
4 tablespoons chopped
  almonds

In a large mixing bowl, combine flour and brown sugar. Cut in butter until mixture forms fine crumbs. Reserve 1 cup crumb mixture for topping. Press remainder over bottom of ungreased 8-inch-square baking pan. Bake for 12–15 minutes at 350° or until lightly browned.

    In mixer bowl, thoroughly cream together cream cheese and granulated sugar. Add egg, amaretto, and vanilla; beat well. Spread batter over partially baked crust. Combine almonds with reserved crumb mixture; sprinkle over batter. Bake for 20–25 minutes. Cool and cut into squares. Yields 16 cookies.

Dining on Deck (Vermont)

Oatmeal Carmelitas

8 ounces (about 32) light
  candy caramels
5 tablespoons light cream
1 cup all-purpose flour
1 cup quick-cooking rolled
  oats
½ cup chopped pecans

½ teaspoon baking soda
  sugar
¾ cup margarine, melted
½ teaspoon salt
1 (6-ounce) package
  semisweet chocolate chips

Melt caramels in cream in top of double boiler. Cool slightly. Set aside. Heat oven to 350°. Combine flour with remaining ingredients except chocolate chips and pecans. Press ½ of crumbs in bottom of ungreased 11x7-inch or 9-inch-square pan. Bake for 10 minutes. Remove from oven. Sprinkle with chocolate chips and pecans. Spread carefully with caramel mixture. Sprinkle with remaining crumbs. Bake for 15–20 minutes longer until golden brown. Chill 1–2 hours. Cut into bars. Makes about 2 dozen.

More Than Sandwiches (Massachusetts)

Frosted Carrot Bars

4 eggs	1 teaspoon salt
2 cups sugar	1½ cups oil
2 cups flour, sifted	3 cups grated carrots
2 teaspoons baking powder	1½ cups grated coconut
2 teaspoons cinnamon	1½ cups walnuts, chopped

Beat eggs until light. Gradually add sugar. Sift flour, baking powder, cinnamon, and salt. Add flour mixture alternately with oil. Fold in carrots, coconut, and walnuts. Spread in 2 greased 13x9x2-inch pans. Bake at 350° for 25–30 minutes. Cool and frost.

CREAM CHEESE FROSTING:

1 (3-ounce) package cream cheese, softened	2½ cups powdered sugar
	1 teaspoon vanilla
1 tablespoon light cream	⅛ teaspoon salt

Blend together cream cheese and cream. Add the sugar and more cream, if necessary, to make frosting spreadable. Add vanilla and salt and beat well.

A Hancock Community Collection (New Hampshire)

STAN SHEBS, WIKIPEDIA.ORG

The site was first dubbed Mystery Hill, but is now called America's Stonehenge. Though there is no cultural heritage between it and Stonehenge in England, it is an archaeological site consisting of a number of large rocks and stone structures scattered around roughly 30 acres within the town of Salem, New Hampshire. A number of hypotheses exist as to the origin and purpose of the structures. It is usually attributed to a mixture of land-use practices of local farmers in the 18th and 19th centuries, as well as construction of structures by owner William Goodwin in the 1930s. Other claims that the site has pre-Columbian origins. Open to the public, you can go see for yourself.

Half-Way-to-Heaven Bars

A brown-sugar meringue crowns these chocolate chip bars, transforming them from the mundane to the ethereal. Perfect for holiday gift-giving.

½ cup (1 stick) butter	2 cups flour
½ cup sugar	¼ teaspoon salt
½ cup brown sugar	¼ teaspoon baking soda
2 egg yolks	1 teaspoon baking powder
1 tablespoon water	1 (12-ounce) package
1 teaspoon vanilla extract	chocolate chips

In large bowl, cream together butter and sugars; add egg yolks, water, and vanilla. Mix well. Mix together flour, salt, baking soda, and baking powder. Add to butter mixture. Preheat oven to 350°. Lightly grease 15-inch jellyroll pan. Pat dough into pan. Sprinkle evenly with chocolate chips.

TOPPING:

2 egg whites	1 cup brown sugar

In small bowl of mixer, beat egg whites until stiff. Gradually beat in brown sugar. Spread mixture over top of chocolate chips. Bake 20–25 minutes. Cool, then cut into bars. Yields 4½ dozen bars.

All Seasons Cookbook (Connecticut)

The Amish believe that photographs in which they can be recognized violate the biblical commandment, "Thou shalt not make to thyself a graven image. . . ." Agreeing to pose for photographs is an act of pride, so visitors are asked to refrain from taking photos of the Amish.

Napoleon Crèmes

FIRST LAYER:

½ cup butter
¼ cup sugar
¼ cup cocoa
1 teaspoon vanilla

1 egg
2 cups graham cracker or
   vanilla wafer crumbs
1 cup flaked coconut

Mix butter, sugar, cocoa, and vanilla in double boiler and cook until butter melts. Beat egg slightly and stir into mixture. Boil until thick. Add graham cracker crumbs (or vanilla wafer crumbs) and coconut. Pour into a buttered 9x9-inch pan.

SECOND LAYER:

1 (3-ounce) package instant
   vanilla pudding
½ cup butter, softened
3 tablespoons milk

2 cups sifted powdered sugar
1 (6-ounce) package chocolate
   chips

Beat first 4 ingredients together and pour over First Layer. Cool until firm. Melt chocolate chips and spread over top. Cut into pieces when firm, but not hard.

The Dinner Bell Rings Again! (Pennsylvania)

Gillie Whoopers

¾ cup sifted flour
¼ teaspoon baking powder
¼ teaspoon salt
2 tablespoons cocoa
¾ cup sugar
½ cup shortening

2 eggs
1 teaspoon vanilla
½ cup walnuts
1 package miniature
   marshmallows

Combine flour, baking powder, salt, cocoa, and sugar. Blend in shortening, eggs, and vanilla. Add walnuts. Spread in greased baking pan and bake at 350° for 20 minutes. Take from oven; sprinkle miniature marshmallows over the top, keeping away from sides. Put back into oven for 3 minutes.

FROSTING:

½ cup brown sugar
¼ cup water
2 squares baking chocolate

3 tablespoons butter
2 tablespoons vanilla
1½ cups powdered sugar

Combine brown sugar, water, and chocolate. Boil for 3 minutes; take from burner and add butter, vanilla, and powdered sugar (enough to make smooth icing). Spread over marshmallows and let cool. Cut in squares.

All-Maine Cooking (Maine)

The Ultimate Brownies

1 (4-ounce) package Baker's German Sweet Chocolate
5 tablespoons butter, divided
1 (3-ounce) package cream cheese, softened
1 cup sugar, divided
3 eggs, divided

1 tablespoon plus ½ cup all-purpose flour, divided
1½ teaspoons vanilla, divided
½ teaspoon baking powder
¼ teaspoon salt
½ cup coarsely chopped nuts
¼ teaspoon almond extract

Melt chocolate and 3 tablespoons butter in saucepan over very low heat, stirring constantly; cool. Cream remaining butter with cheese until softened. Gradually add ¼ cup sugar, creaming until fluffy. Blend in 1 egg, 1 tablespoon flour, and ½ teaspoon vanilla. Set aside. Beat remaining 2 eggs until thick and light. Gradually beat in remaining ¾ cup sugar. Add baking powder, salt, and remaining ½ cup flour. Blend in cooled chocolate mixture, nuts, remaining 1 teaspoon vanilla, and almond extract.

Spread half of chocolate batter in greased 8- or 9-inch square pan. Top with cheese mixture. Spoon remaining chocolate batter onto cheese mixture. With spatula, swirl through batter to marble. Bake at 350° for 35–40 minutes. Cool; cut into bars. Makes about 20.

Wonderful Good Cooking from Amish Country Kitchens (Pennsylvania)

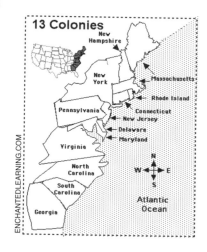

13 Colonies

The Thirteen Colonies were British colonies on the Atlantic coast of North America, which declared their independence in the American Revolution and formed the United States of America. The colonies, whose territory ranged from what is now Maine (then part of the Province of Massachusetts Bay) to the north and Georgia to the south, were Delaware, Pennsylvania, New Jersey, Georgia, Connecticut, Massachusetts, Maryland, South Carolina, New Hampshire, Virginia, New York, North Carolina, and Rhode Island. Each colony had a paid colonial agent in London to represent its interests. It is interesting to note that Pennsylvania is the only original colony not bordered by the Atlantic Ocean.

Cheesecake Fudge Nut Brownies

1 pound cream cheese	2 teaspoons vanilla
¼ pound butter	2 teaspoons lemon juice
1 cup sugar	1 egg

Grease and lightly flour the 10x12-inch cookie sheet.

Soften the cream cheese and butter; combine, then add the sugar, vanilla, and lemon juice. When they are well mixed, beat in 1 egg until the mixture is smooth.

2 cups all-purpose flour	¼ pound butter
2 teaspoons baking powder	8 eggs
1 teaspoon salt	4 cups sugar
1 pound unsweetened chocolate	1 tablespoon vanilla
	1 cup chopped walnuts

Make the fudge part separately by combining the flour, baking powder, and salt. Melt the chocolate and butter together over a low flame. Beat the eggs, sugar, and vanilla together, add the flour mixture, and finally fold in the melted chocolate.

Spread a thin layer of the brownie mix over the bottom of the cookie sheet. Pour the cheesecake mix in, then "plop" the rest of the brownie on top. To get a marbled effect, trail a rubber spatula through the two top layers, but don't overdo, or the finished product will be muddy.

Sprinkle the top with walnuts, then bake for half an hour at 350°.

The Loaf and Ladle Cook Book (New Hampshire)

 New Hampshire boasts that it has four nicknames: The Granite State, for its extensive granite formations and quarries; Mother of Rivers, for the rivers of New England that originate in its mountains; White Mountain State, for the White Mountain Range; and Switzerland of America, for its beautiful mountain scenery.

Mint Brownies

1 package Duncan Hines
  Brownie Mix
½ cup plus 6 tablespoons
  margarine, softened
2 cups powdered sugar

2 tablespoons crème de
  menthe (green)
1 (6-ounce) package chocolate
  chips

Preheat oven to 350°. Follow instructions on box for brownies and bake only 15 minutes in an 11x16-inch jellyroll pan. Refrigerate.

Combine ½ cup softened margarine with powdered sugar and crème de menthe. Ice brownies and refrigerate.

Melt remaining 6 tablespoons margarine and chocolate chips together; mix thoroughly. Dribble or spread over iced brownies. Refrigerate; cut into small squares. Yields 5 dozen.

Philadelphia Main Line Classics (Pennsylvania)

Brownie Crisps

½ cup butter
1 ounce unsweetened
  chocolate
1 teaspoon instant coffee
½ cup sugar

1 egg
¼ teaspoon vanilla
¼ teaspoon salt
¼ cup flour
½ cup finely chopped nuts

Melt butter and chocolate over low heat in a heavy saucepan. Stir until smooth. Add instant coffee and stir to dissolve. Remove from heat and stir in sugar, then egg and vanilla. Mix thoroughly. Add salt and flour; mix until smooth. Pour into a greased 15x10-inch jellyroll pan and spread evenly. Sprinkle with nuts. Bake in a 375° oven on center rack exactly 15 minutes, reversing position of pan once during baking to insure even browning. Remove from oven and without waiting, cut carefully with a sharp knife. Immediately, before cookies cool and harden, remove them with a wide spatula. Cool on rack. Store in airtight container. Yields 5 dozen.

Boston Tea Parties (Massachusetts)

Candy Crispies

1 cup sugar
1 cup corn syrup
1 cup thin cream
½ (4-ounce) package
  cornflakes

½ (3½-ounce) package Rice
  Krispies
1 cup shredded coconut
1 cup salted peanuts

Cook sugar, syrup, and cream together until it forms a soft ball in cold water (236°). Stir only until sugar is dissolved. Crush cornflakes coarsely and mix with Krispies, coconut, and peanuts. Pour hot syrup over mixture and blend together. Press into a flat, buttered pan. Cut into squares when almost cold.

Mennonite Community Cookbook (Pennsylvania)

Meltaway Nut Squares

These are not very sweet and are good for a coffee or tea.

1 stick butter, softened
1 stick margarine, softened
1 cup sugar
2 egg yolks

2 cups flour
1 cup chopped nuts
½ cup seedless jam

Preheat oven to 325°. Cream butter, margarine, and sugar. Add egg yolks and flour; blend well. Fold in nuts. Spoon ½ of the mixture in the bottom of a lightly buttered 8-inch square pan; top with jam and cover with the remaining dough. Bake 1 hour. Cool before cutting.

Home Cookin' is a Family Affair (Connecticut)

Chocolate Marshmallow Slices

1 (12-ounce) package
  HERSHEY'S Semisweet
  Chocolate Chips (2 cups)
½ cup butter or margarine

1 (10½-ounce) package
  mini marshmallows (6 cups)
1 cup finely chopped nuts
Additional chopped nuts

In medium saucepan over low heat, melt chocolate chips and butter, stirring constantly until blended. Remove from heat; cool 5 minutes. Stir in marshmallows and 1 cup nuts; do not melt marshmallows. On wax paper, shape mixture into 2 rolls, 2 inches in diameter. Wrap in foil; chill 15 minutes. Roll in additional chopped nuts. Wrap; chill overnight.

Cut rolls into ¼-inch slices. Store in airtight container in cool, dry place. Makes about 3 dozen slices.

HERSHEY'S Fabulous Desserts (Pennsylvania)

Milton Hershey built the town of Hershey, Pennsylvania, around his chocolate industry. In 1900, the company began producing milk chocolate in bars, wafers and other shapes. With mass-production, Hershey was able to make milk chocolate, once a luxury item for the wealthy, affordable to all. In 1907 production began on a flat-bottomed, conical milk chocolate candy which Mr. Hershey decided to name HERSHEY'S KISSES. At first, they were individually wrapped in little squares of silver foil, but in 1921 machine wrapping was introduced. That technology was also used to add the familiar "plume" at the top to signify to consumers that this was a genuine HERSHEY'S KISS Chocolate. In 1924, the company even had it trademarked. Today, The Hershey Company is the leading North American manufacturer of chocolate products. Hershey is popularly called "Chocolatetown, USA." It is also referred to as "The Sweetest Place on Earth." Even the street lamps are shaped like KISSES.

Almond Butter Crunch

Before starting to make this candy, have all ingredients ready. This candy cooks and cools rapidly.

1 cup chopped, toasted almonds
½ cup butter (1 stick) no substitute

1 cup sugar
2 cups (12-ounce package) chocolate bits, melted
Chopped almonds for topping

Lightly toast almonds, blanched or unblanched, in a slow oven, 250°. Cool. Put through medium blade of food chopper. Measure ½ cup of almonds; set aside.

In saucepan, mix butter and sugar. Stir and cook over high heat until mixture melts and becomes a brown liquid; do not burn. Stir constantly. When mixture is liquid and "smokes," it is nearly ready to remove from heat. Add ½ cup chopped almonds. Stir quickly and pour onto buttered marble or cookie sheet; spread to ⅛-inch thickness. Mark in squares. Have ready in double boiler the chocolate which has been melted over warm, not hot, water. Spread chocolate over candy and sprinkle with chopped almonds. Cool until chocolate hardens; with a spatula, flop candy over and repeat with chocolate and nuts. Break candy into pieces when cold. Makes about 1¼ pounds.

Memories from Brownie's Kitchen (Maine)

Apricot Nut Snowballs

No-bake and oh, so easy.

6 ounces dried apricots
¼ cup apricot jam
1 tablespoon sugar

1 cup chopped nuts
1 cup sweetened coconut
Powdered sugar

Put all ingredients in food processor, except powdered sugar, and pulse until a mass is formed. Form balls using a rounded teaspoon and roll in powdered sugar. Chill, covered loosely, in refrigerator.

Note: Wet hands with water when rounding cookies.

The Island Cookbook (Rhode Island)

Creamy Nutcracker Fudge

Perfect for holidays.

4½ cups sugar
1½ cups half-and-half
¼ cup butter
Dash of salt
1 (12-ounce) package semisweet chocolate pieces

4 (1-ounce) squares
  unsweetened chocolate,
  chopped
1 (7-ounce) jar marshmallow
  crème
1 cup chopped nuts

Combine first 4 ingredients in heavy 3-quart saucepan. Bring to full rolling boil for 6 minutes, stirring frequently. Add chocolate and marshmallow crème. Beat until melted. Add nuts. Pour into buttered 13x9-inch pan. Let stand several hours before cutting. Store in cool place. Makes 4 dozen.

Connecticut Cooks (Connecticut)

Chocolate Peanut Butter Balls

Kids and grown-ups love these!

3 cups creamy peanut butter
2 pounds powdered sugar
3 sticks butter, melted
2 cups (12-ounces) chocolate
  chips

4 ounces German sweet
  chocolate
1 square paraffin wax

Mix peanut butter, sugar, and butter thoroughly. Form into balls and freeze. Melt chocolate chips, German chocolate, and wax in double boiler. Dip frozen balls in chocolate. Keep refrigerated until serving. Yields 8 dozen.

It's Our Serve (New York)

Ricotta Balls

Fried dough is almost synonymous with Italian celebration desserts.

1 pound ricotta cheese
1 tablespoon baking powder
1 teaspoon vanilla extract
3 eggs

1 cup flour
2 cups vegetable oil for deep
 frying
Powdered sugar for dusting

Combine ricotta, baking powder, vanilla, eggs, and flour, and mix well. In a deep fryer or large pot, heat the oil to 325°. Working in batches, drop teaspoonful-size balls of dough into oil and fry until golden brown, 2–3 minutes, turning once. Drain on paper towels. Sprinkle with powdered sugar while hot and serve immediately. Makes 12 servings.

The Long Island Holiday Cookbook (New York)

Truffles

Great for Christmas.

1 (12-ounce) package
 semisweet chocolate chips
¾ cup sweetened condensed
 milk

1 teaspoon vanilla
⅛ teaspoon salt
½ cup cocoa or 1 cup
 chopped, flaked coconut

In double boiler over hot, not boiling water, melt chocolate chips. Stir in condensed milk, vanilla, and salt until well mixed. Refrigerate mixture about 45 minutes or until easy to shape. With buttered hands, shape mixture into 1-inch balls. Roll balls in cocoa or coconut. Yields 36 truffles.

Connecticut Cooks III (Connecticut)

COMMONWEALTH MEDIA SERVICES / THE PENNSYLVANIA TOURISM OFFICE

U.S. Brig Niagara in Erie, Pennsylvania, is a reconstruction of an early 19th-century warship of the United States Navy. On September 10, 1813, nine small ships defeated a British squadron of six vessels in the Battle of Lake Erie. This pivotal event in the War of 1812 secured the Northwest Territory, opening supply lines.

Wet Bottom Shoo Fly Pie

1 cup all-purpose flour
¾ cup brown sugar
1½ tablespoons shortening
1 cup molasses

1 egg, beaten
1 teaspoon baking soda
1 cup boiling water
1 deep 9-inch pie shell

Mix flour, sugar, and shortening until crumbly. Save ½ cup for the top. Mix remaining crumbs with molasses, egg, and soda dissolved in water. Pour this mixture into unbaked pie shell. Sprinkle crumbs on top. Bake at 375° for 45 minutes. This makes a very wet bottom pie.

From Mother's Cupboard (Pennsylvania)

Apple Pan Dowdy

White bread
Melted butter
4 large green apples

½ cup dark brown sugar
½ teaspoon cinnamon
½ cup water

Remove crust from bread and slice into fingers. Dip each finger into melted butter and line bottom and sides of a baking dish with fingers. Peel and core apples. Slice. Place in center of bread fingers. Sprinkle apples with mixture of the sugar and cinnamon. Add ½ cup water and cover the top with a layer of well-buttered fingers of bread. Sprinkle top with additional sugar. Cover and bake 1 hour in a 350° oven. Serve hot with whipped cream. Serves 6.

Recipes from Smith-Appleby House (Rhode Island)

The shoo fly pie is a molasses pie considered traditional among the Pennsylvania Dutch. "Wet bottom" shoo fly pie is most common and consists of a layer of sweet, gooey molasses beneath a crumb topping. In contrast, a "dry bottom" shoofly pie is more thoroughly mixed into a cake-like consistency. Its distinctive flavor and texture is quite alluring to tourists in the Dutch Country of Lancaster County.

The song "Shoo Fly Pie and Apple Pan Dowdy" was first performed by June Christy singing with Stan Kenton and his orchestra in 1945. Dinah Shore's 1946 version of the song was her first top ten hit.

Schnitz Pie

Since apple trees, which grow abundantly in eastern Pennsylvania, produced more apples than could be eaten fresh in most households, the German settlers dried much of their fruit. It was a home operation. The apples were peeled and cut into slices (schnitz means to cut into pieces), then laid on a roof or on racks above a heat source to dry.

Most apples dried in 24–48 hours, depending upon the thickness of the slices, the temperature of the heat source, and the temperature and humidity of the weather. Once dried, the sweet slices were stored in a dry container for use at any time of the year.

Today, Schnitz Pie is usually served at the lunch that follows the Sunday morning church service. It is traditionally part of the main course at the snack meal of the day when either potato soup or bean soup is on the menu. Schnitz is now prepared commercially in Pennsylvania, so it is available to those without their own source of fresh apples.

3 cups dried apples
2¼ cups warm water
1 teaspoon lemon extract

⅔ cup brown sugar
1 (9-inch) unbaked pie shell,
**   plus top crust**

Soak apples in the warm water, then cook over low heat until soft. Mash apples and add lemon and sugar.

Pour into unbaked pie shell. Cover with top crust. Seal edges. Bake at 425° for 15 minutes, then at 350° for 30 minutes. Serve warm. Makes 1 (9-inch) pie.

The Best of Amish Cooking (Pennsylvania)

Dutch Apple Pie

3 cups sliced apples
1 (9-inch) pie shell, unbaked
1 cup sugar
3 tablespoons flour
½ teaspoon cinnamon
1 egg, beaten
1 cup light cream
1 teaspoon vanilla
½ cup chopped nuts
1 tablespoon butter

Place apples into unbaked pie shell. Mix together sugar, flour, and cinnamon. Combine egg, cream, and vanilla; add sugar mixture, mixing well. Pour over apples, then sprinkle with nuts and dot with butter. Bake at 350° for 45–50 minutes, until apples are tender.

An Amish Kitchen (Pennsylvania)

Red Inn Apple Pie

This unusual recipe appears to have no crust. However, the custard forms a kind of crust under the apples. It is delicious and so easy to make!

7 Granny Smith apples, pared
  and thinly sliced
Pinch of cinnamon
Pinch of nutmeg

CUSTARD:
2 eggs
1 cup sugar
½ cup Bisquick
¾ cup milk

CRUMBLE:
1 cup Bisquick
⅓ cup brown sugar
½ cup walnuts
3 tablespoons butter (hard)
Heavy cream

Butter a 10-inch pie plate. Sprinkle the sliced apples with cinnamon and nutmeg and mix together. Place the apples in the pie plate.

Beat together the ingredients for the custard and pour it over the apples. Mix together the ingredients for the crumble and cut in the butter. Sprinkle this over the apples and press down lightly. Bake in a preheated oven at 325° for 1 hour. Serve with whipped cream. Serves 6–8.

A recipe from The Red Inn, Provincetown
A Taste of Provincetown (Massachusetts)

Crunchy Caramel Apple Pie

30 caramels, unwrapped
3 tablespoons water
5 or 6 large apples
1 (9-inch) pie shell, unbaked
¾ cup flour

½ teaspoon cinnamon
Dash of nutmeg
¼ cup sugar
½ cup butter
½ cup chopped walnuts

Melt caramels with water in saucepan over low heat. Slice half the apples into pie shell. Pour half caramel sauce over apples. Repeat. Mix flour, spices, and sugar in bowl with butter until crumbly. Stir in nuts. Sprinkle over pie. Bake at 375° about 45 minutes. I like to use Blushing Golden apples when made in the fall.

What's Cooking at Trinity (Pennsylvania)

New England Blueberry Pie

3½ cups blueberries
¾ cup sugar
⅛ teaspoon salt
¼ teaspoon cinnamon

3 tablespoons flour
Butter
Pastry crust for a 2-crust
  (9-inch) pie

Mix blueberries and all other ingredients (except butter) in a large bowl. Line a shallow pie plate with crust. Pour in berry mixture. Dot with 5–6 small pieces of butter. Moisten edge of crust with water.

Roll top crust to fit plate. Spread lightly with shortening and sprinkle with flour. Fold over and cut 3 or 4 small slits on the fold. Place over berries. Unfold and press down around the edge. Trim crust close to the edge of the plate and press again around the edge with floured tines of a fork. Hold pie over sink and pour about ¼ cup milk over crust, letting surplus drain off. Bake at 475° for 15 minutes. Reduce heat to 350° for 15 minutes longer. If frozen berries are used, increase last baking time to 30 minutes.

Homespun Cookery (New Hampshire)

Lemon Cream Pie with Apricot Sauce

PIE:

1 envelope unflavored gelatin
⅔ cup sugar, divided
¼ teaspoon salt
2 eggs, separated
6 tablespoons cold water
6 tablespoons lemon juice
2 teaspoons grated lemon peel
1 cup heavy cream, whipped
1 (9-inch) graham cracker crust or baked pastry crust

Combine gelatin, ⅓ cup sugar, and salt in saucepan. Beat egg yolks; beat in water and lemon juice; add to gelatin mixture. Mix well. Cook over low heat, stirring constantly until gelatin dissolves and mixture thickens slightly. Remove from heat; add lemon peel. Chill, stirring occasionally, until mixture mounds slightly when dropped from a spoon. Beat egg whites until stiff. Add remaining ⅓ cup sugar gradually and beat until very stiff. Fold into gelatin mixture. Fold in cream. Pour into 9-inch crust. Chill until firm.

SAUCE:

1 (16-ounce) can apricot halves

Drain apricots, reserving ¼ cup syrup. Purée apricots and reserved syrup. Chill. Serve over pie. Garnish with mint leaves. May also be served without the crust as a pudding. Yields 6–8 servings.

The Albany Collection: Treasures & Treasured Recipes
(New York)

 Connecticut, the third smallest state in the nation, is officially called the Constitution State, but most people call it the Nutmeg State, and its residents, "Nutmeggers."

Rhubarb Pie

A Vermont cookbook would be incomplete without a rule for rhubarb pie. The showing of rhubarb is one of the first true signs of spring. While dirt roads are still making automobiles wallow in mud, and neither daffodils nor apple blossoms have yet shown their beauty, the rhubarb may be spotted in the garden patch. For pie or any other rhubarb concoction, pick the rhubarb when the first stalks come up. By the time its ivory plumes of flowers appear, it will be tough and stringy. Young "strawberry rhubarb" makes the best pie.

FOR A 9-INCH PIE, USE:

3 cups rhubarb
Pastry for a double crust
2 tablespoons flour
1½ cups sugar
⅛ teaspoon each of
  cinnamon and nutmeg

1 egg, well beaten
2 tablespoons butter cut
  into 12 bits

Use the youngest, tenderest "strawberry rhubarb"—the kind that needs no peeling. Discard leaves and lower ends of stalks and cut into ½-inch pieces.

Line a 9-inch pie tin with pastry. Leave a good margin of pastry to be turned up over the top crust and crimped with a fork so that no juice will run out. I dislike any drippings in the oven, because I resent spending time cleaning it, so I always place a cookie sheet under fruit pies just in case they drip. In my experience, they have never failed to do so.

Sift flour, sugar, and spice together. Scatter ¼ cup of this mixture over the lower crust. Add half of the rhubarb, half of the remaining sugar mixture, then the rest of the rhubarb and the last of the sugar and spice. Heap the rhubarb slightly toward the center of the pie; it will sink while baking.

Pour the beaten egg over the pie and dot it with bits of butter. Set the top crust in place and gash it well so that steam can escape. Bake at 450° for 15 minutes. Reduce the heat to 350° and continue baking until the fruit is tender and the crust is brown and puffed—about 40 minutes longer. If it browns too quickly, cover it with a tent of aluminum foil, but remove the tent during the last 10 minutes of baking. Enjoy the coming of spring!

Mrs. Appleyard's Family Kitchen (Vermont)

Boston Cream Pie

Boston Cream Pie isn't a pastry at all, and is here purely because of its name.

⅓ cup butter
1 cup sugar
2 eggs, separated
½ teaspoon salt
½ teaspoon vanilla

2 teaspoons baking powder
1½ cups King Arthur Un-
   bleached All-Purpose Flour
½ cup milk
1 recipe chocolate frosting

Preheat your oven to 375°. Cream the butter; add the sugar and cream until light. Add the egg yolks and beat until fluffy. Stir in the salt and the vanilla.

Combine the baking powder with the flour and add this to the batter alternately with the milk. Stir only as much as is necessary to blend the ingredients. Beat the egg whites until they are stiff and fold them into the batter.

Pour the batter into 2 greased, 8-inch cake pans. Bake for 30 minutes. While the batter bakes, prepare the filling.

CREAM FILLING:

⅓–½ cup King Arthur Un-
   bleached All-Purpose Flour
⅔ cup sugar
⅛ teaspoon salt

2 cups milk
2 eggs
1 teaspoon vanilla

Combine the flour, sugar and salt. Scald the milk and pour it over the dry ingredients gradually. Cook until it has thickened. Beat the eggs slightly and add them to the hot, thickened custard. Allow the custard to remain heating for 1 minute. Cool and add the vanilla flavoring.

When the cake layers are cool, put the cooled cream filling between them and top with your choice of chocolate frosting.

The King Arthur Flour 200th Anniversary Cookbook (Vermont)

Turtle Pie

12 caramels, unwrapped
1 (14-ounce) can sweetened
  condensed milk, divided
1 (9-inch) baked pie shell
2 (1-ounce) squares
  unsweetened chocolate

¼ cup butter or margarine
2 eggs
2 tablespoons water
1 teaspoon vanilla extract
Dash of salt
½ cup pecans

Preheat oven to 325°. In a small heavy saucepan, over low heat, melt caramels with ⅓ cup condensed milk. Spread this mixture evenly on bottom of the prepared pie shell.

In a medium saucepan over low heat, melt chocolate with butter or margarine. In large mixer bowl, beat eggs with remaining condensed milk, water, vanilla, and salt. Add chocolate mixture and mix well. Pour into prepared pastry shell; top with pecans. Bake 35 minutes or until center is set. Cool. Chill. May be topped with whipped cream. Refrigerate leftovers.

Asbury Cooks 1799-1999 (New York)

Peanut Butter Pie

⅔ cup powdered sugar
⅓ cup crunchy peanut butter
1 (9-inch) baked pie shell
⅓ cup sugar
1 tablespoon flour

1 tablespoon cornstarch
2 egg yolks, beaten
2 cups milk
1 tablespoon butter
1 teaspoon vanilla

Mix together powdered sugar and peanut butter until it resembles fine crumbs. Sprinkle ½ of mixture in bottom of baked pie shell. Combine sugar, flour, and cornstarch. Add beaten egg yolks. Mix to form a smooth paste. Add milk and cook, stirring constantly until thickened. Remove from heat, and stir in butter and vanilla. Cool slightly; pour into pie shell. Sprinkle crumbs on top. Serve with whipped cream.

200 Years of Favorite Recipes from Delaware County (New York)

White Peach and Raspberry Cobbler

Toward the end of July or the beginning of August, there is nothing better than finding perfectly ripe, fragrant white peaches at a farm stand in Ulster or Dutchess County. At that time in summer, raspberries are sure to be close by. Pick up a good supply of both so you have some left to make this cobbler when you get home.

**3 very ripe peaches, peeled
   and sliced**

**1 cup raspberries
3 tablespoons sugar**

In a 1½ to 2-inch shallow, flameproof casserole, combine the peaches and raspberries with sugar. Preheat oven to 350°.

BATTER:
½ cup sugar
1¼ cups flour
2 teaspoons baking powder

**1 tablespoon unsalted butter,
   melted**
½ cup milk

In a bowl, combine sugar, flour, and baking powder and mix in butter and milk. Put casserole over medium-low heat and gently heat the fruit, stirring it gently as the sugar melts and the peaches and raspberries begin to give up their juice. When fruit has softened, drop batter by tablespoonfuls into the casserole. Place cobbler in oven and bake for about 35 minutes, until fruit is bubbling and top is firm and lightly browned. Serve on its own or with whipped cream or vanilla ice cream. Serves 6–8.

The Hudson River Valley Cookbook (New York)

Bogberry Apple Tart

Great warm with ice cream! (and cold, every time you pass through the kitchen!)

6 apples, peeled and sliced	½ cup brown sugar
1½ cups whole cranberries	½ cup white sugar
½ cup chopped nuts	2 eggs
1 teaspoon cinnamon	½ teaspoon vanilla
⅛ teaspoon salt	½ cup butter, melted
¼ cup white sugar	1 cup flour

Grease a 9-inch pie pan or 8-inch square pan. Layer apples in pan; alternate cranberries with apples. Sprinkle nuts, cinnamon, salt and ¼ cup sugar over fruit. Mix together sugars, eggs, vanilla, butter, and flour. Pour this mixture over apples and berries, spreading evenly to cover (mixture will run down through the fruit.) Bake in 325° oven for 45 minutes or until knife inserted into the center comes out clean. Serves 4-8.

Savory Cape Cod Recipes & Sketches (Massachusetts)

Old White Church Apple Crisp

¾ cup Quaker Oats	1 teaspoon cinnamon
¾ cup brown sugar	4–6 large Cortland or
½ cup butter or margarine	Macintosh apples (or one
½ cup flour	half of each kind)

Prepare apples as for pie; slice thin.

Combine other ingredients. Sprinkle over apples. Bake 35–40 minutes at 350°. Serve with cream. Serves 6–8.

Come Savor Swansea (Massachusetts)

Apple-Raisin Brown Betty

2½ cups packed soft
   stale-bread cubes, divided
4 cups finely chopped tart
   apples
¾ cup seedless raisins
⅔ cup packed brown sugar
¼ teaspoon nutmeg

½ teaspoon cinnamon
¼ cup butter or margarine,
   melted
2 tablespoons lemon juice
⅓ cup water
Cream

Sprinkle ⅓ of bread cubes in greased 1½-quart casserole. Mix next 5 ingredients. Spread half the mixture on top of bread and repeat layers. Cover with remaining bread. Drizzle with butter mixed with juice and water. Cover and bake at 375° for 40 minutes. Uncover and bake 20 minutes longer. Serve warm with cream. Serves 6.

Wonderful Good Cooking from Amish Country Kitchens (Pennsylvania)

Apple Dumplings

2 cups water
1½ cups sugar
¼ teaspoon cinnamon
¼ teaspoon nutmeg
8 drops red food coloring
¼ cup margarine
2 cups flour
2 teaspoons baking powder

1 teaspoon salt
¾ cup shortening
½ cup milk
6 apples, peeled and cored
Sugar and cinnamon for
   sprinkling
Additional butter

Cook first 5 ingredients 5 minutes to make a syrup. Remove from heat and add margarine; set aside. Sift together flour, baking powder, and salt. Cut in shortening till crumbly. Add milk. Stir just till flour is moistened. On a lightly floured surface, roll to 12x18 inches. Cut 6 (6-inch) squares. Place an apple on each square. Sprinkle with sugar and cinnamon, and dot with butter. Moisten edges and pinch together. Place in ungreased 9x13-inch pan, 1 inch apart. Pour syrup over dumplings. Bake in 375° oven for 35–40 minutes.

Society of Farm Women of Pennsylvania Cookbook (Pennsylvania)

Down East Blueberry Crisp

4 cups fresh blueberries
2–4 tablespoons sugar
2 teaspoons lemon juice
¼ cup margarine
¼ cup packed brown sugar

⅓ cup all-purpose flour
¼ teaspoon cinnamon
Dash of salt (optional)
¾ cup old-fashioned rolled
  oats

Preheat oven to 375°. Place blueberries in a greased (margarine) baking dish. Sprinkle with sugar and lemon juice. In a medium bowl, combine margarine, brown sugar, flour, cinnamon, and salt; mix until crumbly. Stir in rolled oats and sprinkle evenly over blueberries. Bake in 375° oven for 35–40 minutes. Serve warm. Yields 6–8 servings.

A Taste of New England (Massachusetts)

Cherry Walnut Delight

1¼ cups flour
¾ cup brown sugar
½ cup margarine, softened
¾ cup flaked coconut
¾ cup chopped walnuts
1 (8-ounce) package cream
  cheese, softened

½ cup sugar
1 egg
1 teaspoon vanilla
1 (1 pound 5-ounce) can
  cherry pie filling
½ cup chopped walnuts
  (for topping)

Combine flour, brown sugar, and butter; blend to fine crumbs. Add coconut and walnuts; mix. Reserve ½ cup crumb mixture and press the rest into bottom of a greased 9x13-inch pan. Bake at 350° for 12–15 minutes or until lightly browned. Beat cream cheese until fluffy. Add sugar, egg, and vanilla. Spread over baked layer and bake 10 minutes. Put cherry filling over cream cheese. Sprinkle with walnuts and crumb mixture. Bake for 15 minutes.

The Parkview Way to Vegetarian Cooking (Maine)

Strawberries Brûlée

1 (8-ounce) package cream
  cheese, softened
1½ cups dairy sour cream
6 tablespoons granulated
  sugar

2 pints fresh strawberries,
  hulled, sliced, and
  sweetened to taste
1 cup packed brown sugar

Beat cream cheese until fluffy. Add sour cream and granulated sugar, blending thoroughly. Arrange berries in a 9x12-inch glass baking dish. Spoon cream cheese mixture over berries. Bake in a 300° oven for 10 minutes; remove and sprinkle with brown sugar. Place on lowest broiler rack, broiling until sugar bubbles and browns lightly (about 5 minutes). Serve at once. Makes 6–8 servings.

Great Island Cook Book (New Hampshire)

Strawberry Delight

1½ cups graham cracker
  crumbs
⅓ cup butter, melted
2 (8-ounce) packages cream
  cheese, softened
1½ cups powdered sugar

1½ (8-ounce) containers
  whipped topping
8 cups sliced strawberries
1 cup sugar
3 tablespoons cornstarch
½ cup water

Combine cracker crumbs and butter; pat in bottom of 9x13-inch pan. Beat cream cheese and powdered sugar. Fold in whipped topping. Spread on top of graham cracker crust.

Mash enough berries to measure 1 cup. Stir together sugar and cornstarch in saucepan. Gradually stir in water and crushed berries. Cook over medium heat, stirring constantly, until mixture thickens and boils. Boil and stir 1 minute. Cool. Spread remaining berries on cream cheese mixture. Pour chilled berry mixture over top. Chill.

River Brethren Recipes (Pennsylvania)

Vanilla Bread Pudding with Butter Rum Sauce

6 eggs
2 cups milk
½ pound sugar
2 teaspoons ground cinnamon
½ cup raisins

2 teaspoons vanilla extract
1 loaf French bread,
  approximately
½ cup walnuts
½ cup brown sugar

In a large bowl, mix together the eggs, milk, sugar, cinnamon, raisins, and vanilla. Cut up enough French bread in small cubes to absorb the mixture. Pour mixture into a greased deep baking pan and top with ½ cup walnuts and ½ cup brown sugar. Bake in oven for 45 minutes at 350°.

BUTTER RUM SAUCE:
½ cup butter, melted
¾ cup powdered sugar

¼ cup Meyer's dark rum

Combine all ingredients and cook over medium heat for 15 minutes. To serve, cut bread pudding into squares and serve warm topped with heated rum sauce.

A recipe from Muriel's Restaurant, Newport
A Taste of Newport (Rhode Island)

Since the 1600s, Mystic Seaport has been a legendary maritime destination and a center of shipbuilding. In fact, between 1784 and 1919—the golden age of American maritime enterprise—more than 600 vessels were constructed along the Mystic River. This historic area is now Connecticut's most popular tourist attraction. The nationally acclaimed "living museum" preserves America's maritime culture and history, and features a restored 19th-century village, authentic whaling ships, and working craftspeople.

Amaretto Cream Puffs

CREAM PUFFS:

½ cup butter
1 cup water
1 cup flour

4 eggs
¼ teaspoon salt

Preheat oven to 450°. Grease a large cookie sheet. Bring butter and water to boil and add flour. Stir until it forms a ball. Remove from heat and cool slightly. Beat eggs in 1 at a time. Beat well and add salt. Drop by teaspoonfuls on cookie sheet, 2 inches apart. Bake at 450° for 15 minutes; lower heat to 350° for 10–25 minutes. Remove immediately and cool on rack.

CREAM FILLING:

1 cup heavy cream
4 teaspoons sugar

¼ cup amaretto

Whip cream until stiff and add sugar and amaretto.

SAUCE:

20 ounces frozen red
  raspberries in syrup,
  thawed

2 teaspoons cornstarch
1 tablespoon water

Place raspberries and syrup in blender. Purée for 10 seconds. Press through sieve. In a small saucepan, mix cornstarch with 1 tablespoon water. Add purée. Heat, stirring, until mixture thickens and starts to boil. Cool.

ASSEMBLY:

Slit Cream Puffs, fill with Cream Filling, and pour Sauce over each one before serving. Serves 8.

Just Desserts (Pennsylvania)

Mousse Amaretto

5 eggs, separated
½ cup sugar
Pinch of salt
1 teaspoon vanilla
1 cup milk

1 envelope gelatin
2 tablespoons cold water
1 pint heavy cream, whipped
Amaretto

Beat egg yolks with sugar until mixture is light yellow. Add salt. Add vanilla to milk and bring to boil. Add milk to yolks, mixing thoroughly. Heat over low heat, stirring constantly, but do not bring to boil. Soften gelatin in cold water, add to milk and strain mixture through a fine sieve. Cool on a bowl of ice, then fold in cream. Whip egg whites until stiff; fold into gelatin mixture. Add 2–3 ounces amaretto. Pour into serving bowl and chill. Before serving, float a tablespoon or two of amaretto on top of each portion.

The Cookbook AAUW (New York)

Hazelnut Cups

1 cup milk
⅓ cup sugar
1½ tablespoons cornstarch
1 egg yolk, beaten
½ cup chocolate chips
1 tablespoon hazelnut liqueur
1 tablespoon butter, room
  temperature

½ teaspoon vanilla extract
½ cup heavy cream
⅓–½ cup powdered sugar
1 teaspoon almond extract
¼ cup grated roasted
  hazelnuts
2 packages small phyllo cups
Grated chocolate for garnish

In microwave-safe bowl, combine milk, sugar, and cornstarch. Cook on high power for 2 minutes, stir mixture, then cook for an additional 2 minutes. Add 3 tablespoons of the milk mixture to the egg yolk, stirring in one tablespoon at a time. Add egg mixture, chocolate chips, and hazelnut liqueur to milk mixture. Cook on high power for 1 minute, then stir. Add butter and vanilla and allow pudding to cool. Whip heavy cream with powdered sugar and almond extract. Add hazelnuts. Fill each phyllo cup with 1 tablespoon of the pudding mixture and top with 1 tablespoon of whipped cream. Sprinkle with chocolate. Makes 30 cups.

Delicious Developments (New York)

Funnel Cake

2 eggs	½ teaspoon salt
2 cups flour	Oil
2 cups milk	Powdered sugar
1 teaspoon baking powder	

Mix all ingredients, except oil and sugar. Heat oil and drop batter in hot oil 2 tablespoons at a time. Deep fry. Cook on both sides. Drain and shake powdered sugar on top.

Fellowship Family Favorites Cookbook (New York)

Pennsylvania Dutch Funnel Cakes

⅔ cup milk	1 teaspoon baking powder
1 egg, beaten	¼ teaspoon salt
1¼ cups all-purpose flour	Fat for frying
2 tablespoons sugar	Powdered sugar or molasses

Beat milk with egg. Blend dry ingredients and gradually add the milk mixture, beating constantly until batter is smooth. Holding finger over the bottom of a ⅜- or ½-inch funnel, fill with batter. Holding funnel as near surface of fat as possible, remove finger and drop batter into deep fat heated to 375° using a circular movement from center outward to form a spiral cake about 3 inches in diameter. Immediately replace finger on bottom of funnel and form other cakes. Fry cakes until they are puffy and golden brown, turning them once. Remove from fat with a slotted spoon to absorbent paper to drain. Sift powdered sugar lightly over cakes or drizzle with molasses and serve at once. Yields 2 dozen cakes.

Philadelphia Homestyle Cookbook (Pennsylvania)

Baklava

1 pound phyllo pastry sheets
¾ pound sweet butter, melted
1 pound walnut meat, finely chopped

5 teaspoons sugar
1 teaspoon cinnamon
Dash of cloves
Syrup

Place sheets of phyllo pastry in a 13x9x2-inch pan; brush each sheet evenly with butter. When 10 or 12 sheets are in place, combine walnuts, sugar, cinnamon, and cloves. Spread ⅓ of this mixture over top sheet. Place another 5 or 6 buttered phyllo sheets on top of nut mixture. Sprinkle with another ⅓ of nut mixture and repeat with buttered phyllo sheets and final ⅓ nut mixture. Spread remaining phyllo sheets on top, carefully buttering each second sheet.

With sharp knife, cut baklava into diamond-shaped pieces. Heat remaining butter (there should be ½ cup) until very hot and beginning to brown and pour evenly over the baklava. Sprinkle top with a few drops of cold water. Bake at 350° for 30 minutes. Reduce temperature to 300° and bake one hour or longer. Makes 30–36 servings.

SYRUP:
3½ cups water
3 cups sugar
1 teaspoon lemon juice

1 cinnamon stick
4 cloves
Orange and lemon slices

Combine ingredients in a saucepan. Bring to a boil and simmer 20 minutes; strain. Cool and pour over Baklava.

Hudson Valley German-American Society Cookbook (New York)

Pull Me Up

(Terra-Me-SU)

24 ladyfingers in halves
1½ teaspoons orange extract,
    divided
3 tablespoons finely ground
    coffee beans
2 tablespoons water
1 cup very strong coffee
1 (16-ounce) container
    mascarpone cheese

½ cup plus 2 tablespoons
    powdered sugar, divided
½ teaspoon salt
3 ounces dark chocolate,
    grated, divided
1½ cups whipping cream,
    whipped, divided

Place 6 ladyfinger halves in a flat casserole dish. In a small bowl, stir
½ teaspoon orange extract with coffee beans, water, and strong coffee. Brush onto ladyfinger halves. In a separate bowl, place mas-
carpone, ½ cup powdered sugar, salt, 1 teaspoon orange extract, and
2 ounces chocolate and mix well. Fold ⅔ of the whipped cream into
mixture. Spoon ⅓ cheese mixture over ladyfingers. Add a layer of
ladyfingers, brush with coffee mixture, and spoon on ⅓ cheese mixture. Repeat. Top with last 6 halves. Brush with coffee mixture.

Mix remaining whipped cream and 2 tablespoons powdered sugar
together. Spread on top layer. Sprinkle remaining chocolate on
whipped cream. Refrigerate 2 hours before serving.

My Italian Heritage (New York)

Banana Split
(Original Walgreens Recipe)

In 1909, Charles Rudolph Walgreen opened a soda fountain along one wall of his drugstore on Chicago's South Side to boost business. The fountain, with its trademark Banana Splits, proved to be a tremendous drawing card, attracting customers who might otherwise have been just as satisfied having their pharmaceutical needs fulfilled at some other drugstore in the neighborhood. And some came just for the Splits. During the summer months, customers would often surround the soda fountain counter, sometimes three or four persons deep, while Walgreens soda jerks peeled bananas and dipped ice cream.

1 banana
1 scoop vanilla ice cream
1 scoop chocolate ice cream
1 scoop strawberry ice cream
2 ounces crushed pineapple
2 ounces chocolate syrup
2 ounces strawberry topping
Whipped cream for garnish

Chopped mixed nuts for
  garnish
Shaved chocolate bark for
  garnish
3 stemmed cherries for
  garnish
2 Nabisco wafers

Split banana lengthwise and place halves parallel on a Banana Split dish. Place vanilla ice cream between the banana halves. To the left of the vanilla place chocolate ice cream, and to the right place strawberry ice cream. Ladle pineapple over vanilla ice cream, chocolate syrup over chocolate ice cream, and strawberry topping over strawberry ice cream.

Garnish with whipped cream. Sprinkle with chopped nuts and chocolate shavings. Place 3 stemmed cherries at top and arrange wafers at either end. Serve with a long-handled spoon. Makes 1 Banana Split.

The Banana Split Book (Pennsylvania)

Using 33,000 bananas, 2,500 gallons of ice cream, 600 pounds of nuts, and lots of other toppings, the world's longest banana split was created in Selinsgrove, Pennsylvania, in 1988. The treat measured 4.55 miles long and is recorded in the *Guinness Book of World Records*.

Three Layer Sherbet Ices

LAYER 1:

1 package orange-flavored Jell-O

1 cup boiling water

½ cup sugar

1 cup orange juice

1 cup nectar drink

LAYER 2:

1 package lemon-flavored Jell-O

1 cup boiling water

½ cup sugar

1 cup orange juice

1 cup pineapple juice

LAYER 3:

1 package raspberry-flavored Jell-O

1 cup boiling water

½ cup sugar

1 cup orange juice

1 cup dark grape juice

Place ingredients for each layer in 3 separate pans. Mix ingredients in each pan and freeze. After frozen, place each layer in blender separately, blending well and pouring into large loaf pan, one layer on top of the other. To avoid uneven layers, freeze each layer for half an hour before adding the next. Completed sherbet should be well frozen before cutting into slices.

Culinary Creations (New York)

Contributing Cookbooks

GWEN McKEE

A grand view of boats at their moorings from the only pedestrian drawbridge in America, at picturesque Perkins Cove, Ogunquit, Maine.

Listed below are the cookbooks that have contributed recipes to this book, along with copyright, author, publisher, city, and state. The information in parentheses beneath each recipe indicates the BEST OF THE BEST cookbook in which the recipe originally appeared.

The Albany Collection: Treasures & Treasured Recipes ©1997 Women's Council, Albany Institute of History & Art, Albany, NY

All-Maine Cooking ©1967 Down East Books, Camden, ME

All Seasons Cookbook ©1988 by Connie Colom, Mystic Seaport Stores, Mystic, CT

Amish Cooking, Herald Press, Scottdale, PA

Another Blue Strawbery ©1983 by James Haller, The Harvard Common Press, Boston, MA

Apple Orchard Cookbook ©1992 by Janet M. Christensen and Betty Bergman Levin, Lee, MA

The Art of Asian Cooking ©1990 Museum of Fine Arts, Boston, MA

As You Like It ©1993 Williamstown Theatre Festival Guild, Williamstown, MA

Asbury Cooks 1799-1999, Asbury United Methodist Church, Croton on Hudson, NY

The Banana Split Book ©2004 by Michael Turback, Camino Books, Inc., Philadelphia, PA

The Bed & Breakfast Cookbook ©1991 by Martha W. Murphy, Narragansett, RI

Bed & Breakfast Leatherstocking Welcome Home Recipe Collection, Bed & Breakfast Leatherstocking Assn., Utica, NY

Berkshire Seasonings, Junior League of Berkshire County, Pittsfield, MA

The Best of Amish Cooking ©1988 Good Books, Intercourse, PA

The Best of Busy Bee #2 ©1987 by Betty Claycomb, Laurel Group Press, Scottdale, PA

The Best of Mennonite Fellowship Meals ©1991 Good Books, Intercourse, PA

Best of the Sweet Potato Recipes Cookbook ©1992 Penndel, PA

The Best from Libby Hillman's Kitchen ©1993 by Libby Hillman, Countryman Press, Woodstock, VT

Best Recipes of Berkshire Chefs ©1993 Berkshire House Publishers, Lee, MA

Betty Groff's Country Goodness Cookbook ©1987 by Betty Groff, Pond Press, Mount Joy, PA

Betty Groff's Up-Home Down-Home Cookbook ©1987 Betty Groff, Pond Press, Mount Joy, PA

Beyond Chicken Soup ©1996 Jewish Home of Rochester Auxiliary, Rochester, NY

Birthright Sampler, Birthright of Johnstown, Inc., Johnstown, PA

The Black Hat Chef Cookbook ©1991 by Chef Rene, Lou Reda Productions, Inc., Easton, PA

The Bloomin' Cookbook, DuBoistown Garden Club, South Williamsport, PA

The Blue Strawbery ©1978 by James Haller, The Harvard Common Press, Boston, MA

Bobbie's Kitchen, Kolmetz Family, Farport, NY

Boston Tea Parties ©1987 Museum of Fine Arts, Boston, MA

Bountiful Harvest Cookbook ©1987 Lancaster Bible College Women's Aus, Lancaster, PA

Bridgehampton Weekends ©2000 by Ellen Wright, William Morrow/Harper Collins, New York, NY

The Bronx Cookbook ©1997 The Bronx County Historical Society, Bronx, NY

Bucks Cooks ©1950 Trinity Church, Solebury, PA

Bucks Cooks II ©1983 Trinity Church, Solebury, PA

Cape Cod's Night at the Chef's Table ©1993 The Provincetown AIDS Support Group, Provincetown, MA

A Cape Cod Seafood Cookbook ©1985 by Margaret Deeds Murphy, Parnassus Imprints, Hyannis, MA

Cape Collection—Simply Soup, Association for the Preservation of Cape Cod, Orleans, MA

Celebrating 200 Years of Survival & Perseverance, Redfield Bicentennial Cookbook Committee, Williamstown, NY

Celebrities Serve ©1991 International Tennis Hall of Fame, Newport, RI

The Central Market Cookbook ©1989 Good Books, Intercourse, PA

Champagne...Uncorked! The Insider's Guide to Champagne ©1996 by Rosemary Zarly, RMZ Publications, New York, NY

Chefs and Artists, Back Mountain Memorial Library, Dallas, PA

The Chef's Palate Cookbook ©1992 by Jayne Pettit, Quechee, VT

Chris Sprague's Newcastle Inn Cookbook ©1992 by Chris Sprague, The Harvard Common Press, Boston, MA

Christmas Memories Cookbook ©1985 by Lois Klee and Connie Colom, Mystic Seaport Stores, Mystic, CT

City Tavern Cookbook ©2003 by Walter Staib, Philadelphia, PA

Classic New England Dishes from Your Microwave ©1991 by Millie Delahunty, Down East Books, Camden, ME

Come Savor Swansea ©1992 First Christian Congregational Church, Swansea, MA

Connecticut Cooks ©1982 American Cancer Society, Wallingford, Ct

Connecticut Cooks II ©1985 American Cancer Society, Wallingford, CT

Connecticut Cooks III ©1988 American Cancer Society, Mystic, CT

Convertible Cooking for a Healthy Heart ©1991 Joanne D'Agostino, Easton, PA

The Cookbook AAUW, American Assn. of University Women, Jamestown, NY

The Cookbook II, Worcester Art Museum, Worcester, MA

Cooking Down the Road, and at Home, Too, by Joan E. Prins, Hudson Falls, NY

Cooking with the Groundhog ©1958 Punxsutawney Area Hospital Aux. Punxsutawney, PA

Cooking with H.E.L.P., York, ME

The Country Innkeepers' Cookbook ©1992 by Wilf & Lois Copping, Country Roads Press, Castine, ME

Country Inns and Back Roads Cookbook, Berkshire House Publishers, Lee, MA

Cuisine a la Mode, by Les Dames Richelieu du Rhode Island, Woonsocket, RI

Culinary Creations ©1998 Bnos Zion of Bobov, Brooklyn, NY

A Culinary Tour of the Gingerbread Cottages, by Joan Davis, Carolina Beach, NC

Delicious Developments ©1994 Friends of Strong Memorial Hospital, Rochester, NY

Dining on Deck ©1986 by Linda Vail, Williamson Publishing, Charlotte, VT

Dinner Bell, Lancaster County Society of Farm Women #22, Millersville, PA

Dinner Bell Encore, Lancaster County Society of Farm Women #22, Millersville, PA

The Dinner Bell Rings Again!, Lancaster County Society of Farm Women #22, Millersville, PA

Dishing It Out, Members of the New Paltz Ballet Theatre, Inc., New Paltz, NY

Divine Recipes Fit for a Pennsylvania Grape Queen, North East PA Grape Queen, North East, PA

The East Hampton L.V.I.S. Centennial Cookbook ©1994 Ladies Village Improvement Society, Inc., East Hampton, NY

The Eater's Digest, Scranton Preparatory School Parents' Club, Scranton, PA

The Ellis Island Immigrant Cookbook by Tom Bernardin, New York, NY

Extending the Table ©1991 by Joetta Handrich Schlabach, Herald Press, Scottdale, PA

Fabulous Feasts from First United, First United Methodist Church, Warrensburg, NY

Family & Company ©1992 Junior League of Binghamton, NY

Famous Dutch Kitchen Restaurant Cookbook ©2004 by Jane and Michael Stern, Rutledge Hill Press, Nashville, TN

Famous Woodstock Cooks ©1997 by Joanne Michaels and Mary Barile, JMB Publications, Woodstock, NY

Favorite New England Recipes, by Sara B.B. Stamm, Country Roads Press, Castine, ME

Favorite Recipes from Quilters ©1992 by Louise Stoltzfus, Good Books, Intercourse, PA

Fellowship Family Favorites Cookbook, Word of Life Fellowship, Schroom Lake, NY

The Festival Cookbook ©1987 by Phyllis Pellman Good, Good Books, Intercourse, PA

The Fine Art of Holiday Cooking ©1992 University of Connecticut, School of Fine Arts, Storrs, CT

The Fine Arts Cookbook II ©1981 Museum of Fine Arts, Boston, MA

Foods of the Hudson ©1993 by Peter G. Rose, The Overlook Press, Woodstock, NY

Fortsville UMC Cookbook, Cookbook Committee, Fortsville, UMC, Ganesvoort, NY

Friend's Favorites, The Friends of the Dover Library, Dover Plains, NY

The Frog Commissary Cookbook ©1985 by Steven Poses, Anne Clark, and Becky Roller, Camino Books, Inc., Philadelphia, PA

From Amish and Mennonite Kitchens ©1994 Good Books, Intercourse, PA

From Ellie's Kitchen to Yours ©1991 by Ellie Deaner, Framingham, MA

From the Inn's Kitchen, by Deedy Marble, The Governor's Inn, Ludlow, VT

From Mother's Cupboard, Anna Mary Wenger, Lititz, PA

The Gardner Museum Café Cookbook ©1985 by Lois McKitchen Conroy, The Harvard Common Press, Boston, MA

Gather Around Our Table, St. Catherine of Siena School and Church, Albany, NY

George Hirsch Living It Up! ©2000 by George Hirsch, M. Evans & Co., NY, Southampton, NY

Good Maine Food ©1974 by Marjorie Mosser, Down East Books, Camden, ME

Grandmother's Cookbook ©1990 by Elizabeth Rose von Hohen, Doylestown, PA

Great Grandmother's Goodies, Pennsylvania's State Federation of Negro Women's Clubs, Inc., Erie, PA

Great Island Cook Book ©1965 New Castle Island Church Guild, New Castle, NH

Great Lake Effects ©1997 Junior League of Buffalo, NY

Great Taste of Parkminster, Parkminster Church, Rochester, NY

The Hammersmith Farm Cookbook, Hammersmith Farm, Newport, RI

A Hancock Community Collection, The Guild, Hancock, NH

The Happy Cooker, Cobble Hill, Elizabethtown, NY

The Harlow's Bread & Cracker Cookbook ©1989 by Joan S. Harlow, Down East Books, Camden, ME

Hasbro Children's Hospital Cookbook, Hasbro Children's Hospital Nursing Staff, Providence, RI

The Heart of Pittsburgh ©1998 Sacred Heart Elementary School, Pittsburgh, PA

The Heart of Pittsburgh II ©2004 Sacred Heart Elementary School, Pittsburgh, PA

Heritage Cooking by Mary Pauplis, Hudson, MA

Heritage Fan-Fare ©1992 Heritage Plantation of Sandwich Museum Store, Sandwich, MA

Home Cookin' is a Family Affair, Windsor Junior Women's Club, Windsor, CT

Homespun Cookery, by Marie Carter Durant, Boscawen, NH

Hospitality ©1991 North Shore Medical Center, Salem, MA

The Hudson River Valley Cookbook ©1995 by Wally Malouf with Molly Finn, Harvard Common Press, Boston, MA

Hudson Valley German-American Society Cookbook, Kingston, NY

In Good Taste, Delaware Valley Arts Alliance, Narrowsburg, NY

In the Village, St. John's Church, New York, NY

Inncredible Edibles ©2003 PA Tourism & Lodging Assn., Winters Publishing, Greensburg, IN

It's Our Serve ©1989 Junior League of Long Island, Roslyn, NY

J. Bildner & Sons Cookbook ©1993 by Jim Bildner, The Harvard Common Press, Boston, MA

Just Desserts ©1988 The Shipley School, Bryn Mawr, PA

The King Arthur Flour 200th Anniversary Cookbook ©1990 The Baker's Catalogue, Norwich, VT

La Cocina de la Familia ©1998 La Bodega de la Familia, New York, NY

Ladies of the Church, Trinity Evangelical Lutheran Church, Lititz, PA

Laurels to the Cook ©1988 Talua Rock Girl Scout Council, Inc., Johnstown, PA

The Legal Sea Foods Cookbook ©1988 Legal Sea Foods, Allston, MA

The Loaf and Ladle Cook Book ©1979 by Joan S. Harlow, Down East Books, Camden, ME

The Long Island Holiday Cookbook ©2000 Newsday Books, Melville, NY

The Lymes' Heritage Cookbook ©1991 Lyme Historical Society/Florence Griswold Museum, Old Lyme, CT

The Maine Collection ©1993 Portland Museum of Art Guild, Portland, ME

Maine's Jubilee Cookbook ©1969 Edited by Loana Shibles and Annie Rogers, Down East Books, Camden, ME

The Marlborough Meetinghouse Cookbook, Congregational Church of Marlborough, CT

The MBL Centennial Cookbook ©1988 MBL Associates, Woods Hole, MA

Measures of Love, by Beverly White and Terri Foster, Springville, NY

Memories from Brownie's Kitchen ©1989 by Mildred "Brownie" Schrumpf, Magazines, Inc., Bangor, ME

Mennonite Country-Style Recipes & Kitchen Secrets ©1987 by Esther H. Shank, Herald Press, Scottdale, PA

Mennonite Community Cookbook ©1978 by Mary Emma Showalter, Herald Press, Scottdale, PA

Merrymeeting Merry Eating, Mid Coast Hospital, Brunswick Aux., Brunswick, ME

Moosewood Restaurant Daily Special ©1995 Moosewood Restaurant, Ithaca, NY

Moosewood Restaurant Book of Desserts ©1997 Moosewood Restaurants/Random House, Ithaca, NY

More Than Delicious, Erie Art Museum, Erie, PA

More Than Sandwiches, Sandwich Junior Women's Club, Sandwich, MA

Moveable Feasts Cookbook ©1992 by Ginger Smyle, Mystic Seaport Stores, Mystic, Ct

Mrs. Appleyard's Family Kitchen ©1977 Vermont Life Magazine, Montpelier, VT

My Italian Heritage, August E. Corea, Editor, East Rochester, NY

My Own Cookbook ©1982 by Gladys Taber, Parnassus Imprints, Marstons Mill, MA

Off the Hook ©1988 Junior League of Stamford-Norwalk, Darien, CT

The Original Philadelphia Neighborhood Cookbook ©1988 by Irina Smith & Ann Hazan, Philadelphia, PA

Our Best Home Cooking, Knights of Columbus #4812, Pittsford, NY

Our Daily Bread, and then some..., The Eldred Family Home School, Auburn, NY

Our Favorite Recipes, Pitcher Hill Community Church, North Syracuse, NY

Our Volunteers Cook, Courtland Memorial Hospital Aux, Inc., Cortland, NY

The Parkview Way to Vegetarian Cooking, Parkview Memorial Hospital Aux., Brunswick, ME

Pennsylvania State Grange Cookbook (Green), Pennsylvania State Grange, Lemoyne, PA

Pennsylvania's Historic Restaurants and Their Recipes ©1996 by Dawn O'Brien and Claire Walter, John F. Blair, Publisher, Winston-Salem, NC

Perennials, Falmouth Garden Club, Falmouth, MA

Peter Christian's Favorites ©1987 by Shirley Edes and Julia Philipson, Down East Books, Camden, ME

Philadelphia Homestyle Cookbook, Norwood-Fontbonne Academy, Philadelphia, PA

Philadelphia Main Line Classics, Junior Saturday Club, Wayne, PA

Plum Crazy ©1973 by Elizabeth Post Mirel, Parnassus Imprints, Marstons Mills, MA

Proulx/Chartrand 1997 Reunion Cookbook, Central Square, NY

Provincetown Seafood Cookbook ©1975 by Howard Mitcham, Parnassus Imprints, Marston Mills, MA

Recipes from the Children's Museum at Saratoga, Saratoga Springs, NY

Recipes from a New England Inn ©1992 by Trudy Cutrone, Country Roads Press, Castine, ME

Recipes from Smith-Appleby House, Historical Society of Smithfield, RI

Recollections and Collections ©1982 by Alfred D. Pellegrini, Hershey, PY

The Red Lion Inn Cookbook ©1992 by Sizi Forbes Chase, Berkshire House Publishers, Lee, MA

Rhinebeck Community Cookbook Desserts of Good Taste, by Andrea Farewell, Rhinebeck, NY

Rhode Island Cooks ©1992 American Cancer Society, New England Division, Pawtucket, RI

River Brethren Recipes, Sonlight River Brethren School, Mount Joy, PA

RSVP ©1982 The Junior League of Portland, ME

Sandy Hook Volunteer Fire Co. Ladies Aux. Cookbook, Sandy Hook, CT

Savor the Flavor, Holy Cross Ladies Society, Buffalo, NY

Savory Cape Cod Recipes & Sketches ©1992 by Gail Cavaliere, Gift Barn, N. Eastham, MA

Seafood Secrets Cookbook ©1990 by Ainslie Turner, Mystic Seaport Stores, Mystic, CT

Seafood Expressions ©1991 by Normand Leclair, N. Kingston, RI

Sharing Our Best, St. Paul's Lutheran Church, Saratoga Springs, NY

Sharing Our Bounty Through 40 Years, Messiah Lutheran Church, Rochester, NY

Signature Recipes, Susquehanna Valley Chef's Assn., York, PA

Simply...The Best ©2000 by Kitty Ledingham, Lake George, NY

Simply in Season ©22005 by Mary Beth Lind & Cathleen Hockman-Wert, Herald Press, Scottdale, PA

Society of Farm Women of Pennsylvania Cookbook, Glen Rock, PA

The Specialties of the House, Ronald McDonald House of Rochester, NY

Susie's Cook Book, Hatfield Quality Meats, Inc., Hatfield, PA

A Taste of Cape Cod ©1994 Shank Painter Publishing Co., Provincetown, MA

A Taste of Hallowell ©1992 by Alice Arlen, Hallowell, ME

A Taste of New England ©1990 Junior League of Worcester, Inc., Worcester, MA

A Taste of Newport, Shank Painter Publishing Co., Provincetown, MA

A Taste of Providence ©1989 Shank Painter Publishing Co., Provincetown, MA

A Taste of Salt Air & Island Kitchens, Ladies Auxiliary of the Block Island Volunteer Fire Dept. Block Island, RI

Tasting the Hamptons ©1998 by Katherine Hartnett, Sag Harbor, NY

Tasty Temptations from the Village by the Sea, Holy Redeemer Guild, W. Chatham, MA

The Teaching Chef ©1984 Indiana University of PA, Indiana, PA

Temple Temptations, Temple Shaaray Tefila, New York, NY

There Once Was a Cook... ©1985 The Wesley Institute, Pittsburgh, PA

Thou Preparest a Table Before Me, Women of the WELCA, The Lutheran Church of the Good Shepherd, Roosevelt, NY

Three Rivers Cookbook I ©1973 Child Health Assn. of Sewickley, PA

Three Rivers Cookbook II ©1978 Child Health Assn. of Sewickley, PA

Three Rivers Cookbook III ©1990 Child Health Assn. of Scwickley, PA

Three Rivers Renaissance Cookbook IV ©2000 Child Health Assn. of Sewickley, PA

Thru the Grapevine ©1983 The Junior League of Elmira-Corning, Elmira, NY

Tony Clark's New Blueberry Hill Cookbook ©1990 Down East Books, Camden, ME

Traditional Portuguese Recipes from Provincetown, Shank Painter Publishing Co., Provincetown, MA

Treasured Greek Recipes, Philoptochos Society of St. Sophia Greek Orthodox Church, Albany, NY

Trinity Catholic School Cookbook, Trinity Catholic School, Oswego, NY

200 Years of Favorite Recipes from Delaware County, Delaware County Senior Council, Delhi, NY

Uncle Billy's Downeast Barbeque Book ©1991 by Jonathan St. Laurent and Charles Neave, Dancing Bear Books, W. Rockport, ME

Uncork New York! Wine Country Cookbook, New York Wine & Grape Foundation, Penn Yan, NY

Venison Cookbook, Public Opinion, Chambersburg, PA

Vermont Kitchens Revisited ©1990 Vermont Kitchen Publications, Burlington, VT

Visions of Home Cook Book, York Hospital, York, ME

Washington Street Eatery Cook Book ©1993 by LuAnn Neff, Greenland, NH

The Way to a Man's Heart, Beth Israel Sisterhood, Washington, PA

What's Cooking at Moody's Diner ©1989 by Nancy Moody Genthner, Moody's Diner, Waldoboro, ME

What's Cooking at Stony Brook, The Staff at University Hospital, Stony Brook, NY

What's Cooking at Trinity, Trinity Evangelical Lutheran Church, Wexford, PA

White Dog Café Cookbook, by Judy Wicks and Kevin Von Klause, Philadelphia, PA

The Whole Valley Cookbook ©1980 Wyoming Historical and Geological Society, Wilkes-Barre, PA

Wild Game Cookbook & Other Recipes ©1997 by Joseph Lamagna, Yonkers, NY

Wonderful Good Cooking from Amish Country Kitchens ©1974 by Johnny Schrock and Fred J. Wilson, Herald Press, Scottdale, PA

Index

The Empire State Building is a 102-story landmark Art Deco skyscraper in New York City at the intersection of Fifth Avenue and West 34th Street. Its name is derived from the nickname for New York, The Empire State. The Empire State Building opened on May 1, 1931, and was the first building to have more than 100 floors. The building houses 1,000 businesses, and has its own zip code, 10118.

INDEX